The Supreme Court

The Supreme Court

HELENA SILVERSTEIN

Student Guides to American Government and Politics
Brian Lloyd Fife, Series Editor

 GREENWOOD

An Imprint of ABC-CLIO, LLC
Santa Barbara, California • Denver, Colorado

Library of Congress Cataloging-in-Publication Data

Names: Silverstein, Helena, author.
Title: The Supreme Court / Helena Silverstein.
Description: Santa Barbara, California : Greenwood, An Imprint of ABC-CLIO,
    LLC, [2021] | Series: Student guides to American government and politics
    | Includes bibliographical references and index.
Identifiers: LCCN 2020026565 (print) | LCCN 2020026566 (ebook) | ISBN
    9781440873003 (hardcover) | ISBN 9781440873010 (ebook)
Subjects: LCSH: United States. Supreme Court—History. | United States.
    Supreme Court—Rules and practice.
Classification: LCC KF8742 .S545 2021 (print) | LCC KF8742 (ebook) | DDC
    347.73/26—dc23
LC record available at https://lccn.loc.gov/2020026565
LC ebook record available at https://lccn.loc.gov/2020026566

ISBN: 978-1-4408-7300-3 (print)
        978-1-4408-7301-0 (ebook)

25 24 23 22 21   1 2 3 4 5

This book is also available as an eBook.

Greenwood
An Imprint of ABC-CLIO, LLC

ABC-CLIO, LLC
147 Castilian Drive
Santa Barbara, California 93117
www.abc-clio.com

This book is printed on acid-free paper ∞

Manufactured in the United States of America

For my brothers,
Dubi and David

Contents

Preface

The promise of the rule of law in the United States is symbolized in many ways. The Constitution of the United States begins with the sentiment of democracy: "We the People." The iconic emblem of Lady Justice stands as the objective and impartial arbiter of law. She is blindfolded so as not to be biased by particulars and holds a set of scales as a representation of her dedication to the fair weighing of evidence and arguments. Nominees to the U.S. Supreme Court pledge neutrality and fairness by saying they will act like umpires tasked with impartially calling balls and strikes. And whether sitting on the bench of the highest court in the United States or in a state court, judges wear simple black robes thought to signify their uniform obligation to adhere to the rule of law.

Law's promise is further embodied in admirable principles pronounced in the U.S. Constitution and its Bill of Rights and additional amendments, such as freedom of speech, free exercise of religion, freedom of the press, voting rights, due process provisions, and equal protection guarantees. Outlining a framework of governance designed, in part, to avoid tyranny, the Constitution separates authority among governing bodies to limit the concentration of power, while identifying liberties retained by individuals against government intrusion.

Praise and respect for the rule of law and the Constitution are widespread, part of the prevailing narrative often used to describe the U.S. system. Law, as the narrative goes, provides order, predictability, and protection; at the same time, it ensures liberty, equality, and self-governance. Self-governing individuals are free to pursue aspirations and dreams within the constraints of rules they have adopted and given to themselves. While personal freedom and individualism are highly valued in this arrangement, no one is thought to be above the law.

The stories Americans tell, however, are often idealized versions of the realities in which they live. Whether, to what extent, and through what mechanisms law's promise is realized (or approximated) are matters some-times neglected or, when told, prone to exaggeration. In the context of the rule of law, this tendency to idealize is magnified. This owes partly to a pressing need to maintain faith in the law, for when the rule of law is threatened or fails, the risk of crisis and chaos is genuine.

At the center of understanding and seeking to enact law's promise in the United States is the institution charged with interpreting the Constitu-tion. The U.S. Supreme Court is, in many ways, a paradox: an enormously powerful arm of government, though largely powerless when it was first established; a highly respected body, though the majority of likely voters cannot name any of the justices on the Court; a panel of judges structured to be insulated from politics, yet at the center of the tug-of-war of partisan battles; an institution described as pivotal in the experiment of American democracy, while criticized for being counter-majoritarian; and an institu-tion that is often credited with bringing about substantial change to the fabric of American life and governance despite being reliant on other gov-ernment institutions to implement its rulings.

This book offers an introduction to the U.S. Supreme Court, one of the most intriguing, complicated, and controversial elements of the U.S. legal and political system. It does so by situating the Supreme Court (a) within the judiciary itself, where it stands at the pinnacle of the federal court sys-tem and a separate but important influence on state court systems; (b) within the trinity of institutional branches—legislative, executive, and judicial—that compose our federal system; and (c) within the historical, political, and cultural contexts that have shaped the evolution of the Court since the time of the Constitutional Convention. Understanding the Court and the rule of law it is charged with protecting means understanding its functions and authority, its structure and processes, its inputs and out-puts, its place in the American political system and culture, and its strengths and weaknesses.

The chapters are organized as follows. The introduction places the Supreme Court in historical context, broadly tracing how the Court emerged as "the least dangerous branch" during the Founding Era and grew over more than two hundred years into the formidable institution it is today. Chapter 1 explains the development of and controversy over judi-cial review, the primary source of the Supreme Court's power. Chapter 2 explores the competing approaches used by the Court to interpret the Constitution and the debates over constitutional interpretation. Chapter 3 situates the Court at the pinnacle of the structure of the federal judicial system and provides an overview of the procedures used by the Court to select, hear, and decide cases. Chapter 4 focuses on the justices, the ways they are selected to serve on the Court, and the impact of the judicial nom-ination and confirmation processes. Chapter 5 delves into the factors thought to influence the decisions made by the Supreme Court, including factors internal to the Court itself as well as those external pressures that might affect decision making. Chapter 6 looks at the Court through the lens of the public and the media, exploring how the institution is received and perceived by the public and how it is portrayed in the media. Chapter 7 explores the implementation and impact of Court decisions, examining ongoing debates about whether and to what extent the Court contributes to social change. The book concludes by looking forward and offering a brief assessment of the future of the Court during a time of increasing political polarization.

My ability to write this volume has its foundations in a wide and deep network of support. Special thanks to Michael McCann for his wisdom, mentorship, and friendship; to Susan Burgess, a role model, booster, and all-around good egg; and to Linda Cornett, an ever-present companion. Thanks to Bruce Murphy for many thoughtful conversations about law and politics, Brian Fife for his invitation to contribute to this series, Kevin Hillstrom for his editorial guidance, and Lafayette College for its institutional support. My gratitude goes to some who have departed, as I remain ever indebted to Stuart Scheingold for imparting his knowledge and a critical lens and hold close the memory of my father, Zelchka. A thousand thanks for the enduring encouragement of the mothers in my life, Lillichka and Roberta, and the inspiration provided by my brothers, Dubi and David.

And, of course and as always, to Wayne. One, two.

Introduction

"The judicial Power of the United States, shall be vested in one supreme Court, and in such inferior Courts as the Congress may from time to time ordain and establish."

Article III, Section 1, U.S. Constitution

The U.S. Supreme Court's term begins each year on the first Monday in October and runs until late June or early July. Every year, as October nears, a flurry of news stories appears identifying what are expected to be the most important cases in the upcoming term. Will the Supreme Court decide that it is a violation of an individual's right against cruel and unusual punishment to be executed if that person currently suffers from dementia and no longer remembers committing the crime? Does the Constitution's prohibition against the imposition of excessive fines for criminal conduct apply just to the federal government or also to states?

As the term unfolds, the Court accepts additional cases while announcing decisions in others. Does the presence on public land of a ninety-three-year-old World War I monument shaped like a cross endorse and establish religion? No. Can the executive branch of the federal government bar transgender people from serving in the military while a challenge to such a ban winds its way through the judicial system? Yes.

When June arrives and the Supreme Court's term nears completion, anticipation increases as people await news of the remainder of the Court's decisions. And when the term concludes in early summer, another flurry of news stories appears summarizing what are deemed the most consequential cases decided by the Court since the previous October.

Summer is typically quieter with the Court on recess, though attention to the Supreme Court is heightened in presidential election years when the outcomes of those contests can have significant implications for the composition of the highest bench. Even more heightened is the attention given to the Court when there are vacant seats to be filled.

Consider the end of the 2017–18 Supreme Court term and the summer months that followed. In June 2018 alone, the Court handed down decisions governing labor unions, travel bans for visitors from several Muslim-majority countries, abortion, privacy, taxation, redistricting, voting rights, religious freedom, and sexual orientation discrimination. In most of these decisions, the nine-member Court was closely divided, ruling by margins of 5–4 on a wide range of cases. On Wednesday, June 27, 2018—the final day of the Court's term—Supreme Court Justice Anthony M. Kennedy announced his retirement. Within two weeks, President Donald J. Trump nominated Justice Kennedy's replacement: Brett Kavanaugh, a judge on the U.S. Court of Appeals for the District of Columbia Circuit. Over the next few months, the country witnessed one of the most contentious confirmation fights in Supreme Court history, as accusations of sexual assault against Kavanaugh resulted in an FBI investigation and a dramatic and emotional televised confirmation hearing.

Of course, not all Supreme Court terms are created equal. Some are far more momentous than others. And while the makeup of the bench can have a marked influence on the law, relatively few Supreme Court nomination and confirmation episodes have turned into historic fights. Still, the Supreme Court, whether handing down rulings that are momentous or mundane and whether composed through processes that are dramatic or ordinary, matters a great deal in American politics.

Moreover, in times of increasingly partisan and divisive politics, the Supreme Court's central role, but unique function, in the American political system is both notable and complicated. The Court reflects the partisan battles that take place in the other branches of government. Indeed, the Court sometimes serves as an avatar of partisan divisions: rulings by the Court are often characterized as being divided along party lines, and justices are frequently described either as having been appointed by a Republican or Democrat or as being part of the "liberal" or "conservative" bloc, or both. At the same time, though, its structural independence and relative insulation from Congress, the presidency, and electoral politics, as well as its role as the head of the "judicial" branch of the federal government, make the Supreme Court, in theory at least, uniquely positioned to resist and rise above the rough-and-tumble of politics.

It is the uniqueness of the Supreme Court and its positioning and function in the American system of governing, politics, and democracy that animate this guide to its history, operations, character, and role in American life.

THE SUPREME COURT: THEN TO NOW

When discussing the U.S. Supreme Court and its authority and place in the trinity that makes up the federal government, the Court is often described as an institution that was firmly established at the time of the founding. Common descriptions of the federal government note the creation of separate and "coequal" branches, each equipped with the ability to check the other branches so that no one arm will become too powerful. The Constitution—drafted in 1787 and in effect since 1789—delineates these separate branches and vests each with distinct yet overlapping authority. Article I of the Constitution identifies the legislative branch and vests it with multiple powers to make law; Article II prescribes those powers held by the executive branch; and Article III establishes federal judiciary authority, stating that "[t]he judicial Power of the United States, shall be vested in one supreme Court, and in such inferior Courts as the Congress may from time to time ordain and establish." Article III also establishes life tenure for federal judges and identifies the types of cases over which the federal courts have jurisdiction.

Article III does not, however, provide many specifics on the structure and authority of the Court. It does not fix the number of judges who will serve on the Supreme Court or other federal courts. Importantly, it does not explicitly grant to the Supreme Court the power of judicial review— that is, the power to decide whether the actions of other government bodies are inconsistent with the Constitution.

This is not to say that the role of the federal judiciary was a complete mystery at the time of the Constitutional Convention and after the Constitution's ratification. But three aspects of this initial ambiguity are worth noting. First, there was considerable uncertainty about the extent of the Court's power and the reach of its authority relative to the other branches and the states. Second, there was substantial worry about creating a federal judiciary that would have too much power. And third, because the Constitution created the federal judiciary but left unaddressed many details about how it would operate, the Supreme Court in particular and the federal courts in general have changed significantly since the time of the founding.

THE FOUNDING ERA

Article III of the Constitution gives Congress explicit authority to structure key aspects of the federal judicial system, such as creating the lower federal courts, and some of the ambiguity surrounding the U.S. judiciary was clarified when Congress passed the Judiciary Act of 1789. This Act, though amended since President George Washington signed it into law, continues to provide the framework for the federal court system. Below the U.S. Supreme Court, it includes federal trial courts (known as District Courts) and appeals courts (known as Circuit Courts). The Judiciary Act established the Office of the Attorney General to represent the United States in cases brought against it. In its original iteration, this law also specified the number of justices who would serve on the Supreme Court: one chief justice and five associate justices.

What the Act did not and could not specify is respect for the Supreme Court as an institution, nor could the Act reverse the distrust toward courts and judges held by many Americans at the time of the founding. Suspicion that judicial authority would morph into judicial tyranny—a misgiving that was a legacy of British colonial rule—was amplified by concern that creating a central judicial system would diminish the power of states. In particular, Anti-Federalists favored a limited federal judiciary. They privileged states' rights over the central government and worried that federal courts would interfere with the authority of states to govern themselves.

That apprehension was common both before and after the passage of the 1789 Judiciary Act. So common was it that in 1788, following the Constitutional Convention and when efforts to persuade states to ratify the document were underway, Alexander Hamilton famously sought to persuade skeptics to accept a judiciary as part of the newly proposed structure of the federal government. He did so in The Federalist Papers by arguing that the judicial branch would be the weakest of the three:

> Whoever attentively considers the different departments of power must perceive, that, in a government in which they are separated from each other, the judiciary, from the nature of its functions, will always be the least dangerous to the political rights of the Constitution; because it will be least in a capacity to annoy or injure them. The Executive not only dispenses the honors, but holds the sword of the community. The legislature not only commands the purse, but prescribes the rules by which the duties and rights of every citizen are to be regulated. The judiciary, on the contrary, has no influence over either the sword or the purse; no direction either of the strength or of the wealth of the society; and can take no active resolution whatever. It may truly be said to have neither FORCE nor WILL, but merely judgment; and must ultimately depend upon the aid of the executive arm even for the efficacy of its judgments. (Hamilton 2009, 392)

Though the Judiciary Act created a broader structure for the federal courts than that favored by Anti-Federalists, the power and prestige of the Supreme Court remained muted in its early years. Today an appointment to the Supreme Court is highly coveted, but in its nascent days it was not especially prized. John Jay, confirmed as the first chief justice of the Supreme

Court in 1789, left the position to become governor of New York in 1795. When President John Adams sought to place John Jay back into the position of chief justice six years later, Jay declined the nomination, bemoaning the limited power and stature of the Court. Repeated efforts to place the federal judiciary on "proper footing," Jay complained, proved "fruitless":

> I left the bench perfectly convinced that under a system so defective it would not obtain the energy, weight, and dignity which are essential to its affording due support to the national government; nor acquire the public confidence and respect which, as the last resort of the justice of the nation, it should possess. Hence I am induced to doubt both the propriety and the expediency of my returning to the bench under the present system. (quoted in Cushman 2013, 3)

THE MARSHALL COURT'S BROAD LEGACY

Jay was hardly alone in his views about the constrained authority and improper footing of the Supreme Court. Among those who shared his views was John Marshall. It was Marshall who, owing to Jay's refusal to return to the role of chief justice, was appointed to the seat by President John Adams just before Adams left office in 1801. Marshall, like the president who appointed him, was a member of the Federalist Party, which pressed for a robust national government. While President Adams lost the election of 1800 to Thomas Jefferson and the political forces that favored a limited central government and strong states' rights, Marshall's ascendancy to the high court provided a platform to advance Federalist values and policy.

Over the ensuing thirty-four years, Chief Justice Marshall played what has arguably been the most pivotal role in the nation's history in shaping and advancing the Court's position, power, and prestige. Most important was Justice Marshall's 1803 ruling in *Marbury v. Madison*, which established the Court's power of judicial review. Writing on behalf of a unanimous Court, Marshall found a section of Congress's 1789 Judiciary Act to be inconsistent with the language in Article III of the Constitution. In so finding, the Court held in *Marbury v. Madison* that when a law passed by Congress conflicts with the Constitution, the Constitution prevails. Marshall further explained that because it is the role and responsibility of the judicial branch to interpret law, it is also the role and responsibility of the Court to declare a Congressional statute (or portion thereof) unconstitutional upon finding that it runs afoul of the Constitution. As will be discussed further in chapter 1, by asserting the power of judicial review in *Marbury v. Madison*, Chief Justice Marshall put the federal judiciary on much firmer ground as a strong third branch of the federal government.

In later cases, Marshall fortified the Federalist vision. He did so by leading a Court that handed down rulings expanding the power of the central government and reinforcing the supremacy of federal law and the Constitution over that of state laws. Marshall gave broad interpretation to Congress's constitutional authority to make all laws necessary and proper for carrying out its delegated powers (*McCulloch v. Maryland* 1819) and to regulate interstate commerce (*Gibbons v. Odgen* 1824). Following the logic of *Marbury v. Madison*, Marshall also propelled the idea of the supremacy of federal authority, much to the dismay of Anti-Federalists and advocates of state rights, by emphasizing the importance of the Constitution's so-called Supremacy Clause. This clause, found in Article VI, states, "This Constitution, and the Laws of the United States which shall be made in Pursuance thereof; and all Treaties made, or which shall be made, under the Authority of the United States, shall be the supreme Law of the Land; and the Judges in every State shall be bound thereby, any Thing in the Constitution or Laws of any State to the Contrary notwithstanding." Marshall interpreted this clause to hold not only that state laws in conflict with the Constitution cannot stand but also that it is for the federal courts—not state courts—to determine when such a conflict exists (*Fletcher v. Peck* 1810).

As much of a Federalist as Marshall was, however, the Court's 1833 ruling in *Barron v. Baltimore* rejected an effort to *nationalize* the Bill of Rights. Nationalizing—or *incorporating*—the Bill of Rights would require states to abide by those provisions. The case involved a claim by John Barron that the city of Baltimore had violated his Fifth Amendment rights by taking his property without just compensation. In a unanimous opinion for the Court, Marshall rejected Barron's claim by holding that the protections afforded by the Bill of Rights only restricted the federal government and did not apply to state and local governments. The Constitution, Marshall wrote, was established for the people of the United States, not for the government of individual states. As such, the Court concluded that the restraints on government and individual protections articulated in the Bill of Rights, including those in the Fifth Amendment, are restraints only on the federal government, not on state governments. Given the holding in *Barron*, the reach of the provisions in the Bill of Rights was significantly curtailed and would remain so until after the passage of the Fourteenth Amendment in 1868.

THE TANEY COURT AND DRED SCOTT

Roger B. Taney succeeded John Marshall as chief justice after the latter's death in 1835. Though the Taney Court was marked by moderation of the Federalist positions that Marshall advocated, it has become most well known for its notorious ruling in *Dred Scott v. Sandford* (1857).

Dred Scott was a slave who sued for his freedom, arguing that he should be declared legally free because he had lived for a period in a territory that banned slavery. Chief Justice Taney, writing the opinion for the Court, not only denied Dred Scott's claim for freedom but also declared that neither Scott nor any other African American—including those held in slavery and those who were free—could be a citizen of the United States. While a state could decide to grant state citizenship to those of African descent, Taney argued that the Constitution prohibits those of African descent from holding national citizenship and, in turn, from suing in federal court. Taney further ruled that Congress did not have the authority to make slavery illegal in the U.S. territories and deemed unconstitutional the Missouri Compromise, a law passed by Congress in 1820 that permitted slavery in some territories while banning it in others. According to the Court's *Dred Scott* ruling, Congress's prohibition of slavery in certain territories went beyond its legislative authority and interfered with the constitutionally protected property rights of slave owners.

Though welcomed by the Southern states and supporters of slavery, the decision in *Dred Scott* proved highly polarizing. Northern states, abolitionists, and Republicans condemned the decision and the Court that issued it. Among the vocal opponents of the ruling was Republican Abraham Lincoln, who would go on to win the presidential election of 1860 and issue the Emancipation Proclamation in 1863 ordering the freedom of slaves in Confederate states. Regarded by many as among the Court's most infamous decisions, *Dred Scott v. Sandford* undermined the status, prestige, and influence that Marshall had previously garnered for the Court.

FROM RECONSTRUCTION THROUGH THE *LOCHNER* ERA

In the months and years immediately following the Civil War, three amendments—which have come to be called the Reconstruction Amendments—were added to the Constitution. The Thirteen Amendment, ratified in 1865, abolished slavery. The Fourteenth Amendment, enacted in 1868, reversed the *Dred Scott* ruling by establishing that all persons born or naturalized in the U.S. are U.S. citizens and citizens of the state in which they reside. The Fourteenth Amendment also granted key rights as follows: "No State shall make or enforce any law which shall abridge the privileges or immunities of citizens of the United States; nor shall any State deprive any person of life, liberty, or property, without due process of law; nor deny to any person within its jurisdiction the equal protection of the laws." The last of the Reconstruction Amendments—the Fifteenth, ratified in 1870—holds that the right to vote cannot be denied because of race, color, or previous condition of servitude.

In the late 1800s and into the 1900s, however, the Court's interpretation of the Reconstruction Amendments did little to help secure African Americans the equality and liberty promised in the words of the Amendments. Instead, with few exceptions, the Court supported ongoing, institutionalized discrimination on the basis of race. Of particular notoriety, in *Plessy v. Ferguson* (1896) the Court permitted racial segregation in railway cars as long as the separate accommodations were themselves equal. Ruling in this way, the Court produced the "separate but equal" doctrine and a precedent that provided constitutional cover to a whole host of state and local "Jim Crow" laws that segregated the races in theaters, hotels, restaurants, schools, and more.

The Fourteenth Amendment's Privileges or Immunities Clause and Due Process Clause, as well as their specific application to states, were seen by some Americans as a vehicle for nationalizing the Bill of Rights. In the 1873 decision in the *Slaughterhouse Cases*, though, the Court closed the door on using the Privileges or Immunities Clause to do this. The ruling considered but rejected a challenge to a Louisiana law establishing a monopoly in the operation of slaughterhouses. In its holding, the Court rejected the argument that the explicit guarantees in the Bill of Rights are included in the privileges and immunities of U.S. citizens set out in the Fourteenth Amendment.

In later cases, though, the Court slowly and selectively opened the door to using the Due Process Clause to nationalize the Bill of Rights. In 1897, the Court for the first time incorporated one of the guarantees of the first Ten Amendments into the Fourteenth Amendment. In *Chicago, Burlington & Quincy Railroad Company v. Chicago*, the Court held that just compensation for a government taking of property required by the Fifth Amendment is also required under the Fourteenth Amendment mandate that states provide due process of law. In *Gitlow v. New York* (1925), the Court found that the Fourteenth Amendment due process right requires states to respect First Amendment guarantees of freedom of speech and press. Even though the Court concluded in that case that New York had not violated Benjamin Gitlow's freedom of speech by convicting him under a criminal anarchy statute, the Court notably held, "For present purposes, we may and do assume that freedom of speech and of the press which are protected by the First Amendment from abridgment by Congress are among the fundamental personal rights and 'liberties' protected by the due process clause of the Fourteenth Amendment from impairment by the States" (*Gitlow v. New York* 1925, 666). Though *Gitlow* did not delineate the other "fundamental personal rights and 'liberties'" incorporated by the Due Process Clause, it served as a foundational ruling for future cases to do so.

While the first quarter of the twentieth century is notable for the emergence of the incorporation doctrine, one of the most salient characteristics of this period of the Court's history is its treatment of economic regulation and protection of "freedom of contract." At the outset of the twentieth century, with the industrial revolution and rapid expansion of business and corporate activities, the Court's focus shifted substantially to cases involving government efforts to regulate businesses and the marketplace. In that shift, the Supreme Court rejected most government regulation of the economy based on the view that individual liberty includes the right of employers to enter into contracts with employees. The Court elevated protection for "freedom of contract" by grounding it in the language of the Fifth and Fourteenth Amendments that government may not deprive "any person of life, liberty, or property, without due process of law." From 1897 to 1937, the Court routinely struck down federal and state laws that sought to regulate the economy in favor of workers and consumers (including, e.g., minimum wage laws, maximum work hour laws, and child labor laws). This became known as the Lochner Era, named after a 1905 Supreme Court decision in *Lochner v. New York* that struck down a maximum work-hour law for bakery employees.

The Supreme Court's protection of economic liberty and freedom of contract during this Era came under serious criticism, though—especially with the onset of the Great Depression. Following the stock market crash in 1929 and the ensuing economic depression that devastated America, public and political support for government regulation of the economy increased. After his election in 1932, President Franklin Delano Roosevelt put forward a series of federal programs known as the New Deal, which included such things as public works projects to grow jobs and provide support for the unemployed, regulations of banks and the financial industry, and monetary reform policies. As popular as many of these programs were, however, the conservative-majority Supreme Court used the freedom of contract philosophy to declare key components of the New Deal unconstitutional. Much to the chagrin of Roosevelt, the Court overturned the National Industrial Recovery Act and the Agricultural Adjustment Act—two central New Deal programs—in 1935 and 1936, respectively.

West Coast Hotel Co. v. Parrish in 1937 is typically seen as marking the end of the Lochner Era. In that case, the Supreme Court dramatically reversed course from its previous rulings by affirming the constitutionality of a state minimum wage law. The decision came down shortly after President Roosevelt had proposed a bill to increase the number of justices on the Supreme Court from its nine-member total. If adopted, the bill would have given the president the authority to appoint new justices to the bench for every member of the Court over seventy-and-a-half years of age. While Congress never voted on the proposed bill, Roosevelt's controversial "court-packing plan" is often credited with having pressured the Supreme Court to move away from the shield that the Lochner Era approach provided to freedom of contract.

CAROLENE PRODUCTS *THROUGH THE WARREN COURT*

A year after "the switch in time that saved nine," as the change brought about by opinion in *West Coast Hotel Co. v. Parrish* came to be called, the Court handed down another momentous ruling in *United States v. Carolene Products Company*. The ruling affirmed that the Lochner Era, with its heightened protection for "freedom of contract," was over. The Court held that, moving forward, it would only declare government regulation of the economy unconstitutional if the regulation is unreasonable or lacks a rational foundation. At that same time, though, the Court signaled a willingness to give heightened protection for other individual liberties, like free speech and assembly. In addition, the Court indicated its inclination to defend the civil rights of racial minorities and other minority groups. The Court articulated these leanings almost in passing, stating them in a footnote in the opinion. In that note—now famously called *Carolene Products* Footnote 4—the Court suggested it would give "searching judicial inquiry" or "exacting judicial scrutiny" to government regulation that restricts the liberties protected by the Bill of Rights and the Fourteenth Amendment and to regulations based on "prejudice against discrete and insular minorities" (*United States v. Carolene Products Company* 1938, 152 n.4). Though Footnote 4 did not define what searching judicial scrutiny would entail, the Court implied that it would require the government to provide something stronger than merely a "reasonable" interest to justify unequal treatment of certain groups or restrictions of certain liberties.

In the three decades that followed, the Court's decisions did, indeed, increasingly take up and give extra scrutiny to and thus extra protection for key fundamental rights and liberties, though not for liberty of contract. The Court also continued to selectively incorporate other provisions of the Bill of Rights into the Fourteenth Amendment.

These shifts owed in part to substantial change in the Court's membership. By 1940, four of the justices who had voted against Roosevelt's New Deal legislation retired or passed away, giving the president the opportunity to nominate new jurists. During the course of his twelve years in the Oval Office, Roosevelt appointed eight new Supreme Court justices and promoted Associate Justice Harlan Fiske Stone to the position of chief justice. Presidents Harry S. Truman and Dwight D. Eisenhower, who followed Roosevelt, also had opportunities to shape the composition of the bench. They made four and five Supreme Court appointments, respectively.

In 1953, President Eisenhower appointed California Governor Earl Warren to the position of chief justice. That nomination proved historic. Eisenhower had thought that Warren would be a conservative chief justice, but he was mistaken. Led by Warren, the so-called Warren Court, which ran from 1953 to 1969, handed down a host of liberal decisions that greatly changed the complexion of American law.

For example, the Warren Court substantially expanded the rights of the criminally accused. In landmark rulings, the Court held (a) that criminal suspects must be notified of their rights before police interrogation (*Miranda v. Arizona* 1966) and have certain protections against police searches and seizures (*Mapp v. Ohio* 1961) and (b) that criminal defendants have the right to receive legal counsel (*Gideon v. Wainwright* 1963). In several cases, the Warren Court's expansion of the rights of the criminally accused proceeded by way of incorporating Fifth and Sixth Amendment protections into the Fourteenth Amendment. For instance, in *Benton v. Maryland* (1969) the Court ruled that states must respect an individual's right against being tried twice for the same crime.

In other landmark decisions, the Warren Court widened protections under the First Amendment by identifying various forms of political action and symbolic expression as speech (e.g., *Tinker v. Des Moines Independent Community School District* 1969); giving the press increased protection against accusations of libel (*New York Times Co. v. Sullivan* 1964); and extending free speech rights to expression identified as "obscene" (*Roth v. United States* 1957). Offering further protection for individual liberty, the Warren Court held that the Constitution's explicit protections for certain rights imply a personal right to privacy (*Griswold v. Connecticut* 1965). This ruling would provide the foundation for later courts to find constitutional protection for abortion and intimate sexual relations.

Perhaps the most momentous series of rulings during Warren's tenure concerned civil rights. In the landmark *Brown v. Board of Education of Topeka* (1954), a unanimous Court declared racial segregation in public schools to be unconstitutional. According to the Court, *Plessy*'s "separate but equal doctrine" has no place in public school education because segregating students based on race is inherently unequal. The Court further supported the expansion of civil rights in 1964, holding that Congress had the authority under the Constitution's Commerce Clause to prohibit race discrimination in public accommodations (*Heart of Atlanta Motel v. United States* 1964). Three years later, the Court struck down a Virginia law that prohibited interracial marriage (*Loving v. Virginia* 1967).

THE MODERN COURTS: BURGER, REHNQUIST, AND ROBERTS

Many of the rulings handed down by the Warren Court generated considerable backlash. Republican Richard M. Nixon's 1968 run for the presidency capitalized on this criticism by pledging to appoint jurists who would "strictly construct" the Constitution. As political scientist Henry J. Abraham explains, Nixon promised judges "who would see 'their duty as interpreting law and not making law'; who would follow a 'properly conservative' course of judging that would, in particular, protect society's 'peace forces' against the 'criminal forces'; who would 'see themselves as caretakers of the Constitution and servants of the people, not superlegislators with a free hand to impose their social and political viewpoints upon the American People'" (Abraham 1992, 298–99). Later Republican candidates and presidents, including Ronald Reagan, George H. W. Bush, George W. Bush, and Donald Trump, would similarly pledge to staff the bench with strict constructionists. The results of these promises have influenced the composition of the Court and the character of its rulings.

Since Warren's departure from the bench in 1969, the Supreme Court has been presided over by chief justices appointed by Republican presidents, Nixon, Reagan, and Bush 43, respectively. The Burger Court, the Rehnquist Court, and the Roberts Court have each in turn pulled back from the left-leaning tendencies of the Warren Court. For example, the Court in a series of cases narrowed the reach of the rights of the criminally accused, including the *Miranda* requirement as well as rights against unreasonable searches and seizures. The Court has begun to question and limit the extent of Congress's power to regulate interstate commerce, while protecting state's rights. The Court extended speech rights to corporations in *Citizens United v. Federal Election Commission* (2010), while narrowing civil rights protections for individuals by limiting the reach of the Voting Rights Act of 1965 in *Shelby County v. Holder* (2013). And in the landmark *District of Columbia v. Heller* (2008), the Court for the first time interpreted the Second Amendment of the Constitution as providing an individual right to bear arms that limits government's ability to enforce gun control legislation. In 2010, the Court went on to nationalize the Second Amendment, holding that states must also abide by the Second Amendment right to keep and bear arms for individual self-defense, given the Fourteenth Amendment Due Process Clause (*McDonald v. The City of Chicago* 2010).

The more rightward-leaning decisions of these Courts, though, have hardly been uniform. In 1973, for example, the Burger Court ruled in *Roe v. Wade* that the Constitution affords women a right to an abortion. While the Rehnquist and Roberts Courts have narrowed the reach of that right and expanded the ability of states to regulate and restrict abortion, calls for the Court to overturn *Roe v. Wade* have yet to be realized as of early 2020. In 1974, *United States v. Nixon* limited the presidential claim of executive privilege (the power asserted by the executive branch to withhold information) and required Nixon to obey a subpoena demanding delivery of audio recordings taken in the White House Oval Office. Though the Supreme Court has, since the 1970s, been less solicitous than the Warren Court of the rights of the criminally accused, some of the landmark rulings of the Warren Court, including *Miranda*, remain. In other cases, the Court has extended the rights of some criminal defendants. It held in

Graham v. Florida (2010), for instance, that life imprisonment without the possibility of parole is cruel and unusual punishment when imposed on minors for non-homicide offenses.

Perhaps the most noticeable aspect of the Court in the modern era is its increasing polarization. In 2017, two leading legal analysts declared that since 2010 the Court had become more sharply divided along partisan lines than ever before. They described it as "the first period in which the Court has been sharply divided between substantial blocs of Justices from each of the two major political parties" (Devins and Baum 2017, 309). What's more, each distinct bloc of justices on the recent Court is more uniform ideologically than in the past.

Recent fights over the selection of justices have laid bare both the politicization and the polarization of the Supreme Court. To be sure, controversy in the nomination and confirmation process is not new. Of the 162 Court nominations made by the president between 1789 and 2017, 37 were unsuccessful. Eleven of these were rejected in Senate roll-call votes, while most of the rest, in the face of committee or Senate opposition to the nominee or the president, were withdrawn by the president, or were postponed, tabled, or never voted on by the Senate. The 37 unconfirmed nominations, however, included those of 6 individuals who were later renominated and confirmed (see McMillion and Rutkus 2018, Summary).

But with televised confirmation hearings, the advent of the cable news and the twenty-four-hour news cycle, and the rise and influence of social media, contentious battles over the judicial selection process have become highly visible. The unsuccessful nomination of Robert Bork in 1987 and the televised spectacles over the confirmations of Justices Clarence Thomas in 1991 and Brett Kavanaugh in 2018—both of which were dominated by allegations of sexual misconduct—have been striking for an institution that is mythologized as being above politics.

CONCLUSION: THE SUPREME COURT THEN AND NOW

The assertion and development of the Supreme Court's power that was ultimately cemented by the establishment of judicial review has not always been welcome. Resistance to the growing prominence and power of the Supreme Court specifically and the federal judiciary in general is a key part of understanding the Supreme Court from the Founding Era to the present day. That resistance has ebbed and flowed over time, has come from both sides of the political aisle, and has manifest in different forms. This resistance—from other branches of government, the media, and the public—have shaped not only the Supreme Court as an institution but also the rulings it has handed down and, in turn, the way the Constitution has been interpreted.

Chronology

The following chronology highlights key events in the development of the Supreme Court as an institution and identifies notable cases addressing separation of powers, federalism, individual liberties, and civil rights.

1787

Constitutional Convention meets in Philadelphia and drafts the U.S. Constitution, including Article III, which establishes the U.S. Supreme Court and gives Congress the authority to establish lower federal courts. The final draft of the Constitution is signed on September 17, 1787.

1788

The U.S. Constitution is formally ratified on June 21 after nine of the thirteen states agree to its adoption.

1789

The Judiciary Act of 1789 is signed into law by President George Washington. Officially titled "An Act to Establish the Judicial Courts of the United States," the statute creates the structure of the federal court system, including thirteen judicial districts composed of thirteen district courts and three circuit (appeals) courts. The Act sets the number of Supreme Court justices at six, including one chief justice and five associate justices.

On September 24, the same day that the Judiciary Act was signed into law, President George Washington nominates John Jay to serve as the first chief justice of the Supreme Court.

1790

The Supreme Court convenes its first public session, at the Royal Exchange in New York City.

1791

The first Ten Amendments to the Constitution, known as the Bill of Rights, are ratified.

1793

The Supreme Court rules in *Chisholm v. Georgia* against the state of Georgia's claim that, as a sovereign state, it is immune from a lawsuit to which it did not consent brought by a citizen in federal court. The ruling angers and mobilizes supporters of states' rights to propose a constitutional amendment overturning the decision.

1795

The ruling *Chisholm v. Georgia* is reversed by ratification of the Eleventh Amendment, which states that "[t]he Judicial power of the United States shall not be construed to extend to any suit in law or equity, commenced or prosecuted against one of the United States by Citizens of another State, or by Citizens or Subjects of any Foreign State."

1801

On February 4, John Marshall, after being confirmed by the Senate in January 1801, officially begins his service as the fourth chief justice, starting a term of office that will last until 1835.

The Judiciary Act of 1801 becomes law, creating new judicial circuits and new judgeships, and eliminating the requirement that Supreme Court justices also serve on the lower appeals courts, a practice called "circuit riding." President John Adams, about to leave office when the Act was passed, uses it to stack the courts with Federalists. The appointment of what became known as the "Midnight Judges" sets up the conflict that would lead to *Marbury v. Madison*.

1803

The Supreme Court hands down its ruling *Marbury v. Madison*, declaring portions of the Judiciary Act of 1789 unconstitutional and thereby establishing its authority to determine whether laws passed by Congress are consistent with the Constitution. In later cases, the Court expands its "judicial review" authority by applying it to executive branch actions and laws and actions by states.

1804

The House of Representatives votes to impeach Justice Samuel Chase, making Chase the first (and, to date, only) justice to be impeached.

1805

The Senate acquits Justice Chase of impeachment charges.

1810

The Court issues its ruling in *Fletcher v. Peck*, using judicial review to overrule for the first time a state law found to be inconsistent with the Constitution.

1819

The Court expands federal authority in *McCulloch v. Maryland*, upholding the constitutionality of Congress's decision to charter a national bank.

1824

In *Gibbons v. Ogden*, the Marshall Court further enhances the authority of the federal government over states through a broad interpretation of Congress's authority to regulate interstate commerce.

1857

The Court ruling in *Dred Scott v. Sandford* holds that African Americans are not and were not intended by the Framers to be citizens of the United States, and declares the Missouri Compromise unconstitutional holding that Congress does not have authority to regulate the slave status of the new territories. The divisive and controversial decision escalates the growing conflict between the North and South that would ultimately lead to the Civil War.

1861

The Civil War begins on April 12 when Confederate forces open fire on Fort Sumter.

1863

On January 1, President Abraham Lincoln declares in The Emancipation Proclamation "that all persons held as slaves" in Southern states are "forever free."

1865

The surrender of the Confederate army at the Appomattox Courthouse on April 9 ends the Civil War.

The Thirteenth Amendment, the first of the Civil War Amendments, is ratified on December 6, abolishing slavery and involuntary servitude.

1866

In *Ex parte Milligan*, the Supreme Court declares unconstitutional the use of military tribunals to try civilians when civilian courts are available to hold such trials.

1868

Ratification of the Fourteenth Amendment adds equality to the Constitution and requires states to respect due process rights. The Amendment provides that "[n]o State shall make or enforce any law which shall abridge the privileges or immunities of citizens of the United States; nor shall any State deprive any person of life, liberty, or property, without due process of law; nor deny to any person within its jurisdiction the equal protection of the laws."

1869

Congress passes the Judiciary Act of 1869, returning the number of Supreme Court justices to nine (where it has since remained) after it had expanded to ten in 1863 to allow President Lincoln to appoint new justices and then reduced down to eight in 1867 to stop President Johnson from selecting new justices. The Act also provides benefits to retiring federal judges who meet certain conditions, for the first time offering justices an incentive to step down from the bench.

1870

The Fifteenth Amendment—the final Civil War Amendment—is ratified, stating that the right to vote cannot be denied on the grounds of race, color, or previous condition of servitude.

1873

In its holding in the *Slaughterhouse Cases*, the Court rejects the argument that the explicit guarantees in the Bill of Rights are incorporated into the privileges and immunities of U.S. citizens that the Fourteenth Amendment prohibits states from abridging.

1883

The Court rules in the *Civil Rights Cases* that Congressional authority to enforce the Fourteenth Amendment is limited to regulating "state action" and does not extend to prohibiting private racial discrimination in public conveyances, hotels, theaters, restaurants, and other places of public accommodation.

1895

The decision in *Pollock v. Farmers' Loan and Trust Company* declares a direct federal income tax unconstitutional.

1896

The Court ruling in *Plessy v. Ferguson* establishes the "separate but equal" doctrine, providing support for Jim Crow laws and widespread racial segregation.

1897

The Court in *Chicago, Burlington & Quincy Railroad Company v. Chicago* holds that the Fifth Amendment requirement of just compensation for a government taking of property applies to states as well through the Fourteenth Amendment Due Process Clause.

1898

Williams v. Mississippi upholds literacy tests as a condition of voting.

1905

The Supreme Court hands down *Lochner v. New York*, finding unconstitutional a New York state law that imposed maximum works hours in a bakery. The ruling marks the beginning of the "Lochner Era," during which time the Supreme Court interprets the Fifth and Fourteenth Amendment Due Process Clause as protecting the "freedom of contract" and limiting government regulation of the economy.

1908

The "freedom of contract" upheld in *Lochner* is used in *Adair v. United States* to overturn federal legislation protecting labor union membership. In *Adair*, the Court declares unconstitutional a law that made it illegal for employees to be fired for being members of a labor union.

In *Muller v. Oregon*, the Court upholds a labor law that limits the number of hours women can work in laundries. Unlike other legislation the Court deems too restrictive of the "freedom of contract," in *Muller* the Court finds that it is within the state's power to give women special protection because their health, as mothers, is an object of the public interest.

1913

The Sixteenth Amendment is ratified, giving Congress the power to impose a federal income tax and effectively reversing *Pollock v. Farmers' Loan and Trust Company*, the 1895 Court decision that ruled a federal income tax unconstitutional.

The Seventeenth Amendment, providing for the direct election of U.S. senators, is ratified.

1914

Providing foundation for the "exclusionary rule," the Court in *Weeks v. United States* interprets the Fourth Amendment's guarantee against unreasonable search and seizure as requiring evidence obtained in violation of that guarantee to be excluded from federal trials.

1916

Louis Brandeis becomes the first Jewish justice to serve on the Supreme Court, nominated by President Woodrow Wilson and confirmed after contentious Senate hearings.

1918

Hammer v. Dagenhart invalidates a federal child labor law that had banned the interstate shipment of products made with child labor. Declaring the Keating-Owen Child Labor Act unconstitutional, the Court holds that Congressional authority to regulate interstate commerce does not extend to the regulation of production.

1919

The Eighteenth Amendment is added to the Constitution, banning the manufacture, sale, and transportation (but not consumption) of alcohol.

1920
Women win the right to vote with the ratification of the Nineteenth Amendment.

1921
Former president William Howard Taft becomes chief justice. No other U.S. president has served on the Court.

1923
Relying on *Lochner*'s freedom of contract, *Adkins v. Children's Hospital* invalidates federal minimum wage legislation for women.

1925
In *Gitlow v. New York*, the Court finds that the Fourteenth Amendment Due Process Clause "incorporates"—that is, requires states to respect— First Amendment guarantees of freedom of speech and press. *Gitlow* becomes a foundational precedent for future cases that incorporate or "nationalize" other fundamental rights and liberties contained in the Bill of Rights.

1927
The Court upholds forced sterilization of institutionalized women under Virginia's "Eugenical Sterilization Act" in *Buck v. Bell*.

1930
The Senate denies confirmation of John J. Parker, nominated to the Court by President Herbert Hoover.

1931
In *Near v. Minnesota*, the Court holds that the Fourteenth Amendment Due Process Clause requires states to guarantee First Amendment protections for freedom of the press and that prior restraint on the press—the prohibition of publication in advance—is unconstitutional.

1932
The Court holds in *Powell v. Alabama* that Fourteenth Amendment Due Process includes the right to be represented by counsel in death penalty cases.

1933
The adoption of the Twenty-first Amendment, which repeals the Eighteenth Amendment, marks the end of the Prohibition Era.

1935
In *Railroad Retirement Board v. Alton Railroad Co.*, the Court invalidates the Railroad Pension Act of 1934.

In *Schechter Poultry Corp. v. United States*, the Court rules the National Industrial Recovery Act unconstitutional.

1937

Following a series of Court rulings overturning key components of President Franklin Delano Roosevelt's New Deal legislation, the president counters with a plan to grow the size of the Supreme Court, pressing Congress to pass a law that would add up to six new justices (one for each sitting justice older than seventy). Though never enacted, the threat is credited with successfully pressuring the Court to uphold laws regulating the economy, called "the switch in time that saved nine." Several significant Court decisions follow, reversing earlier ones and increasing federal regulatory authority.

West Coast Hotel Co. v. Parrish affirms the constitutionality of a state minimum wage law for women and reverses the holding in *Adkins v. Children's Hospital*.

National Labor Relations Board v. Jones & Laughlin Steel Corp. upholds the National Labor Relations Act, affirming Congressional authority to regulate labor relations as part of its interstate commerce power.

1938

In *United States v. Carolene Products*, the Supreme Court upholds a federal regulation governing transport of skim milk in interstate commerce using a deferential level of scrutiny. But in the famous footnote four, the Court signals the possible future use of more exacting judicial scrutiny for legislation that restricts protections in the Bill of Rights and the Fourteenth Amendment or that involves prejudice against "discrete and insular minorities."

1942

The Court ruling in *Wickard v. Filburn* further extends Congressional authority to regulate the economy under its interstate commerce power, allowing a farmer to be penalized for overproduction of wheat even where the wheat was being used for the farmer's personal consumption.

1943

West Virginia State Board of Education v. Barnette rules that compelling public school students to salute and pledge allegiance to the flag violates First and Fourteenth Amendment freedom of speech guarantees.

1944

Smith v. Allwright holds all-white primaries unconstitutional.

In *Korematsu v. United States*, the Court upholds an executive order issued after the bombing of Pearl Harbor that led to the relocation and internment in camps of anyone of Japanese ancestry, including Japanese Americans.

1947

Everson v. Board of Education finds that the Fourteenth Amendment Due Process Clause requires states to respect First Amendment guarantees against government establishment of religion, but concludes that using public funds to reimburse parents for the cost of transportation to private schools, including religious schools, does not violate the Establishment Clause.

1949
In *Wolf v. Colorado*, the Court holds that the Fourth Amendment guarantee against unreasonable search and seizure applies to states through the Fourteenth Amendment Due Process Clause, but does not apply the exclusionary rule to states.

1951
Ratification of the Twenty-second Amendment limits the term of office a president can serve.

1952
Youngstown Sheet & Tube Co. v. Sawyer invalidates President Harry Truman's order that U.S. steel mills be seized and kept running, limiting the reach of executive authority even during time of war.

1953
Earl Warren, former California governor, becomes chief justice, beginning a tenure marked by a significant extension of constitutional protection for civil rights and civil liberties.

1954
The Court declares racial segregation in public school unconstitutional in *Brown v. Board of Education of Topeka* (*Brown I*), overturning *Plessy*'s "separate but equal doctrine" as it applies in public school education.

1955
The Court in *Brown II* outlines implementation guidelines for *Brown I*, mandating that desegregation proceed with "all deliberate speed."

1957
In the combined cases of *Roth v. United States* and *Alberts v. California*, the Court rules that obscenity is not protected speech under the First Amendment.

1961
In *Mapp v. Ohio*, the Court overturns *Wolf v. Colorado* finding that Fourth Amendment protection against unreasonable search and seizure, applicable to the states through the Fourteenth Amendment, requires states to abide by the exclusionary rule.

1962
In *Baker v. Carr*, the Court finds legislative redistricting questions to be justiciable—subject to Court review—and generates the test for distinguishing a justiciable legal question from a nonjusticiable "political question."

The Court declares in *Engel v. Vitale* that state-sponsored, non-denominational prayer in public school violates the First Amendment Establishment Clause.

1963

Gideon v. Wainwright establishes that the right to legal counsel in criminal cases protected by the Sixth Amendment applies to criminal defendants accused of felonies in state courts. Finding that the Fourteenth Amendment right to due process incorporates the Sixth Amendment's guarantee of counsel, the Court rules that state courts must provide legal counsel for defendants who cannot afford to hire their own.

1964

Ratification of the Twenty-fourth Amendment makes poll taxes illegal.

New York Times Co. v. Sullivan expands protection for freedom of the press, holding that evidence of "actual malice" is needed to prove a press statement has libeled or defamed a public figure. Actual malice requires showing "that the statement was made with knowledge of its falsity or with reckless disregard of whether it was true or false."

Reynolds v. Sims invalidates Alabama apportionment of state legislative districts on the grounds that it violates the Fourteenth Amendment Equal Protection Clause. The ruling holds that consistency with the principle of "one person, one vote" requires, where possible, that state legislative districts consist of roughly equal populations.

The Fifth Amendment right against self-incrimination is incorporated into the Fourteenth in *Malloy v. Hogan*, making the right applicable to states.

The Court further supports the expansion of civil rights and Congressional authority in *Heart of Atlanta Motel v. United States*, holding that under the Interstate Commerce Clause, Congress has authority to pass the Civil Rights Act of 1964, which prohibits race discrimination in public accommodations.

1965

The ruling in *Griswold v. Connecticut* declares constitutional protection for a general right to privacy, rejecting a Connecticut ban on birth control.

1966

South Carolina v. Katzenbach affirms the constitutionality of the Voting Rights Act of 1965 under Congressional authority to enforce the Fifteenth Amendment.

In *Miranda v. Arizona*, the Court rules that Fifth and Fourteenth Amendment protection against self-incrimination mandates that criminal suspects be notified of their rights prior to police interrogation.

1967

Ratification of the Twenty-fifth Amendment delineates the line of presidential succession in cases when the president is deemed "unable to discharge the powers and duties" of the office.

On equal protection and due process grounds, *Loving v. Virginia* strikes down a Virginia law that criminalizes interracial marriage.

Thurgood Marshall becomes the first African American to serve on the Supreme Court.

1968

Duncan v. Louisiana holds that for non-petty crimes and given due process protections of the Fourteenth Amendment, states must provide trial by jury as required by the Sixth Amendment.

After years of resistance to implementing *Brown*, the Court rules in *Green v. County School Board of New Kent County* that delays are no longer tolerable and orders school boards to act now to end school segregation.

United States v. O'Brien upholds a federal prohibition against the burning of military draft cards saying it does not violate First Amendment speech protections.

1969

Tinker v. Des Moines Independent Community School District affirms children's First Amendment speech rights in public schools, holding that wearing arm bands to express opposition to the Vietnam War is protected.

Justice Abe Fortas resigns under impeachment threat.

The Court incorporates Fifth Amendment double jeopardy rights into the Fourteenth Amendment, holding in *Benton v. Maryland* that states may not try someone twice for the same crime.

Warren Burger replaces Earl Warren as chief justice.

The Senate rejects President Richard Nixon's nomination of Clement Haynsworth to the Court.

1970

The Senate rejects President Nixon's nomination of G. Harrold Carswell to the bench.

Following the failed nominations of Haynsworth and Carswell, the Senate confirms President Nixon's appointment of Harry Blackmun to the Court with no dissenting votes.

1971

The Court rules in *New York Times Co. v. United States* against the Nixon administration's effort to prevent the publication of the leaked Pentagon

Papers, a Department of Defense study of U.S. involvement in the Vietnam War classified as "top secret." The Court holds that prevention of publication would constitute prior restraint of the press in violation of the First Amendment.

Ratification of the Twenty-sixth Amendment sets the voting age at eighteen, reduced from twenty-one.

The Court in *Reed v. Reed* for the first time finds a law that discriminates on the basis of gender unconstitutional.

1972

In *Furman v. Georgia*, the Court finds that the death penalty, as carried out in the states, violates the Eighth and Fourteenth Amendment prohibitions against cruel and unusual punishment. Most justices highlight evidence of the arbitrary and racially discriminatory manner of its imposition.

1973

Roe v. Wade holds that the Fourteenth Amendment guarantee of due process and the general right to privacy upheld in *Griswold* protect a women's right to choose abortion. Under the ruling, the state may not ban abortion in the first or second trimesters. Regulation to protect a woman's health is permitted beginning in the second trimester, and regulation to protect the potential life of the unborn is permitted in the third trimester but must include protections to preserve the life or health of the mother.

1974

Rebuffing claims of executive privilege, the Court orders in *United States v. Nixon* that the president obey a subpoena to produce tapes relating to the Watergate break-in and coverup.

President Nixon resigns as a result of Watergate.

1976

Gregg v. Georgia permits the use of capital punishment under certain conditions that limit discretion and require its careful and judicious use.

Craig v. Boren holds that laws discriminating on the basis of gender are subject to "intermediate scrutiny" under the Equal Protection Clause: constitutional only when they advance an important government objective and use means substantially related to achieving that objective.

1978

The Court rejects a voluntary race-based affirmative action plan that uses quotas in *Regents of the University of California v. Bakke*. However, the Court leaves open the possibility that institutions of higher education might use affirmative action to advance diversity if race is not the sole factor in admissions decisions.

1981

Sandra Day O'Connor, nominated by President Ronald Reagan, becomes the first woman to serve on the Court.

1983

On separation of power grounds, *INS v. Chadha* invalidates a Congressional statute allowing one house of Congress to veto an executive action.

1985

Wallace v. Jaffree invalidates under the Establishment Clause a state law mandating a moment of silence or voluntary prayer in public school.

1986

Bowers v. Hardwick holds that the right to privacy does not prohibit states from criminalizing consensual and private acts of homosexual sodomy.

After serving on the Court since 1972, William Rehnquist is confirmed as chief justice.

1987

President Ronald Reagan's nomination of Robert Bork to the Supreme Court is rejected by the Senate by a margin of 42–58.

Douglas Ginsburg, nominated by Reagan after Bork is rejected by the Senate, withdraws his name after his use of marijuana becomes public.

The Senate votes 97–0 to confirm Anthony Kennedy to the Court.

1988

In *Employment Division, Department of Human Resources of Oregon v. Smith*, the Court finds that First Amendment protection for free exercise of religion does not bar the incidental burden imposed on religion by a criminal law that is religiously neutral, generally applicable, and within the constitutional authority of government to enact.

1989

Texas v. Johnson finds flag burning to be protected symbolic speech under the First and Fourteenth Amendments.

1990

Cruzan v. Director, Missouri Department of Health holds that an individual's right to refuse medical treatment protected by the Fourteenth Amendment does not extend to an individual's parents seeking to act on behalf of their children.

1992

Following contentious confirmation hearings around sexual harassment allegations, the Senate confirms Clarence Thomas to the Court by a 52–48 margin.

Planned Parenthood of Southeastern PA v. Casey reaffirms the "central holding of *Roe*" that the Constitution protects a woman's right to abortion, but modifies the conditions under which states can regulate abortion. The modifications allow states to regulate abortion throughout pregnancy on behalf of the woman's health and to protect the state's interest in the potential life of the unborn, as long as the regulations do not impose "an undue burden" on women.

1995

United States v. Lopez invalidates federal legislation restricting firearm possession in school zones on the grounds that the regulation exceeds Congressional interstate commerce authority.

1996

United States v. Virginia invalidates the exclusion of women from Virginia Military Institute, an all-male undergraduate military academy, and finds the state's creation of an alternative women's-only military school to violate equal protection.

1997

The ruling in *Clinton v. Jones* finds the Constitution does not give a sitting president immunity from civil litigation.

1998

Clinton v. City of New York declares unconstitutional the Line Item Veto Act. Under the Act, the president would be allowed to veto specific line items in budget bills rather than requiring that a presidential veto apply to the entire bill.

2000

The controversial Court ruling in *Bush v. Gore* determines the outcome of the 2000 presidential election. The Court finds the ongoing recount of contested ballots in Florida unconstitutional and, by a 5–4 margin, rules that the limited remaining time foreclosed the possibility of a constitutional recount.

United States v. Morrison invalidates the Violence Against Women Act on the grounds that the law exceeds Congressional interstate commerce authority.

2002

Atkins v. Virginia declares that capital punishment for mentally disabled defendants constitutes cruel and unusual punishment in violation of the Eighth and Fourteenth Amendments.

2003

Lawrence v. Texas overturns *Bowers v. Hardwick*, finding that constitutional protections for privacy and due process extend to decisions by same-sex couples to engage in private, consensual sexual activity.

Gratz v. Bollinger invalidates the race-based affirmative action used in undergraduate admissions at the University of Michigan because it awards an automatic number of extra points to all minority applicants, effectively assuring admission.

Grutter v. Bollinger upholds the race-based affirmative action used in admissions for the University of Michigan Law School. The Court holds that seeking diversity in higher education is a compelling government interest and that, unlike the automatic points awarded in undergraduate admissions, the Michigan Law School gives individualized consideration to each applicant to determine how they might contribute to diversity.

2004

A plurality of the Court in *Hamdi v. Rumsfeld* rules that Fifth Amendment due process rights extend some protections for U.S. citizens held as "enemy combatants," including the right not be held indefinitely without charge and the right to challenge the detention in front of a neutral decision maker.

2005

Roper v. Simmons concludes that capital punishment for defendants who committed crimes under the age of eighteen violates the Eighth Amendment prohibition against cruel and unusual punishment.

Kelo v. New London holds that the Fifth Amendment does not prohibit government seeking to improve a city's economy from taking private property with just compensation in order sell that for private development.

After the death of Chief Justice William Rehnquist, President George W. Bush appoints John Roberts as chief justice.

2006

Hamdan v. Rumsfeld rules that the trial of Osama bin Laden's former chauffeur, who was captured and held as a terrorist suspect, is illegal, in part because Salim Ahmed Hamdan was tried before a military commission not specifically authorized by any act of Congress.

2008

District of Columbia v. Heller holds that the Second Amendment protects a personal, individual right to keep and bear arms.

2009

Sonya Sotomayor, nominated by President Barack Obama, becomes the first Latina justice to serve on the Court.

2010

Citizens United v. Federal Election Commission extends certain First Amendment freedom of speech protections to corporations, including labor unions, holding that corporate and union funding of independent political broadcasts or advertising in candidate elections cannot be restricted.

McDonald v. The City of Chicago extends the holding in *District of Columbia v. Heller* by finding that states must respect Second Amendment rights.

2012

The Court upholds most provisions of the Affordable Care Act in *National Federation of Independent Business v. Sibelius*, including an individual mandate requiring most Americans to have health insurance, which the Court affirms under Congress's authority to tax. The Court invalidates a provision penalizing states that refused to expand Medicaid programs.

2013

In a victory for advocates of marriage equality, *United States v. Windsor* declares unconstitutional Section 3 of the 1996 Defense of Marriage Act. Section 3, which defined marriage as a union between a man and a woman, effectively withheld the federal benefits and regulations associated with marriage from same-sex marriages.

Shelby County v. Holder declares unconstitutional a key portion of the Voting Rights Act. In particular, the Court invalidates the formula for determining which states must receive Justice Department or a federal court clearance prior to modifying voting procedures.

2015

Obergefell v. Hodges recognizes the constitutional right of same-sex couples to marry.

2016

Senate Majority Leader Mitch McConnell declares that the Senate will not hold confirmation hearings for anyone President Barack Obama might nominate to fill the opening on the Supreme Court created by Justice Antonin Scalia's death. McConnell holds to his promise, and Merrick Garland, appointed by Obama, never receives a Senate hearing, leaving the seat available for the next president.

2017

President Donald Trump nominates Neil Gorsuch to the seat that had been filled by Justice Scalia. In order to ensure Gorsuch's confirmation, the Senate votes to end the availability of the filibuster for Supreme Court candidates. Gorsuch wins confirmation on April 7 by a 54–45 margin.

2018

The Court upholds President Trump's travel ban on those coming to the U.S. from countries that are predominantly Muslim in *Trump v. Hawaii*.

Brett Kavanaugh, nominated to replace retiring Justice Anthony Kennedy, is confirmed after contentious hearings that include allegations of sexual misconduct.

2019
Rucho v. Common Cause uses the political questions doctrine to conclude that the judiciary is not the appropriate body to resolve complaints about partisan gerrymandering.

1

Judicial Review

"It is emphatically the province and duty of the Judicial Department to say what the law is."
          —Chief Justice John Marshall, *Marbury v. Madison*

"[J]udicial review is a deviant institution in the American democracy."
          —Alexander Bickel, *The Least Dangerous Branch*

In 1788, when Alexander Hamilton characterized the judiciary as the "least dangerous" branch of the federal government, he emphasized the structural limits on the courts, especially its lack of enforcement power. At the same time, though, Hamilton identified what the Constitution did not explicitly enumerate and what has become the bedrock of Supreme Court authority: the power to decide whether the laws and actions of other government bodies violate the Constitution. This chapter traces the origins, development, critiques, and defenses of judicial review, a power that one commentator has characterized as transforming the "least dangerous branch of American government" into "the most extraordinarily powerful court of law the world has ever known" (Bickel 1962, 1).

THE EARLY ORIGINS OF JUDICIAL REVIEW

In defending the idea that the judicial branch has the authority to declare invalid those legislative acts that conflict with the Constitution,

Hamilton argued in The Federalist Papers that it is the "peculiar province" of the courts to interpret the law and, therefore, to interpret the Constitution. It is the courts of justice, Hamilton (2009) urged, "whose duty it must be to declare all acts contrary to the manifest tenor of the Constitution void. Without this, all the reservations of particular rights or privileges would amount to nothing" (393). Moreover, rebuffing the claim that vesting the Supreme Court with judicial review upends the balance of power by making the judiciary the superior branch, Hamilton insisted that it is the power of the people that is superior. "[W]here the will of the legislature, declared in its statutes, stands in opposition to that of the people, declared in the Constitution, the judges ought to be governed by the latter rather than the former. They ought to regulate their decisions by the fundamental laws, rather than by those which are not fundamental" (394).

In making this case, Hamilton was not fabricating a novel power. Prior to the Constitutional Convention, many state courts exercised this power in reviewing state legislative acts in light of their own constitutions and charters. In addition, discussion of this power at the Constitutional Convention suggests both knowledge of and support for it. "[T]he number of delegates who spoke favorably of judicial review indicates that it largely had become an accepted product of a written constitution with a separation of powers. Fifteen delegates from nine of the twelve states that sent delegates spoke about judicial review of federal legislation in almost two dozen different instances" (Prakash and Yoo 2003, 952).

After the Constitution was ratified, judicial review was exercised in a number of instances, both by state and federal judiciaries. But it was in 1803, when the Supreme Court handed down its decision in *Marbury v. Madison*, that the authority of the federal courts to exercise judicial review took root.

MARBURY V. MADISON AND ITS AFTERMATH

The landmark precedent on which judicial review is grounded emerged out of the presidential election of 1800. Thomas Jefferson, a Republican and staunch supporter of states' rights, defeated President John Adams, a Federalist who favored strengthening the central government. Just prior to departing office, the Federalist-dominated Congress passed a law that enlarged the federal bench by creating forty-two new judicial positions. In an effort to preserve some Federalist power in the wake of its electoral defeat, Adams appointed, and the lame-duck Senate confirmed, Federalists to these positions. William Marbury, whom Adams nominated as Justice of the Peace for the District of Columbia, was among these "Midnight Judges," so called because Adams is said to have finalized the signing and sealing of the commissions the night before his term of office ended. But Marbury and some others did not receive the signed commissions authorizing their appointments. Upon assuming office, President Jefferson, outraged by these last-minute political maneuvers, refused to order his secretary of state to convey the undelivered commissions. William Marbury sued Secretary of State James Madison, asking the Supreme Court to order the delivery of his commission.

Chief Justice John Marshall took the opportunity presented in the case of *Marbury v. Madison* to establish the Court's authority to review the Constitution. Marbury's petition to the Supreme Court sought a writ of mandamus (i.e., an order from the Court) commanding the delivery of the commission. Writing the unanimous opinion for the Court, Chief Justice Marshall argued that Marbury had a right to the commission because it had been signed and sealed by President Adams. However, the Court declined to order that the commission be delivered. Marshall argued that the Court did not have the authority to issue writs of mandamus, even though Section 13 of the Judiciary Act of 1789 explicitly delegated that authority to the Court. According to Marshall, Section 13 of the Act was inconsistent with the provisions of Article III of the Constitution. As Marshall construed it, issuing a writ of mandamus is an act of original jurisdiction (the authority to hear a case in its first hearing, rather than on appeal from a lower court), but the Constitution grants the Supreme Court original jurisdiction in only a handful of cases that do not include writs of mandamus.

But Marshall went further than simply declining to issue the writ of mandamus sought by Marbury. Finding that the language of the Judiciary Act conflicted with the delegation of authority in the Constitution, Marshall concluded that an act of Congress "repugnant" to the Constitution cannot stand: "Certainly all those who have framed written Constitutions contemplate them as forming the fundamental and paramount law of the nation, and consequently the theory of every such government must be that an act of the Legislature repugnant to the Constitution is void. This theory is essentially attached to a written Constitution, and is consequently to be considered by this Court as one of the fundamental principles of our society" (*Marbury v. Madison* 1803, 177).

In ruling this way, Marshall plainly echoed the line of reasoning offered by Hamilton in the Federalist Papers. As Marshall asserted, "It is emphatically the province and duty of the Judicial Department to say what the law is. Those who apply the rule to particular cases must, of necessity, expound and interpret that rule. If two laws conflict with each other, the Courts must decide on the operation of each" (137).

Declaring that it is the province of the courts to exercise judicial review and finding Section 13 of the 1789 Judiciary Act unconstitutional, Marshall took hold of the authority that would define the Supreme Court. Quite notably, he did so in a way that acknowledged Marbury's right to the commission but did not seek to compel the new Jefferson administration to honor that right. Knowing that Jefferson and Madison may well have defied an order from the Supreme Court, Marshall avoided issuing one. In so doing, he sidestepped a likely confrontation between the Supreme Court and the president that the latter would probably win.

The Marshall Court did not wield the power of judicial review to routinely declare acts of Congress unconstitutional. To the contrary, during Marshall's tenure as chief justice, the Court did not declare any other federal legislation unconstitutional. The Court did, however, use the power of judicial review to affirm the constitutionality of laws passed by Congress. It is one of the important, albeit underplayed, characteristics of judicial review that its exercise often functions to *confirm* the constitutionality of legislation in the face of legal challenges. Marshall used this function in a way that advanced his Federalist vision. In *McCulloch v. Maryland* (1819), for example, the Marshall Court upheld the constitutionality of Congress's decision to charter the Second Bank of the United States.

At the same time, the Marshall Court expanded the reach of judicial review and, in turn, the authority of the federal judiciary. Importantly, the Court exercised this power in several cases in which it reviewed whether state laws and state court rulings interfered with the Constitution. For example, in *Fletcher v. Peck* (1810) the Supreme Court first extended the reach of judicial review to rule a state law unconstitutional. In *Martin v. Hunter's Lessee* (1816), the Supreme Court held that it has authority over state courts when it comes to interpreting the Constitution, federal laws, and federal treaties. In the *Martin* case, the Virginia State Supreme Court argued that its own ruling upholding a Virginia state law against a federal treaty could not be reviewed by the U.S. Supreme Court. Virginia contended that allowing the U.S. Supreme Court to review a state supreme court ruling would interfere with state sovereignty—the authority of states to govern themselves. But the high Court rejected this argument in a unanimous opinion written by Justice Joseph Story. The Supremacy Clause of the U.S. Constitution, Story argued, makes federal law "the supreme law of the land," and when state court interpretations of federal law conflict with U.S. Supreme Court interpretations, the latter prevails.

The foundation set during the Marshall era made the Supreme Court the institution that exercises the final authority to review whether actions of governmental officials are consistent with the Constitution. While the Supreme Court did not rule another act of Congress unconstitutional until the Taney Court's decision in *Dred Scott v. Sandford* (1857), later Courts have had more opportunity (and, in some cases, proclivity) to find federal legislation unconstitutional. In just over a two-hundred-year period, from

Marbury v. Madison to 2013, the Supreme Court overturned 186 acts of Congress (O'Brien 2014, 30). In addition, and over that same period, the Court overturned 990 state laws and 119 municipal ordinances (O'Brien 2014, 30).

THE DEBATE OVER JUDICIAL REVIEW

Whether in response to *Marbury v. Madison, McCulloch v. Maryland, Martin v. Hunter's Lessee,* or any of a multitude of cases handed down by Supreme Courts since the time of Marshall's tenure, controversy over the fact of judicial review has continued. There is, perhaps, no better indicator of this than when the Supreme Court finds it necessary to reiterate its authority to exercise the power and to demand that its rulings be followed.

Consider, for example, the Supreme Court's 1958 opinion in *Cooper v. Aaron,* a ruling announced four years after the landmark Supreme Court declaration in *Brown v. Board of Education of Topeka* (1954) that segregation based on race in public schools violates the Constitution. Resistance to desegregating public schools in the wake of *Brown* was rampant and often led by state governors, legislators, and other public officials. In one such incident, efforts to desegregate the all-white Central High School in Little Rock, Arkansas, led to rioting and violence after Arkansas Governor Orval Faubus ordered his state's National Guard to prevent integration. That act of defiance and ensuing disorder ultimately led President Dwight D. Eisenhower to send a thousand U.S. Army paratroopers to assist with the Little Rock School Board's plan to integrate the high school. When the school board later asked the Supreme Court to permit delay of its desegregation plans in the face of the unrest, the Court refused to do so. In its unanimous decision in *Cooper v. Aaron,* the Court insisted that its authority to review the Constitution must be respected.

Noting that the case "necessarily involves a claim by the Governor and Legislature of a State that there is no duty on state officials to obey federal court orders resting on this Court's considered interpretation of the United States Constitution" (*Cooper v. Aaron* 1958, 4), the Court issued a sharp rebuke to state officials. Defending its authority, the Court said, "It is necessary only to recall some basic constitutional propositions which are settled doctrine" (17), including the Supremacy Clause of the Constitution and John Marshall's holding in *Marbury v. Madison*. "This decision declared the basic principle that the federal judiciary is supreme in the exposition of the law of the Constitution, and that principle has ever since been respected by this Court and the Country as a permanent and indispensable feature of our constitutional system. It follows that the interpretation of the Fourteenth Amendment enunciated by this Court in the *Brown* case is the supreme law of the land, and Art. VI of the Constitution makes it of binding effect on the States 'any Thing in the Constitution or Laws of any State to the Contrary notwithstanding'" (18).

Through their opinion in *Cooper v. Aaron*, the justices scolded those public officials who defied the Court by refusing to implement the *Brown* ruling. "No state legislator or executive or judicial officer can war against the Constitution without violating his undertaking to support it. Chief Justice Marshall spoke for a unanimous Court in saying that: 'If the legislatures of the several states may at will, annul the judgments of the courts of the United States, and destroy the rights acquired under those judgments, the constitution itself becomes a solemn mockery'" (18).

When the Supreme Court uses *Marbury v. Madison* in the reproachful way it did in *Cooper v. Aaron*, that typically signals an institution on the defensive. The Court *was* on the defensive in the years after *Brown*, with Southern officials questioning and attacking the asserted authority of judicial review. Still, while debate over and disagreement with Supreme Court decisions are commonplace, there is also widespread acceptance that the power to review the constitutionality of laws and government actions properly rests with the judiciary and, ultimately, the Supreme Court. The doctrines laid out in *Marbury v. Madison* and its early progeny extending federal judicial review to state laws and state court decisions have, as legal scholar Alexander Bickel wrote in 1962, long held sway: "So long have they been among the realities of our national existence. Settled expectations have formed around them. The life of a nation that now encompasses 185 million people spread over a continent and more depends upon them in a hundred different aspects of its organization and coherence" (Bickel 1962, 14).

Judicial review is, in short, both accepted and resisted, both defended and critiqued. Why, even after over two hundred years of use by the Court and while considered "settled doctrine," does it remain the subject of controversy and debate?

CRITIQUES OF JUDICIAL REVIEW

There are a number of reasons why judicial review has been the target of continued criticism. Some argue that if the Framers of the U.S. Constitution intended to authorize the federal judiciary to have overriding power to review the constitutionality of laws and actions of federal and state officials, that power would have been explicitly delineated in the Constitution. On this view, the Constitution's silence speaks volumes. Others argue, as noted earlier, that the power of judicial review in the hands of the Supreme

Court gives the institution too much power over the legislative and executive branches and infringes on state sovereignty. Still other detractors caution that the exercise of judicial review transforms the Court into a policy-making body and a "super-legislature."

One of the most common criticisms of judicial review that has preoccupied legal analysis, public commentary, political discourse, and judicial opinions takes the form expressed by Alexander Bickel in his influential book *The Least Dangerous Branch*. Bickel described judicial review as a deviant institution (Bickel 1962, 18). "The root difficulty," Bickel explained, "is that judicial review is a counter-majoritarian force in our system" (16). Supreme Court justices are appointed, rather than elected, and can hold their positions for life, unless removed from the bench by the uncommon and challenging process of impeachment. This means that the institution wielding the power of judicial review is insulated from the electoral accountability that voters hold over other governing officials, such as presidents, governors, and federal and state legislators. In other words, voters can boot elected officials from office when their terms end but cannot do the same to federal judges. Thus, according to Bickel, "when the Supreme Court declares unconstitutional a legislative act or the action of an elected executive, it thwarts the will of representatives of the actual people of the here and now; it exercises control, not in behalf of the prevailing majority, but against it. . . . [I]t is the reason the charge can be made that judicial review is undemocratic" (16–17).

Those who critique judicial review in this way often call on the Supreme Court to exercise "judicial restraint" when hearing cases. In other words, the Supreme Court should generally presume that legislation and the actions of elected officials are constitutional unless they plainly are not. Such restraint does not require the jettisoning of judicial review but suggests its limited use.

This critique of judicial review, coupled with advocacy of judicial restraint, is often voiced by the justices themselves. Such an example can be found in Chief Justice John Roberts' dissenting opinion in *Obergefell v. Hodges*, the 2015 Court ruling that found it unconstitutional to deny same-sex couples the right to marry. Roberts lamented the majority ruling in the case, criticizing what he characterized as the Court's lack of restraint and its willingness to interrupt democratic processes. By deciding the meaning of marriage, Roberts protested, "the Court removes it from the realm of democratic decision. There will be consequences to shutting down the political process on an issue of such profound public significance" (*Obergefell v. Hodges* 2015, 2625). Roberts also asserted that "[t]hose who founded our country would not recognize the majority's conception of the judicial role. They after all risked their lives and fortunes for the precious right to govern themselves. They would never have imagined yielding that right on a question of social policy to unaccountable and unelected judges" (2624).

DEFENSES OF JUDICIAL REVIEW

Others have defended judicial review against its critics. In response to the fact that the Constitution does not explicitly authorize the federal courts to exercise judicial review, some have argued—as Chief Justice John Marshall did—that the grant is implicit in Article III and the Supremacy Clause. Supporters also cite evidence that delegates to the Constitutional Convention discussed, largely favored, and expected federal exercise of judicial review. Responding to the concern that judicial review in the hands of the federal judiciary disturbs the balance of powers and undermines state sovereignty, defenders argue that the Supreme Court is constrained by several important checks. Perhaps most significant, the appointment and confirmation processes give the president and the Senate, respectively, a direct voice in who serves on the federal bench, and, through their elected officials, the public retains indirect voice. The constitutional amendment process also provides a check on the Court. If the Court interprets a provision of the Constitution in a manner that runs contrary to what the people want, changing the Constitution through the amendment process is an option (although a challenging one to execute).

While many have echoed the counter-majoritarian criticism of judicial review, others downplay or dismiss this worry. They emphasize that the selection of judges is consistent with the principles of representative democracy because elected officials choose those who serve on the federal bench. Others note that the lack of direct election of federal judges is not unique in the U.S. system; plenty of governing officials who have significant influence are unelected, including vast swaths of the federal bureaucracy.

Relatedly, some argue that judicial review is far from a "deviant" institution in the U.S. system of governing. As constitutional law professor Erwin Chemerinsky explains, the United States is a constitutional democracy, intentionally designed in an anti-majoritarian way. "Indeed, so much of the Constitution was inherently anti-majoritarian. The President is chosen by the Electoral College, not the popular vote. The members of the Senate were chosen by state legislators. Supreme Court Justices and federal judges are chosen by the President and confirmed by the Senate. Of the four institutions of the federal government, only one, the House of Representatives, was elected by the people" (Chemerinsky 2012). Chemerinsky goes further, urging that "[i]t is time to accept that the Constitution is anti-majoritarian and that, of course, judicial review to enforce it also will be counter-majoritarian and that is a good thing" (Chemerinsky 2012).

Chemerinsky is not alone in harboring this viewpoint. But how in a democracy—whether a representative or constitutional one—can such anti-majoritarianism be good? If the value of democracy resides in self-governing rule by the people, shouldn't governing institutions generally reflect and respect majority rule? And if judicial review in the hands of an unelected and unaccountable institution like the Supreme Court undermines democracy, shouldn't that counter-majoritarian difficulty, as Bickel called it, be remedied?

The response to these questions offered by many defenders of the current system goes like this: if democracy is defined by and run simply according to majority rule, it risks falling victim to "tyranny of the majority." Famously discussed by John Stuart Mill in his 1859 book *On Liberty*, tyranny of the majority occurs when governance by majority vote becomes oppressive of minorities or individuals. The will of the people, Mill wrote, "practically means the will of the most numerous or the most active *part* of the people—the majority, or those who succeed in making themselves accepted as the majority; the people, consequently, *may* desire to oppress a part of their number, and precautions are as much needed against this as against any other abuse of power" (Mill 1985, 62). One way to protect against majority tyranny is to set forth, in a manner that cannot be easily undermined by a simple majority vote, certain fundamental principles and rights that protect all persons in the polity.

The Constitution, including the liberties and rights encapsulated therein, can be seen as serving this function. While the Constitution can be amended, it takes super-majorities to do so (requiring support from two-thirds of both houses of Congress and three-fourths of the states); a simple majority is not enough. And, according to this view, what better institution is there to interpret the enduring principles of the Constitution than one that is insulated from simple majority rule? A judiciary composed of judges who do not have to worry about reelection can, the argument goes, best uphold the fundamental values and rights embodied in the document.

Hamilton made this point in Federalist Paper No. 78. He not only defended judicial review and the establishment of a federal judiciary, but also the appointment of judges with lifetime tenure: "This independence of the judges is equally requisite to guard the Constitution and the rights of individuals from the effects of those ill humors, which the arts of designing men, or the influence of particular conjunctures, sometimes disseminate among the people themselves, and which, though they speedily give place to better information, and more deliberate reflection, have a tendency, in the meantime, to occasion dangerous innovations in the government, and serious oppressions of the minor party in the community" (Hamilton 2009, 395).

Even Bickel, who expressed concern about the counter-majoritarian difficulty, put forward a similar point in defending judicial review. Distinguishing between the immediate and pressing needs of governance on the one hand and maintaining longer-term principles on the other hand, Bickel suggested that elected institutions are better suited to the former. An independent judiciary, by contrast, is best suited to upholding the enduring values and principled rules embodied in the Constitution.

CONCLUSION

Debates about judicial review will surely continue. But it is indisputable that long-standing precedent recognizes the authority of the Supreme Court to exercise it. It is also the case that were it to be otherwise, the U.S. system of governance would be quite different.

Even though it is perfectly plain that precedent recognizes this power, the following question remains: how and by what means should the Court exercise that authority? It is to this question that Chapter 2 turns.

2

Constitutional Interpretation

"Because judicial power resides in the authority to give meaning to the Constitution, the debate is really a debate about how to read the text, about constraints on what is legitimate interpretation."
—Supreme Court Justice William Brennan, "The Constitution of the United States: Contemporary Ratification"

Article I, Section 3, of the Constitution states, "No Person shall be a Senator who shall not have attained to the Age of thirty Years, and been nine Years a Citizen of the United States, and who shall not, when elected, be an Inhabitant of that State for which he shall be chosen." At first glance, the minimum age requirement established in this clause appears to be perfectly clear. It seems plain that to be a member of the Senate one must be at least thirty years old. But how clear is this? Should we interpret the age requirement as holding that to be a senator, one must have reached the age of thirty by the moment one takes the oath of office? Or does this eligibility requirement mean that a candidate must have reached the age of thirty by election day? And how should we interpret this language alongside other stipulations in the Constitution? For example, Article I, Section 5, states, "Each House shall be the Judge of the Elections, Returns and Qualifications of its own Members." Does this permit the Senate to increase the minimum age above thirty years? Alternatively, could a state set the minimum age for its senators to something above thirty or establish a maximum age requirement?

11

Interpreting the Constitution becomes more complicated when the provisions include open-ended terms and indefinite concepts. Consider, for example, whether an alcohol sobriety checkpoint that briefly stops all drivers going through it violates the language of the Fourth Amendment: "The right of the people to be secure in their persons, houses, papers, and effects, against unreasonable searches and seizures, shall not be violated, and no Warrants shall issue, but upon probable cause, supported by Oath or affirmation, and particularly describing the place to be searched, and the persons or things to be seized." Under the language of Fourth Amendment, does a person have a right to be secure in their vehicle? Does a very brief stop by police at such a sobriety checkpoint count as a seizure? Is a breathalyzer test a search? Does a police officer need a warrant in order to demand that a driver submit to a breathalyzer? And what counts as unreasonable?

Just as there is no universally agreed-upon answer to the question of what constitutes an "unreasonable search or seizure," there is also no agreed-upon answer to the question of *how* judges should go about interpreting these words. For that matter, there is no consensus about how judges should go about interpreting *any* provision in the Constitution.

While there is little agreement over the legal theory—or jurisprudence—that should guide constitutional interpretation, there are multiple methods that judges have adopted in their efforts to decide what the Constitution means. Some of these jurisprudential approaches have found more favor than others. This chapter outlines some of the main methods of constitutional interpretation.

METHODS OF INTERPRETATION

The varying methods of constitutional interpretation discussed in the following sections are not exhaustive. One account of the multiple approaches to determining constitutional meaning identifies fourteen different methods (Reid 2016). Moreover, though some of the methods described here are mutually exclusive, others are not. For example, most originalists generally oppose interpreting the Constitution as a living or aspirational document. But a living originalist finds value in both approaches. It is worth emphasizing that while the methods discussed here are distinguishable, they sometimes overlap. For example, Justice Antonin Scalia described himself as a textualist first—bound by the words of the Constitution not the intent behind those words—and an originalist second—interpreting the constitutional text based on its original meaning. This contrasts with other textualists who take themselves to be bound by the constitutional text but who interpret those words in light of their present-day meaning.

It is also worth emphasizing that the methods discussed here are methods of *constitutional* interpretation. Judicial bodies also engage in what is called *statutory* interpretation. Because legislative statutes, like the Constitution, may include language that is opaque or subject to multiple interpretations, the "exercise of the judicial power of the United States often requires that courts construe statutes so enacted to apply them in concrete cases and controversies" (Eig 2014, 1). For example, in 2019 the Supreme Court agreed to hear three cases addressing whether the Civil Rights Act of 1964—a federal statute—prohibits discrimination in employment based on sexual orientation and transgender status. Title VII of the 1964 statute, which bans workplace discrimination based on race, color, national origin, and religion, also bans employment discrimination based on "sex." Whether a bar on sex discrimination also includes a ban on discrimination against those who are gay or transgender is the question before the Court in these cases, and that question is one that involves construing the meaning of Title VII (see *Bostock v. Clayton County, Ga., Altitude Express Inc. v. Zarda*, and *R.G. & G.R. Harris Funeral Homes Inc. v. Equal Employment Opportunity Commission*). The Court's ultimate interpretation of the "meaning" of Title VII in these cases may have major legal repercussions for members of the LGBTQ community and the American workplace.

Some approaches to statutory interpretation overlap with methods of constitutional interpretation outlined in this chapter. Those include approaches that give primacy to the importance of the text and structure of the statute and that take legislative history and intent into consideration. But statutory interpretation is distinct from constitutional interpretation and should not be conflated or confused with it.[1]

The methods of constitutional interpretation explained here include (a) stare decisis, (b) originalism, (c) textualism, (d) pragmatism, (e) structuralism, (f) moral arguments, and (g) tradition and history. Keep in mind that while some judges align primarily with one or two approaches to interpretation, court opinions often present a variety of argument types. As constitutional law scholar Philip Bobbitt put it,

> If you were to take a set of colored pencils, assign a separate color to each of the kinds of arguments, and mark through passages in an opinion of the Supreme Court deciding a constitutional matter, you would probably have a multi-colored picture when you finished. Judges are the artists of our field, just as law professors are its critics, and we expect the creative judge to employ all the tools that are appropriate, often in combination, to achieve a satisfying result. Furthermore, in a multi-membered panel whose members may prefer different constitutional approaches, the negotiated document that wins a majority may, naturally, reflect many hues rather than a single bright splash one observes in dissents. (Bobbitt 1984, 93–94)

Let the Decision Stand: Stare Decisis

Legal precedent is composed of the principles and rules set down by previous court decisions. The doctrine of stare decisis holds that judges should, as a rule, take themselves to be bound by relevant precedent. Interpreting the Constitution based on stare decisis—an approach sometimes referred to as doctrinalism—requires judges to reason by analogy from previous precedent.

Respect for precedent—a basic tenet of a common law legal system like the United States—is described as both just and pragmatic by its supporters. The practice of establishing precedent and expecting lower and future courts to follow precedent is said to be just because it affords consistency and predictability to judicial decision making. It is also said to be pragmatic because it reduces the need to continually relitigate similar cases.

The doctrine of stare decisis does not mean that all courts must follow the rules set down by all other courts. Jurisdiction matters in determining the reach and application of stare decisis, as does the relationship between higher (or "superior") courts and lower (or "inferior") courts. The judicial structure in the United States and the individual states is hierarchical, with trial courts situated below midlevel appeals courts, and a high court serving as the supreme court above both trial and intermediate appellate courts. Legal precedent established by the high court is taken to bind the inferior trial and intermediate appeals courts within the particular jurisdiction. Thus, for example, a precedent established by the Supreme Court of Vermont must be followed by trial and appeals courts in Vermont, but not by courts in other state jurisdictions or under federal jurisdiction, over which Vermont has no authority. However, given the federal structure of the United States and the Constitution's Supremacy Clause, a precedent established by the U.S. Supreme Court must be followed by trial and appeals courts at both the state and federal levels.

In contrast with the vertical application of precedent that governs the relationship between superior and inferior courts, there is also a horizontal application of precedent across the same court from past to present. It is this type of precedent that is said to apply, albeit with less force, to the U.S. Supreme Court. As the highest court in the nation, the Supreme Court is not bound to follow the legal rules created in the lower federal courts or in state courts. But according to the doctrine of stare decisis, Supreme Court justices are generally supposed to adhere to the precedents established by previous U.S. Supreme Courts.

Because stare decisis is widely regarded as "a bedrock principle of the rule of law" (Stone 2008, 1537), appeal to precedent is a common method of constitutional interpretation, and it is relatively unusual for the Supreme Court to *directly* overturn its earlier decisions. That said, direct reversals of precedent do happen, and while justices routinely extol the importance of adhering to precedent, they also say that it is not an "inexorable command." Consider *Payne v. Tennessee* (1991), a case that overturned two earlier precedents interpreting the Eighth Amendment's prohibition against cruel and unusual punishment. Writing for the majority, Chief Justice William Rehnquist grounds the Court's rationale for overturning precedent by citing precedents that allow it!

> Adhering to precedent "is usually the wise policy, because, in most matters, it is more important that the applicable rule of law be settled than it be settled right." *Burnet v. Coronado Oil & Gas Co.* (1932) (Brandeis, J., dissenting). Nevertheless, when governing decisions are unworkable or are badly reasoned, "this Court has never felt constrained to follow precedent." *Smith v. Allwright* (1944). *Stare decisis* is not an inexorable command; rather, it "is a principle of policy and not a mechanical formula of adherence to the latest decision." *Helvering v. Hallock* (1940). This is particularly true in constitutional cases, because in such cases "correction through legislative action is practically impossible." *Burnet v. Coronado Oil & Gas Co.* (Brandeis, J., dissenting). (*Payne v. Tennessee* 1991, 827–28, internal citations omitted)

Departures from precedent do not require direct reversals. As political scientists Lee Epstein and Thomas G. Walker explain, while explicit reversals are departures from precedent, "they are not only or even the usual method for extinguishing 'unloved precedents.' The Court also can question, limit, criticize, or otherwise distinguish the unloved precedent—and, in fact, does so in nearly 30 percent of its cases" (Epstein and Walker 2018, 28).

There is, furthermore, considerable debate as to what particular precedents actually establish. If, as discussed earlier, the language of the Constitution is indeterminate and subject to interpretation, the same is true of precedent. And whether a prior court ruling and principle should be taken to apply to a new context can often be a matter of contentious debate and disagreement.

In short, appealing to previous precedent and using prior rules as guideposts are at the heart of how justices interpret the Constitution. But if prior rulings were completely predictive of future court rulings, there would either be routinely unanimous rulings or little need for judges to continue the work of interpreting the Constitution.

Originalism

An historical or "originalist" approach advocates interpreting the Constitution based on its meaning, understanding, or intent at the time its provisions were originally ratified. As Justice Antonin Scalia, perhaps the most prominent proponent of originalism, put it, "the Constitution that I interpret and apply is not living but dead—or, as I prefer to put it, enduring. It means today not what current society (much less the Court) thinks it ought to mean, but what it meant when it was adopted" (Scalia 2002). Or as Thomas Jefferson described it, "on every question of construction, carry ourselves back to the time when the Constitution was adopted, recollect the spirit manifested in the debates, and instead of trying what meaning may be squeezed out of the text, or invented against it, conform to the probable one in which it was past" (Jefferson 1823).

Different brands of originalism offer varying methods for this type of interpretive time travel. One main variant underscores the original *intent* of the Framers, while another focuses on the original *meaning* of the words set down in the text.

Judge Robert Bork, one of the pioneers of originalist jurisprudence, pressed the original intent position by arguing that "the only legitimate basis for constitutional decision" is one in which judges are "bound by the original intentions of those who framed, proposed, and ratified the Constitution" (Bork 1985). Interpreting the Constitution, on this view, requires that a judge asks what was intended by the specific provisions set down in the document and use multiple sources to arrive at an answer, including the constitutional text as well as historical documents (such as records of debate at the Constitutional Convention, letters written by the Framers, the Federalist Papers, etc.). Notably, an original intent approach allows the possibility that the Framers might have intended something that is not clearly spelled out in the document.

Though court rulings often appeal to the original intent of the Framers, an original meaning (or original understanding) approach has become the more common form of originalism in the contemporary era. Original meaning jurisprudence does not search for the intent of those who framed or ratified the Constitution. Instead, it seeks to discern the everyday understanding or public meaning of the text at the time the Constitution was adopted. According to this perspective, it is the ordinary meaning of the words at the time of adoption or amendment that matters, not what the Framers may have intended.

Advocates of these two main strands of originalism argue that this approach to interpretation is the best method for identifying the Constitution's true meaning because it purports to keep justices from imposing readings about what the Constitution *should* protect, based on their own preferences and beliefs. Originalism, advocates argue, constrains judges by binding them to the original intent or meaning of the Constitution, thereby denying judges the authority to infuse the Constitution with values that were not understood to be part of the original document or amendment to the document. It is also said to provide continuity and consistency in the law, as well as respect for rule by the people, by avoiding an approach that allows the meaning of the Constitution to be changed over time by unelected judges who cannot be held accountable by electoral processes.

Critics of originalist jurisprudence dispute these claims, putting forward a number of counter arguments. Among other things, critics note the difficulties or even impossibility of identifying a single or unified original intent or meaning when it comes to interpreting the provisions of the Constitution. Should those searching for original intent focus on the Framers of the Constitution and, if so, what documents provide sufficient evidence of intent? Even if the focus is narrowed to the intentions of the Framers and a set of documents for identifying intent were agreed upon, how should we interpret differences among those Framers? If original meaning is what is sought, what sources will prove sufficiently edifying and illuminating to demonstrate the shared public meaning of such things as "free exercise of religion," "freedom of speech," "due process of law," "probable cause," and so forth? This challenge is especially problematic since it is unlikely that there was consensus about the meaning of these terms, just as there is hardly agreement today on the meaning of the concepts set down in the Constitution.

Even if the original intent or meaning of constitutional provisions could be divined, critics argue that present-day jurists should not be bound so inflexibly to the past. After all, they point out, the Framers themselves were far from perfect protectors of civil rights and liberties. They crafted an instrument, the Constitution, that supported and afforded institutional protection for slavery and the disenfranchisement of women. Moreover, critics suggest that an approach that treats the Constitution as having a meaning fixed by the past and unable to evolve with changing times, circumstances, needs, and interests runs the risk of turning this foundational document into an anachronistic relic that is ill-suited to govern present-day conflicts.

Textualism

A textual approach emphasizes the text of the Constitution. Proponents of textualism focus on the words of the Constitution to derive the common or plain meaning of these terms. Though this sounds simple enough, digging a bit deeper reveals an approach that is not always as plain as it appears.

Those who subscribe to textualism argue that the four corners of the Constitution provide the boundaries of interpretation. Importantly, textualists argue not only that we should look at the text for what the Constitution protects, but also pay close attention to those matters about which the

Constitution is silent. Where the Constitution is silent, the textualist urges that judges should not read into the document what is not there. The textualist, then, reads the Constitution as explicitly protecting certain liberties (e.g., Congress shall make no law respecting an establishment of religion) and the role of judicial interpretation is to stop government intrusion into those protected realms. On this view, "A judge need not decide whether such an extension [of governmental power] is wise or prudent; and as such a non-decider, he is a mere conduit for the prohibitions of the Constitution" (Bobbitt 1984, 31). The corollary of this view is that if the Constitution does not explicitly guarantee a particular liberty—that is, if the Constitution is silent—then governing bodies may exercise their delegated authority. If the Constitution says nothing explicit, for example, about a right to abortion, then the government is permitted to regulate abortion.

While textualists share this outlook about interpretation, there are, nevertheless, different variants of textualism. One relatively uncommon version is the literalist or pure textualist. The classic and oft-cited example of the literalist approach is the version espoused by Justice Hugo Black. He argued that the First Amendment forbids Congress from making absolutely any law restricting speech because the text of the Amendment is unequivocal: "Congress shall make no law . . . abridging the freedom of speech, or of the press." According to Black's literalism, unequivocal protections in the Constitution should be protected unequivocally, even if doing so might cause grave harm (e.g., protecting speech that divulges military secrets).

Two additional and important variants of textualists should be noted: the textualist who relies on the original meaning of the words in the Constitution, and the textualist who relies on contemporary meaning of the words. While these brands of textualist have much in common with each other—namely, that they view what is in the text of the Constitution as setting the outer bounds of interpretation—they diverge quite notably on what sources are to be used to interpret that text. For the textualist who is also an originalist, the words should be interpreted in accordance with what they meant when added to the Constitution. For the contemporary textualist, interpretation is determined by how we understand those words in our current context.

While Justice Black's literalism is not common, his arguments in favor of that approach provide the grounding for the multiple variations of textualism. Proponents of textualism assert that it provides a simple approach that restrains judges from imposing their own views about what the Constitution should say and should protect. Bound to the text and to interpretations of the text tethered to its plain meaning is said to promote value-free judging.

Critics, by contrast, question whether such interpretation is value free or simple. The plain meaning of terms is often up for debate and dispute, leaving room for the imposition of values. As to simplicity, those who suggest the limits of a textualist approach argue that while it may be plain that the First Amendment prohibits regulations of speech, what counts as speech is perhaps not as apparent. Take, for instance, the 1971 case of Paul Robert Cohen, who was convicted of engaging in offensive conduct because he wore a jacket that criticized the military draft using an expletive. The Court, by a 5–4 ruling, held that Cohen's arrest for wearing in a courthouse a jacket bearing the words "F—the Draft" violated his right to free expression. But several justices disagreed with the conclusion that this display amounted to speech. As Justice Harry Blackmun wrote in dissent, "Cohen's absurd and immature antic, in my view, was mainly conduct, and little speech" (*Cohen v. California* 1971, 27).

Pragmatism: Prudence and Balancing

Though judges rely on a variety of the methods discussed earlier in defining the concepts embodied in the Constitution, they often do so while attending to the possible consequences of their interpretations. Consider, for example, the problem a judge faces when "multiple principles bear on the same case," making reliance upon a textual or originalist approach "insufficient to determine the outcome" (Barzun 2018, 1010). Such an instance, as Justice Benjamin Cardozo argued, requires judges to weigh and balance competing social interests (1010). Put otherwise, as much as jurists may be engaged in the foundational task of determining what the principles and procedures in Constitution mean, they are not blind to the pragmatic outcomes of their interpretations. Taking a prudential or pragmatic approach, some judges consider the costs and benefits of competing interpretations and give weight to the interpretation that they judge to produce the best consequences.

There are a number of different ways in which judges have applied a pragmatic approach. "One flavor of pragmatism weighs the future costs and benefits of an interpretation to society or the political branches" (Murrill 2018, 13). Justice Stephen Breyer, for example, illustrated this approach in his dissenting opinion in *District of Columbia v. Heller* (2008). Breyer argued in favor of upholding Washington, D.C.'s ban on possessing handguns in homes and against the majority's conclusion that the handgun ban violated the Second Amendment right to keep and bear arms. Breyer dissented, based in part on prudential grounds, after finding the regulation "a proportionate, not a disproportionate, response to the compelling concerns that led the District to adopt it" (*District of Columbia v. Heller* 2008, 722). In Breyer's pragmatic view,

> [A] legislature could reasonably conclude that the law will advance goals of great public importance, namely, saving lives, preventing injury, and reducing crime. The law is tailored to the urban crime problem in that it is local in scope and thus affects only a geographic area both limited in size and entirely urban; the law concerns handguns, which are specially linked to urban gun deaths and injuries, and which are the overwhelmingly favorite weapon of armed criminals; and at the same time, the law imposes a burden upon gun owners that seems proportionately no greater than restrictions in existence at the time the Second Amendment was adopted. In these circumstances, the District's law falls within the zone that the Second Amendment leaves open to regulation by legislatures. (*District of Columbia v. Heller* 2008, 682)

Another version of pragmatism, prominently expounded by Supreme Court Justice Louis Brandeis (who served on the Court from 1916 to 1939) and legal scholar Alexander Bickel, urges courts to take into account whether or not they should play a role in adjudicating particular matters. Brandeis, for example, "believed the Court should avoid constitutional decision in order to safeguard the Court's own position and to activate the political processes of the legislature. These are not textual or historical or even doctrinal reasons, though they are sometimes embodied in doctrine. They are prudential reasons" (Bobbitt 1984, 63). Similarly, Bickel suggested, in an article titled "The Passive Virtues" (1961), that the Supreme Court has the choice of whether, when, and how much to adjudicate, and lays out prudential considerations for how judges should navigate that choice. The Supreme Court deploys a number of doctrines pertaining to jurisdiction and justiciability (e.g., standing and political questions) that Bickel argues serve the pragmatic end of determining whether the courts should be the arbiters of particular disputes.

Justice Lewis Powell took such an approach in *Frontiero v. Richardson* (1973), a case involving a claim of gender-based discrimination. The Supreme Court ruled that gender-based discrimination in an Air Force policy violated the Fifth Amendment of the Constitution. In an opinion signed by four members of the Court, Justice William Brennan wrote that sex-based discrimination should be viewed with suspicion and receive the highest level of judicial scrutiny. But Justice Powell did not join the majority opinion—even though he agreed that the Air Force policy violated the Constitution. Powell objected to what would have amounted to increasing the level of scrutiny in cases involving gender-based discrimination, and he did so for a pragmatic reason, namely that the states were in the midst of considering adding the Equal Rights Amendment to the Constitution. If ratified, that Amendment would have added to the Constitution the following language: "Equality of rights under the law shall not be denied or abridged by the United States or by any State on account of sex." Powell, writing a separate opinion that concurred in judgment in the case, said this:

> There is another, and I find compelling, reason for deferring a general categorizing of sex classifications as invoking the strictest test of judicial scrutiny. The Equal Rights Amendment, which if adopted will resolve the substance of this precise question, has been approved by the Congress and submitted for ratification by the States. If this Amendment is duly adopted, it will represent the will of the people accomplished in the manner prescribed by the Constitution. By acting prematurely and unnecessarily, as I view it, the Court has assumed a decisional responsibility at the very time when state legislatures, functioning within the traditional democratic process, are debating the proposed Amendment. It seems to me that this reaching out to preempt by judicial action a major political decision which is currently in process of resolution does not reflect appropriate respect for duly prescribed legislative processes. (*Frontiero v. Richardson* 1973, 692, concurring in judgment)

Those who favor a pragmatic approach to constitutional interpretation often emphasize that the role of courts is not only or even necessarily to find the foundational meaning of the document but to resolve disputes in a way that attends to the needs and interests of society. As Judge Richard A. Posner has argued, "All that a pragmatic jurisprudence really connotes . . . is a rejection of a concept of law as grounded in permanent principles and realized in logical manipulations of those principles, and a determination to use law as an instrument for social ends" (Posner 1990, 1670). Opponents counter that a pragmatic method undermines the core function of the appellate judiciary, namely determining what the law means, and replaces that function with a policy-oriented and legislative task—determining how to balance costs and benefits of particular actions.

Structuralism

A structural approach draws on the overall structure of the Constitution in arriving at interpretations of specific provisions. In particular, structuralism gives weight to the Constitution's allocation and division of authority to (a) different branches of the federal government, (b) federal versus state governments, and (c) government versus the people. In other words, interpretations that draw inferences from the broader constitutional delegations of power and authority that make up separation of powers, federalism, and democratic processes are called structural interpretations.

Consider, for example, *Youngstown Sheet & Tube Co. v. Sawyer* (1952), a case challenging President Harry Truman's April 1952 order that U.S. steel mills be seized and kept running to avert their closure in the face of a labor strike. Truman defended his executive order on the grounds of national security. He said that an interruption in steel production would endanger the country, which was engaged in the Korean War. He also put forward a structural defense of his executive order, arguing that because Article II of the Constitution confers on the president the explicit power to faithfully execute the laws and serve as Commander in Chief of the armed forces, the president also has implicit power to take control of steel mills under exigent circumstances created by wartime. The Supreme Court rejected that structural argument, however. Drawing on both a textual and structural argument, it ruled that the executive authority set forth in Article II must not be examined in isolation but, rather, in light of the legislative authority set forth in Article I. As Justice Black explained, "Nor can the seizure order be sustained because of the several constitutional provisions that grant executive power to the President. In the framework of our Constitution, the President's power to see that the laws are faithfully executed refutes the idea that he is to be a lawmaker. The Constitution limits his functions in the lawmaking process to the recommending of laws he thinks wise and the vetoing of laws he thinks bad. And the Constitution is neither silent nor equivocal about who shall make laws which the President is to execute" (*Youngstown Sheet & Tube Co. v. Sawyer* 1952, 587).

Structural arguments are most common in separation of powers cases, like *Youngstown*, and federalism cases, like *McCulloch v. Maryland* (1819). In the latter case, the Court held that Congress has the authority to create a national bank and that states do not have the authority to tax it. When Maryland taxed a branch of the Bank of the United States, the Supreme Court ruled that action unconstitutional. It agreed that states have authority to levy taxes, but ruled that exercising that authority against the national government exceeds state authority.

> The sovereignty of a State extends to everything which exists by its own authority or is introduced by its permission, but does it extend to those means which are employed by Congress to carry into execution powers conferred on that body by the people of the United States? We think it demonstrable that it does not. Those powers are not given by the people of a single State. They are given by the people of the United States, to a Government whose laws, made in pursuance of the Constitution, are declared to be supreme. Consequently, the people of a single State cannot confer a sovereignty which will extend over them. . . . If we apply the principle for which the State of Maryland contends, to the Constitution generally, we shall find it capable of changing totally the character of that instrument. We shall find it capable of arresting all the measures of the Government, and of

prostrating it at the foot of the States. The American people have declared their Constitution and the laws made in pursuance thereof to be supreme, but this principle would transfer the supremacy, in fact, to the States. (*McCulloch v. Maryland* 1819, 429–32)

Structuralism is occasionally deployed in cases involving individual liberties, and advocates of its use suggest that it provides well-founded reasoning for identifying implicit liberties. In *Crandall v. Nevada* (1867), for instance, the Court found implicit in the Constitution an individual's right to travel among the states. It grounded that right in part on the idea that, as citizens of the United States, we each have a right to access the seat of the federal government, a right that requires freedom to cross state lines. In other words, *Crandall* held that a constitutional structure that provides for democratic governance and a citizen's right to participate in that governance must include, even if it's not explicitly granted, a right to travel.

Moral and Philosophical Approaches

Because the Constitution contains certain broad and undefined philosophical concepts—like liberty, equality, and due process—some approaches to constitutional interpretation suggest that defining these concepts is best done by appeal to normative arguments and moral reasoning. To determine, for example, whether a government ban on "obscene" speech violates the First and Fourteenth Amendments, definitions of what counts as "speech" and what counts as "obscene" are required. Another consideration is whether "due process" and "liberty" *should* include protections for engaging in "obscene speech." Some urge what philosopher and constitutional law scholar Ronald Dworkin labeled a "moral reading" of the Constitution (Dworkin 1996). Law professor James E. Fleming, one such advocate who draws on Dworkin's work, describes the approach this way: "By 'moral reading' and 'philosophic approach,' I refer to conceptions of the Constitution as embodying abstract moral and political principles—not codifying concrete historical rules or practices—and of interpretation of those principles as requiring normative judgments about how they are best understood—not merely historical research to discover relatively specific original meanings" (Fleming 2016, 489).

There are, of course, multiple theories within the branch of moral philosophy, so the use of normative reasoning in constitutional interpretation lends itself to numerous interpretations and not a great deal of consensus. As legal scholar David M. O'Brien summarizes: "Professor Ronald Dworkin and other contemporary legal scholars call for 'a fusion of constitutional law and moral theory' or political philosophy. Contemporary legal scholarship is indeed marked by a proliferation of expressly normative theories that would rationalize and guide constitutional interpretation according to 'abstract beliefs about morality and justice,' the 'voice of reason,' 'a moral patrimony' implicit in 'our common heritage,' 'the circumstances and values of the present generation,' 'conventional morality,' 'public morality,' 'constitutional morality,' 'fundamental values,' and 'the essential principles of justice,' or 'the ideas of progress'" (O'Brien 2017, 93–94).

This catalog is certainly wide ranging, though it is only a sampling of how a moral reading might be used in constitutional analysis. And to be clear, it is not just legal scholars who are proponents of such an approach. Justices, too, have advocated for moral readings or relied on philosophical arguments in their opinions. Justice William Brennan's characterization of the Constitution and the duty imposed on those responsible for interpreting it illustrates this approach:

> [T]he Constitution embodies the aspirations to social justice, brotherhood, and human dignity that brought this nation into being. . . . In all candor we must concede that part of this egalitarianism in America has been more pretension than realized fact. But we are an aspiring people with faith in progress. Our amended Constitution is the lodestar for our aspirations. Like every text worth reading, it is not crystalline. The phrasing is broad and the limitations of its provisions are not clearly marked. Its majestic generalities and ennobling pronouncements are both luminous and obscure. This ambiguity of course calls forth interpretation, the interaction of reader and text. (Brennan 1985, 183)

Brennan goes on to argue that the interpretative obligation requires taking account of the Constitution's substantive values and fundamental principles as we come to understand them. In his reading, the Constitution, the Bill of Rights, and the Civil War Amendments form "a sparkling vision of the supremacy of the human dignity of every individual" (Brennan 1985, 188). It is dignity, a term not explicitly in the Constitution, that Brennan sees as the fundamental principle protected by the document's explicit provisions, structure, and spirit. It is human dignity that the Constitution recognizes and protects when it expressly grants rights to the criminally accused, when it authorizes individual freedoms of speech and religious exercise, and when it acknowledges the right to vote and guarantees of equality. Seeing the explicit grants of rights and freedoms as infused with the principle of human dignity leads Brennan to interpret guarantees of freedom of speech and religious exercise as including broader protection for freedom of expression and conscience. He also sees the right to vote as including the principle of "one person, one vote," and to reading the equal protection clause as ensuring that "gender has no bearing on claims to human dignity" (191). It also leads Brennan to a morally grounded argument that the Eighth Amendment ban against cruel and unusual punishment should be interpreted as prohibiting the death penalty in all circumstances, even though this interpretation is at odds with historical practice and the original intent of the Framers.

> I view the Eighth Amendment's prohibition of cruel and unusual punishments as embodying to a unique degree moral principles that substantively restrain the punishments our civilized society may impose on those persons who transgress its laws. Foremost among the moral principles recognized in our cases and inherent in the prohibition is the primary principle that the state, even as it punishes, must treat its citizens in a manner consistent with their intrinsic worth as human beings. . . . The calculated killing of a human being by the state involves, by its very nature, an absolute denial of the executed person's humanity. . . . For me, then, the fatal constitutional infirmity of capital punishment is that it treats members of the human race as nonhumans, as objects to be toyed with and discarded. (192)

Critics of the moral and philosophical approach to constitutional interpretation level a number of charges. Some worry about the power this mode of interpretation gives to judges and, relatedly, how much power it takes away from the public and elected representatives. Critics also question whether judges have the moral and philosophical skill to engage in this type of interpretation, and how to determine whether judges are imposing a reasonable moral reading or merely their own ideological and personal preferences.

Tradition, History, and National Ethos

Somewhat related to the use of moral reasoning is the appeal to long-standing tradition and practices when seeking to interpret abstract constitutional language like "liberty," "due process," and "equality." The turn to prevailing historical and cultural practices, or, relatedly, to characterizations of a shared "national ethos," seeks to ground the meaning of these concepts in traditional and commonly held views.

Take, for example, the Supreme Court ruling in *Washington v. Glucksberg* (1997), which held that the Fourteenth Amendment Due Process Clause does not protect a right to assisted suicide. Writing for the Court, Chief Justice Rehnquist said, "We begin, as we do in all due process cases, by examining our Nation's history, legal traditions, and practices" (*Washington v. Glucksberg* 1997, 710). The opinion proceeds by noting seven hundred years of Anglo-American common law tradition against suicide and assisted suicide and referencing laws at the founding and through the nineteenth and twentieth centuries. With this point of departure, the Court continues its analysis by relying, in part, on the idea that the fundamental liberties guaranteed by the Constitution are those that have been longstanding: "[W]e have regularly observed that the Due Process Clause specially protects those fundamental rights and liberties which are, objectively, 'deeply rooted in this Nation's history and tradition' ('so rooted in the traditions and conscience of our people as to be ranked as fundamental'), and 'implicit in the concept of ordered liberty,' such that 'neither liberty nor justice would exist if they were sacrificed'" (*Washington v. Glucksberg* 1997, 720–21, internal citations omitted).

The corollary of this argument is that liberty claims that challenge tradition and run counter to common historical practice are not deemed fundamental. Because tradition and common practice included laws and customs against suicide, the Court ruled against those arguing in favor of a fundamental right to assisted suicide.

Related to appeals to tradition and historical practice are appeals to a common national ethos or identity. Put slightly differently, it is American tradition and practice, and prevailing notions of what counts as central to American identity, that judges will sometimes rely on in their analyses. Such appeals are exemplified in a series of cases involving the rights of parents to raise their children without undue interference from the government. These cases, including rulings overturning laws that required compulsory public school education, tether broader historical traditions to specific practices and ethos of the United States: "The history and culture of Western civilization reflect a strong tradition of parental concern for the nurture and upbringing of their children. This primary role of the parents in the upbringing of their children is now established beyond debate as an enduring American tradition" (*Wisconsin v. Yoder* 1972, 232).

One of the appeals of turning to history, tradition, and national ethos to interpret the Constitution is that it seems to mitigate some of the concerns about justices imposing their own preferences over those of the public. Supporters say that if something has been central to the history, culture, and tradition of the people, then it likely serves the best interests of the people. On the other hand, critics note that such an approach risks reinforcing outdated or harmful traditions, along with the power relations, exclusions, and marginalization those traditions often embody. Relatedly, critics suggest that an interest in protecting individual and minority rights against tyranny of the majority might not be well advanced by appeals to a national ethos.

THE CONSTITUTION: DEAD OR ALIVE?

The preceding methods illuminate a key divide in jurisprudential debates over constitutional interpretation: whether judges should treat the

Constitution as a living or dead document. Simply put, this dispute goes like this: "originalists" argue that the Constitution means what it meant when its provisions were originally adopted, whereas "living constitutionalists" argue that the document's broadly worded principles should be interpreted in the present, as we come to learn, identify, and better understand the guarantees the Framers sought to protect.

In a 2015 Supreme Court ruling, Justice Anthony Kennedy said the following in speaking to how judges should interpret the Constitution: "The nature of injustice is that we may not always see it in our own times. The generations that wrote and ratified the Bill of Rights and the Fourteenth Amendment did not presume to know the extent of freedom in all of its dimensions, and so they entrusted to future generations a charter protecting the right of all persons to enjoy liberty *as we learn its meaning*" (*Obergefell v. Hodges* 2015, 2598; emphasis added).

Justice Kennedy, whose majority opinion in *Obergefell v. Hodges* held that same-sex couples have a constitutional right to marry under the Fourteenth Amendment of the Constitution, argued that to figure out what the term "liberty" means, judges should certainly be guided by the past, by history, and by tradition. But judges must also "exercise reasoned judgment in identifying interests of the person so fundamental that the State must accord them its respect," and such a method, while respecting and learning from history and the past, does not allow "the past alone to rule the present" (2598). In so arguing, Justice Kennedy was offering a version of living constitutionalism.

It was Kennedy's opinion that prevailed in *Obergefell*, much to the consternation of the four justices who dissented. And among the arguments put forward in dissent was an originalist argument, put quite plainly by Justice Scalia: "When the Fourteenth Amendment was ratified in 1868, every State limited marriage to one man and one woman, and no one doubted the constitutionality of doing so. That resolves these cases" (2628, dissenting opinion). In short, Scalia asserted that the meaning of the Fourteenth Amendment should be located not in how we come, over time, to define liberty and equality—even if those definitions now better approximate justice, fairness, dignity, and democratic values. Rather, the originalist who rejects living constitutionalism insists that justices be bound to interpret the Constitution in line with its original meaning. And if same-sex marriage was widely prohibited when the Fourteenth Amendment was ratified—which it was—then the Fourteenth Amendment does not protect a right to same-sex marriage. This brand of originalist will add and emphasize, as Scalia did in dissent, that if the American people today have come to believe that marriage equality rights should be granted and protected, they should secure those rights through democratic processes—either by passing new laws that give same-sex couples the right to marry or by amending the Constitution.

A few caveats about this divide are in order. First, it should be noted that just as there are different versions of originalism, there are varying brands of living constitutionalists, and a number of the methods of interpretation described earlier (e.g., pragmatism, structuralism, moral arguments) can be consistent with the broader jurisprudence that views the Constitution as living. Justice Brennan's use of moral reasoning, for instance, strongly emphasized reading the Constitution as living and evolving: "Those who would restrict claims of right to the values of 1789 specifically articulated in the Constitution turn a blind eye to the social progress and eschew adaptation of overarching principles to changes of social circumstance" (Brennan 1985, 185).

Second, it is also worth noting that the mere characterization of a divide between viewing the Constitution as living or dead is itself contested. Political scientist Ken Kersch (2016) critiques this binary. Law professor Jack Balkin (2011) argues for "living originalism," maintaining that a genuinely originalist approach must acknowledge that the Framers designed constitutional provisions in abstract and broad terms, thereby intending to leave interpretation of those words open to future generations. And legal scholar James Fleming (2016) argues for "aspirationalism," an approach that takes historical meaning into account while suggesting that constitutional interpretation requires that we aspire to a more perfect document.

Still, the different jurisprudential dispositions—especially an ongoing divide between those who call for a static version of originalism and those who urge adaptability—continue to shape debate over how the Court should interpret the Constitution and, in turn, who should be appointed to the high bench.

CONCLUSION

Though much ink has been spilled on the pages of books and journals debating the relative merits of originalism, textualism, pragmatism, and more, disagreements over approaches to constitutional interpretation are not merely academic. As we will see in later chapters, these disagreements make their way into debates over who should serve on the judiciary and on the Supreme Court in particular, so much so that political polarization of the judiciary is often cast in terms of judicial philosophy. The label "activist judge"—typically used in a disparaging way—has come to be used as criticism for those willing to follow a living approach to interpretation, while the term "judicial restraint" has been adopted by those who purport to "strictly interpret" the Constitution according to text and original meaning. Importantly, disagreements over these varying approaches often morph into allegations that justices are acting illegitimately by inserting their personal and political views into adjudication.

NOTE

1. Though statutory interpretation will not be treated in this discussion, an excellent overview is offered by Eig (2014).

3

Court Structures and Processes

The U.S. Supreme Court is housed in a majestic and formidable building. Located on Capitol Hill in Washington, D.C., the main entrance is reached by climbing forty-four wide marble steps flanked on each side by two large marble sculptures. The Contemplation of Justice—a female figure seated stoically on the left—holds a book of law and a figure of blind justice. Guarding the right is the Authority of Law—a seated male figure displaying a tablet of law and a sword. Atop the high staircase, a portico composed of sixteen Corinthian marble columns stands tall. The columns hold up a pediment—a triangular building element common in classical architecture—decorated with a sculpture showing many figures symbolic of law, dressed in the garb of Ancient Rome. Above the columns and below the sculpture reads the building's inscription: "Equal Justice Under Law." One walks through the columns to arrive at the main, though no longer used, entryway: two bronze doors measuring seventeen feet in height, weighing close to thirteen tons, and featuring sculptures of legal scenes in the Western tradition.

There are other notable features that mark the interior of the Supreme Court building: two marble and bronze spiral staircases climb five stories; leading to the Court Chamber is the Great Hall, a stately corridor that includes busts of all former chief justices; and the Court Chamber itself, with its own set of marble columns, a raised bench, and, adorning the four walls, marble friezes portraying actual or allegorical figures of law. Less well known is a room that sits on the top floor. Originally designed for storage, the room was converted into a gym and now includes a basketball court. Instead of marble columns and a bench, plexiglass backboards mark this court. So, atop the highest court in the land sits the "Highest Court in the Land" (Kay 2018), access to which is heavily restricted by various rules and customs.

But it is what goes on in and on the way to the Court Chamber located on the second floor, where an altogether different set of hoops govern access, that is the subject of this chapter. Though many seek a hearing in that chamber, gaining access is a rarity. In each of the past ten terms—terms that commence on the first Monday in October and typically run through late June—the Court issued an average of only sixty-seven signed opinions in the approximately 7,250 cases submitted annually to it for consideration.[1] How are cases screened for selection and review? What happens to those cases turned away? Can the Court hear and rule on any case it wants? Who writes the judicial opinions issued by the Court? What happens in and beyond the walls of the Court Chamber? In short, how do cases get to and through the Court?

HIERARCHICAL STRUCTURE OF THE COURT SYSTEM

The U.S. Supreme Court sits not only atop a wide and long marble stairway, it also sits at the pinnacle of the federal court system. The United States is a federal system, structured so that there is a division of authority and sovereignty between the national government, on the one hand, and the states, on the other. Under the version of federalism that governs the United States, the national government and the states have their own legislative and executive branches. Likewise, each state has its own court system structured according to the laws and constitutions of the individual state; alongside the state court systems, and in some respects above them, sits the federal judiciary.

The Constitution provides only limited guidance on the structure of the federal judiciary, leaving to Congress considerable authority to design the system. Congress subsequently built a federal judicial structure that, like state systems, is organized hierarchically, with trial courts forming the base and appellate courts situated above the trial courts.

Trial courts handle criminal and civil cases. They decide whether criminal laws (e.g., homicide, assault, theft) have been violated and assess penalties and punishments for such violations. They also adjudicate disputes over civil law (e.g., breach of contract, property disputes) and, in those types of disputes, assess whether compensation is due. Whether handling criminal allegations or civil complaints, trial courts address cases on their first (or original) presentation with the goal of determining the facts and applying the law to the facts as found. As "finders of fact," trial courts hear evidence, testimony, and arguments presented by the competing parties. A single judge presides over trial court cases, and a jury is typically charged with the responsibility of rendering a verdict pertaining to guilt in criminal cases or liability in civil cases. Some types of trials, called bench trials, are handled without a jury, and the judge makes the finding of fact regarding guilt or liability.

By contrast, appellate courts (also called appeals courts and, at the federal level, Circuit Courts of Appeal) hear cases after a trial court has reached a verdict. Because the task of the appeals court is, typically, to give appellate review and not to determine facts, juries are not involved. Instead, a panel of judges hears appeals with the goal of ensuring that the trial court followed applicable legal processes and correctly interpreted and applied the pertinent laws.

Court systems are commonly structured so that there are intermediate appellate courts as well as a court of "last resort" to which rulings from the appellate courts can themselves be appealed. Thus, all states have a high court (most often labeled the "supreme court") that sits at the pinnacle of the state court system. Decisions handed down by a state supreme court are binding on that state and the lower courts within it (unless later overturned by the U.S. Supreme Court).

Like state court systems, the federal judicial system is composed of trial courts, intermediate appellate courts, and a high court. Federal trial courts, called U.S. District Courts, typically include juries and handle criminal and civil cases that involve federal law. Each state, the District of Columbia, and the territories of Puerto Rico, the Virgin Islands, Guam, and the Northern Mariana Islands have at least one U.S. District Court. Because of workload, many states have multiple District Courts. In total, there are presently ninety-four U.S. District Courts. There are, as well, a handful of specialized trial courts charged with such things as handling disputes over international trade and customs laws and claims for money damages against the U.S. government.

The appellate courts positioned between the District Courts and the U.S. Supreme Court are known as U.S. Courts of Appeal. They are also referred to as Circuit Courts because the ninety-four District Courts are divided into twelve regional circuits (labeled One through Eleven and, for the District of Columbia, the D.C. Court of Appeals), and a thirteenth circuit (the Federal Circuit) that hears appeals from the specialized federal trial courts and administrative agencies. Each regional Circuit Court of Appeals has authority to hear challenges to decisions made by the District Courts within the regional circuit. For example, U.S. District Courts in New York, Connecticut, and Vermont are located in the Second Circuit; thus, appeals from those federal trial courts go the Court of Appeals for the Second Circuit. The U.S. Supreme Court serves as the court of last resort for the entire federal judiciary. As such, appeals from any Circuit Court are petitioned to the U.S. Supreme Court.

The U.S. Supreme Court also serves as the court of last resort for state courts, but only when the case heard in state court raises a "substantial" federal question. State courts adjudicate matters pertaining to their own state's laws and constitutions. Of course, sometimes a state law implicates federal law or constitutional rights. For example, when the state of Virginia convicted Mildred and Richard Loving in 1958 of violating a state law that made it illegal for some members of different racial groups to marry each other, that conviction raised a question of whether Virginia's law violated the U.S. Constitution's guarantee of equal protection. The Lovings brought that question first to the Supreme Court of Virginia. Upon losing in that tribunal, they appealed to the U.S. Supreme Court, which issued the landmark ruling declaring state anti-miscegenation laws unconstitutional (*Loving v. Virginia* 1967).

The route of appeal from a state court system to the federal court system goes from the highest state court directly to the U.S. Supreme Court, not to the lower courts in the federal system. In almost all such cases, the U.S. Supreme Court has the discretion to decide whether to hear the case. If the high court declines to hear the case, the decision made by the highest state court remains in force. On matters that fall solely within the province of state law or that are deemed to raise an insubstantial federal question, the court of last resort at the state level has the final word.

CASE SELECTION: JURISDICTION AND JUSTICIABILITY

In 2016, there were over eighty-two million incoming cases in state courts (Courts Statistics Project). By comparison, the number of cases filed in the U.S. District Courts is a drop in the bucket. From October 2015 through September 2016, civil and criminal case filings in the U.S. District Courts amounted to almost 370,000, with another 800,000 filings of bankruptcy petitions (Roberts 2016b, 12–13). As noted earlier, the U.S. Supreme Court hears just a tiny fraction of these cases. How these cases are selected depends a great deal on the discretion of the justices. There are very few mandates that require the Supreme Court to accept and hear specific cases, but some rules, practices, and customs influence whether a case will be taken up by the Court.

Jurisdiction

One of the main rules that governs whether the Supreme Court will select and decide a case is jurisdiction. In the context of a judicial system, jurisdiction refers to whether a particular court has authority to decide a particular matter. As alluded to earlier, America's system of federalism delineates jurisdictional authority between state courts and federal courts. The federal courts only have authority to render legal decisions over matters pertaining to federal law. In legal matters about which federal law is silent, state courts have jurisdiction and federal courts do not. State courts only have jurisdiction over their own state laws, not the laws of other states.

Though the Constitution provides slim guidance on the structure of the federal judiciary, Article III, Section 2, outlines federal court jurisdiction:

> The judicial Power shall extend to all Cases, in Law and Equity, arising under this Constitution, the Laws of the United States, and Treaties made, or which shall be made, under their Authority;—to all Cases affecting Ambassadors, other public Ministers and Consuls;—to all Cases of admiralty and maritime Jurisdiction;—to Controversies to which the United States shall be a Party;—to Controversies between two or more States;—between a State and Citizens of another State;—between Citizens of different States;—between Citizens of the same State claiming Lands under Grants of different States, and between a State, or the Citizens thereof, and foreign States, Citizens or Subjects.

The Eleventh Amendment, ratified in 1795, modifies a portion of Article III by stating that "the Judicial power of the United States shall not be construed to extend to any suit in law or equity, commenced or prosecuted against one of the United States by Citizens of another State, or by Citizens or Subjects of any Foreign State." Otherwise, the jurisdictional listing remains in place and applies not just to the Supreme Court but also to the courts that make up the federal system. But Article III, Section 2, goes on to explain that the Supreme Court only has "original" jurisdiction—that is, the authority to hear a case that has not yet been heard by another court—in a handful of cases, namely those "affecting Ambassadors, other public Ministers and Consuls, and those in which a State shall be Party." In other words, the Supreme Court has authority to act as a trial court, hearing a case in its initial iteration, and an appellate court, hearing a case on appeal. But its authority to act as a trial court is quite limited, and the Court hears original jurisdiction cases infrequently. "Between 1789 and 1959, the Court issued written opinions in only 123 original cases. Since 1960, the Court has received fewer than 140 motions for leave to file original cases, nearly half of which were denied a hearing. The majority of cases filed have been in disputes between two or more states" (Federal Judicial Center).

By and large, then, the Supreme Court functions under its appellate court jurisdiction, hearing disputes brought to it on appeal after a lower federal court or a state supreme court has already heard the case and rendered a decision. Moreover, the Court's appellate jurisdiction is discretionary, conferring on the Court its authority to hear cases, but not mandating that the Court hear such cases. Prior to 1988 there were certain cases that the Court was required to hear—that is, which conferred a right of appeal. But Congress passed the Supreme Court Case Selections Act of 1988, which removed the Court's *mandatory* appellate jurisdiction, leaving to the Court the decision of whether or not to hear cases in virtually all instances.

Justiciability

Though the Supreme Court may have jurisdiction over a particular subject matter (i.e., matters arising under the Constitution, federal laws, or treaties), that alone does not mean there is a case or controversy to be heard by the Court. Because the language of Article III, Section 2, restricts judicial power to "Cases" and "Controversies," the subject matter must be within the scope of the Court's jurisdiction *and* there must be a case or controversy around the subject matter. What it means for there to be a case or controversy is, itself, something the Court has considered and debated over many years. In doing so, the Court has created (and, over the years, modified) a set of "justiciability" doctrines that govern the federal courts by restricting the extent and reach of judicial power.

Justiciability refers to whether a matter or conflict is appropriate for and capable of judicial resolution. For a federal court to arrive at a conclusion on the merits of litigation brought to it, the case must first be deemed justiciable. The Court has held litigation must exhibit several characteristics to be considered justiciable, the sum of which are as follows: there must be a controversy that is real, live, and ongoing, and poses actual harm to the party bringing suit on an issue suitable for resolution in a legal rather than a political venue. In more technical terms, justiciability requires that a suit contain an *adverse relationship*, that the issue at stake be *ripe* and not *moot*, that the party petitioning the Court has *standing* to do so, and that the case does not present a *political question*.

Adverseness

The adverseness component of justiciability requires that there be a real and non-hypothetical conflict or, as the Court has put it, an "honest and actual antagonistic assertion of rights" (*Chicago & G. T. R. Co. v. Wellman* 1892, 345). This means that the federal courts will not issue *advisory opinions* on hypothetical matters or on legislation or policy under consideration but not yet adopted. The Court articulated its position on the non-justiciability of advisory opinions in 1793—and has generally held to that precedent ever since[2]—in reaction to a request from then secretary of state Thomas Jefferson asking for judicial input on international relations with France. On behalf of President George Washington, Jefferson wrote that the Court's guidance "would secure us against errors dangerous to the peace of the US. and their authority ensure the respect of all parties" (Schmidt 2017). The Court declined to offer advice, saying, "The Lines of Separation drawn by the Constitution between the three Departments of Government—their being in certain Respects checks on each other—and our being Judges of a court in the last Resort—are Considerations which afford strong arguments against the Propriety of our extrajudicially deciding the questions alluded to; especially as the Power given by the Constitution to the President of calling on the Heads of Departments for opinions, seems to have been purposely as well as expressly limited to executive Departments" (2017).

The adverseness component of justiciability has also come to mean that litigation in the federal courts is not supposed to permit *collusive suits*. Collusive or contrived suits are those in which the competing parties do not have a real conflict but, instead, have a mutual interest in the case and seek the same outcome. In collusive suits, the parties cooperate to bring litigation typically to test a law and generate a court decision. If the interests of the petitioning and the responding parties to a lawsuit are the same, the Court typically holds that there is no controversy to resolve. Note that the restriction against collusive suits does not prohibit so-called *test cases*, that is, cases that seek to test the constitutionality of a law or policy. Instead, the restriction prohibits those test cases in which the "opposing" parties are not really in opposition.

Ripeness and Mootness

Because justiciability requires that legal intervention be limited to "the protection of concrete, particularized, continuing injuries" (Nichol 1987, 154–55), the Court generally insists that suits present issues that are ripe and not moot. An issue brought forward in a lawsuit prematurely is considered unripe, whereas a conflict that has already been resolved through other means is considered moot. Whether brought too soon or too late, a suit that does not contain an existing and concrete dispute is likely to be dismissed as nonjusticiable.

The rationale of the ripeness doctrine, the Court has said, "is to prevent the courts, through avoidance of premature adjudication, from entangling themselves in abstract disagreements" (*Abbott Laboratories v. Gardner* 1967, 148). The Court sometimes invokes the ripeness doctrine in cases where a law has yet to take full effect or, as in *Poe v. Ullman* (1961), which will be discussed later, when a law has not been implemented for a long time. Ripeness also commonly requires that parties exhaust other remedies (e.g., lower court appeals or administrative remedies) before the Court will rule.

On the flip side, the rationale for the mootness doctrine is to prevent courts from entangling themselves in an issue that has already been resolved through other means. The Court has held "that federal courts are without power to decide questions that cannot affect the rights of litigants in the case before them" (*North Carolina v. Rice* 1971, 246) and has frequently relied on this precedent. For example, the Court reiterated this declaration in *DeFunis v. Odegaard* (1974), a case in which Marco DeFunis Jr., who had been denied admission to the University of Washington Law School, challenged the use of affirmative action in the admissions process. By the time the Supreme Court heard the case, DeFunis had nearly completed his law degree at the University, which had admitted him in 1971 when a state trial court ruled in his favor. Concluding that a decision reached on the merits of the case would not affect DeFunis, the Court dismissed his claim as nonjusticiable.

The Court has carved out several exceptions to the mootness doctrine, recognizing that an unyielding application of the requirement would prove problematic. For example, the Court has held that because some recurring conflicts are inherently short-lived and, as such, not likely to be ongoing by the time the case arrives for its consideration, exceptions to mootness may be warranted. Consider here *Roe v. Wade* (1973), the case in which the Court declared that the Constitution protects a woman's right to choose abortion. The petitioner challenged a Texas law that prohibited most abortions, but by the time the case arrived at the Court, she had given birth. The Court nevertheless reached the merits of the case rather than dismissing the conflict as moot, explaining that

> when, as here, pregnancy is a significant fact in the litigation, the normal 266-day human gestation period is so short that the pregnancy will come to term before the usual appellate process is complete. If that termination makes a case moot, pregnancy litigation seldom will survive much beyond the trial stage, and appellate review will be effectively denied. Our law should not be that rigid. Pregnancy often comes more than once to the same woman, and in the general population, if man is to survive, it will always be with us. Pregnancy provides a classic justification for a conclusion of non-mootness. (*Roe v. Wade* 1973, 125)

Standing

Justiciability further requires that the party petitioning a federal court demonstrate *standing* to sue. To have standing, the party must have a direct stake in the outcome of the litigation, but having a direct stake does not simply mean that the party is interested in or desires a particular outcome. Demonstrating a direct stake entails demonstrating direct injury or harm. More specifically, the Supreme Court held in *Lujan v. Defenders of*

Wildlife (1992) that to establish standing to sue in federal court the plaintiff must show three things. First, the plaintiff must have suffered, or is about to suffer, a concrete and particularized injury to a legally protected interest. Second, the injury must be "fairly traceable" to the action of the defendant. And third, it must be "likely," not "speculative," that a favorable judicial ruling will provide redress for the injury (560–61).

Standing insists that a party presenting a legal challenge in federal court show more than dislike of a law or disagreement with policy, even if the disagreement is grounded in the view that the law or policy in question is unconstitutional. For example, if a public university employs a race-based affirmative action policy in its admissions processes, a U.S. taxpayer who objects to the use of race in admissions on the grounds that it denies equal protection cannot establish standing to sue merely because of that objection or on the grounds of paying taxes. On the other hand, a student denied admission to that public university may be in a better position to establish standing.

In the 1961 ruling in *Poe v. Ullman*, the Supreme Court declined to evaluate the constitutionality of a prohibition on the use of contraceptives on the grounds of both the standing and ripeness doctrines. The Connecticut law in question, which had been on the books since 1879, restricted the use of birth control drugs and devices, and prohibited physicians from giving advice about contraceptives. The plaintiffs—a married couple, a married woman, and their physician, Dr. C. Lee Buxton—were deemed to lack standing because they had not been subject to prosecution. Moreover, the case was deemed unripe because even though Connecticut indicated its intent to prosecute violations of any state law, the Supreme Court noted that with regard to this statute, with one exception, "During the more than three-quarters of a century since its enactment, a prosecution for its violation seems never to have been initiated. . . . Neither counsel nor our own researches have discovered any other attempt to enforce the prohibition of distribution or use of contraceptive devices by criminal process" (501–502). Given the absence of prosecutions, as well as the availability of contraceptives in drug stores, the Court declined to rule one way or another on the constitutionality of the contraception ban, explaining that:

> "The best teaching of this Court's experience admonishes us not to entertain constitutional questions in advance of the strictest necessity." The various doctrines of "standing," "ripeness," and "mootness," which this Court has evolved with particular, though not exclusive, reference to such cases are but several manifestations—each having its own "varied application"—of the primary conception that federal judicial power is to be exercised to strike down legislation, whether state or federal, only at the instance of one who is himself immediately harmed, or immediately threatened with harm,

by the challenged action. "This court can have no right to pronounce an abstract opinion upon the constitutionality of a State law. Such law must be brought into actual or threatened operation upon rights properly falling under judicial cognizance, or a remedy is not to be had here." (503–504, citations omitted)

Four years later, the Supreme Court declared the Connecticut law unconstitutional after Dr. C. Lee Buxton and Estelle Griswold, the executive director of Planned Parenthood League of Connecticut, were found to have standing subsequent to being found guilty of prescribing contraceptives to married couples (*Griswold v. Connecticut* 1965).

Political Questions

In June 2019, the Supreme Court refused to declare partisan gerrymandering unconstitutional. Partisan gerrymandering is the practice of drawing the boundaries of voting districts in order to help the candidates of a particular political party win election. That momentous refusal by the Court to consider partisan gerrymandering allegations in North Carolina and Maryland was not based on a conclusion that such gerrymandering is constitutional. Indeed, the 5–4 majority in *Rucho v. Common Cause* (2019) acknowledged that "[e]xcessive partisanship in districting leads to results that reasonably seem unjust" and is "incompatible with democratic principles" (2506). These observations, the Court nevertheless concluded, do not mean that the solution to the problem "lies with the federal judiciary" (2506). Instead, the Court invoked what is known as the *political questions doctrine* to conclude that the judiciary is not the appropriate body to resolve complaints about this type of electoral manipulation. According to Chief Justice John Roberts, who wrote the majority decision for the Court, "[P]artisan gerrymandering claims present political questions beyond the reach of the federal courts. Federal judges have no license to reallocate political power between the two major political parties, with no plausible grant of authority in the Constitution, and no legal standards to limit and direct their decisions" (2506–07).

When the Court finds that a matter raises a so-called political question, it declares the issue nonjusticiable. For example, the Court has said that sometimes "the judicial department has no business entertaining the claim of unlawfulness—because the question is entrusted to one of the political branches or involves no judicially enforceable rights" (*Vieth v. Jubelirer* 2004, 277, plurality opinion). Moreover, the Court has declared that its authority to act is "grounded in and limited by the necessity of resolving, according to legal principles, a plaintiff's particular claim of legal right" (*Gill v. Whitford* 2018, 1929). Determining whether a political question is at issue involves figuring out whether there is an "appropriate role for the Federal Judiciary" in remedying the presented claims—"whether such claims are claims of *legal* right, resolvable according to *legal* principles, or political questions that must find their resolution elsewhere" (*Rucho v. Common Cause* 2019, 2494).

What it means for something to be a political question has been the subject of sometimes intense disagreement and controversy. *Baker v. Carr* (1962), the landmark case that generated the test for identifying the existence of a political question, was so fraught that, according to one account, "it pushed one Supreme Court justice to a nervous breakdown, brought a boiling feud to a head, put one justice in the hospital, and changed the course of the Supreme Court—and the nation—forever" (Abumrad and Lechtenberg 2016). The drama of that redistricting case aside, a majority of the Court agreed that the presence of one or more of the following six features demonstrates the existence of a political question:

> Prominent on the surface of any case held to involve a political question is found a textually demonstrable constitutional commitment of the issue to a coordinate political department; or a lack of judicially discoverable and manageable standards for resolving it; or the impossibility of deciding without an initial policy determination of a kind clearly for nonjudicial discretion; or the impossibility of a court's undertaking independent resolution without expressing lack of the respect due coordinate branches of government; or an unusual need for unquestioning adherence to a political decision already made; or the potentiality of embarrassment from multifarious pronouncements by various departments on one question. (*Baker v. Carr* 1962, 217)

Agreement that the presence of one of these features creates a nonjusticiable political question does not mean that the justices are always in agreement about when such features are, indeed, present. To the contrary, as in *Rucho v. Common Cause*, the Court was sharply and intensely divided around whether judicially discoverable and manageable standards are available to resolve partisan gerrymandering. Chief Justice Roberts argued for the majority that the Court lacked such standards. The four dissenters in the case disagreed. Writing on behalf of those dissenters, Justice Elena Kagan lamented the majority's conclusion that the political questions doctrine foreclosed judging the merits of the case, calling it an "abdication [that] comes just when courts across the country, including those below, have coalesced around manageable judicial standards to resolve partisan gerrymandering claims. Those standards satisfy the majority's own benchmarks. . . . In giving such gerrymanders a pass from judicial review, the majority goes tragically wrong" (*Rucho v. Common Cause* 2019, 2509, dissenting opinion).

CASE SELECTION: PROCESSES AND AGENDA SETTING

Whether the federal courts have jurisdiction over an issue and whether a matter is justiciable are threshold questions. That is, they must be answered before and in order for the Court to reach a decision on the merits of case—though not necessarily before the Court hears the case. If the Court concludes that a matter is not justiciable or not within its jurisdiction, it will not arrive at a ruling on the case's merits, even while it may, in some instances, issue an opinion in the case explaining the lack of justiciability or jurisdiction.

Moreover, even if a case is justiciable and within the Court's jurisdiction, that does not mean the Court will select the case for review. A number of other factors figure into whether and how cases are selected by the Supreme Court. Some of these factors are governed by rules or conventions, others by politics and discretion.

Process of Certification

Under its discretionary appellate jurisdiction, a case may (but rarely does) come to the Court by way of the *process of certification*. Used infrequently, the process of certification allows a lower court to seek from the Supreme Court clarification on a question of the law. Unlike the common avenue of appeal discussed in the next section, when a question or proposition of law is certified to the Supreme Court, it is the lower court rather than the individual parties to litigation that is seeking the higher court's review.

Writ of Certiorari

Most cases arrive at the Supreme Court when a party to litigation seeks a *writ of certiorari*, which, if granted, is an order telling a lower court to provide its record in a case to the higher court. When a party loses in the state supreme court or in a federal appeals court, that party can petition the high court requesting that it issue a writ of certiorari. Each term, about seven thousand "cert" petitions are filed with the Supreme Court.

Most often—indeed for about 99 percent of cert petitions—the Court's response is dismissal without comment. To a small subset of cert petitions, the Court provides summary consideration, issuing an order without oral argument; to another small subset of cert petitions—about seventy cases a year, or 1 percent of petitions—the Court grants cert and provides full review; and occasionally, the Court will hold a case over to review the following term (Administrative Office of the Court 2018). Full review cases are those that generate the most attention in the news media, in politics, in the classroom, and in scholarship.

Determining whether a case is granted or denied cert begins with the process of considering the cert petition. The petition for cert is a type of legal brief—a written document that elaborates legal arguments in favor of a particular position. The cert petition, in addition to discussing the facts and background of the case, focuses its legal arguments on why the Court should accept the case for review. The opposing party has the option of filing a legal brief—called a brief in opposition—making arguments to explain why the Court should deny cert. Others who have a strong interest in the case, even if they are not parties to it, sometimes have the option of submitting legal briefs, known as "friend of the court" or amicus briefs. At this stage of the process, friends of the court submitting legal briefs make arguments in favor of or against the grant of cert.

When all the briefs related to whether or not the Court should hear the case have been submitted, the Supreme Court's Office of the Clerk distributes copies to the justices. Each justice typically employs four law clerks—commonly recent graduates from leading law schools—who assist with the legal review, research, and analysis of petitions, and—for the cases granted review—the drafting of opinions.

Cert Pool

At the cert stage, law clerks play an especially significant role, reviewing and screening the petitions. Most work in the vetting process through what's called the *cert pool*. Established in the 1970s by Chief Justice Warren Burger, the cert pool was created to manage the expanding workload of the Court. The cert pool functions by randomly assigning each petition to one of the participating justice's law clerks. (Participation in the cert pool is optional for the justices; as of early 2020, all except Justices Samuel Alito and Neil Gorsuch use the pool.) That law clerk reads all the material related to the petition and produces a *pool memo*, summarizing the petition and offering a recommendation as to whether it should be accepted. The pool memo is shared with all the justices who participate in the pool, and the individual justices may ask their own law clerks to provide additional analysis or commentary on the petition. The justices then use the pool memos and whatever additional input their clerks may have provided to arrive at an initial view concerning whether cert should be granted or denied.

Conference

Deciding whether a case is granted cert occurs when the justices meet in *Conference*, typically held on Fridays of the weeks when oral arguments take place. The Conference is closed and private; only the justices are permitted to attend. No transcripts of these meetings are recorded, and notes taken by individual justices need not ever become public. Unlike the records and notes of presidents, which, according to federal law, must all be preserved, the records, files, and notes of justices are unregulated, and individual justices may dispose of them however they wish. Many justices eventually decide to make their papers public, but do not release them until after departing from the Court.

Still, some information is known about the process and norms that guide the Conference deliberations, as well as the process that produces the Court's rulings and written opinions. Prior to Conference, the chief justice produces and circulates to the associate justices the list of cases to be discussed during the Conference. Only those cases that make it to the *discuss list* in advance of Conference are, in fact discussed, but any justice can add a case to the list. In all, only about 20–30 percent of docketed cases make it to the discuss list. Cases on the discuss list do not necessarily receive a grant of cert, but those that do not make it are automatically denied cert.

Conference, over which the chief justice presides, begins with handshakes all around—part of a norm of collegiality—and proceeds to a review of the discuss list to determine which cases should be granted cert. Cases are discussed initially by the chief justice, or, if another justice put the case on the list, by that justice. Discussion proceeds in order of seniority, which is determined by length of service on the Court, except for the chief justice who has seniority over the eight associate justices regardless of length of tenure on the bench. Sometimes the discussion is quite brief, consisting mostly of justices indicating whether they would grant or deny cert. In other instances, discussion is longer. In still other instances, a justice might request that the discussion be extended (or "redistributed") to a later Conference for further consideration.

The *Rule of Four* determines whether cert is granted: at least four justices must vote in favor of granting cert. In addition, four justices must vote to proceed with full review and oral argument. Explaining the logic behind this approach to granting cert, Justice Felix Frankfurter offered this: "The 'rule of four' is not a command of Congress. It is a working rule devised by the Court as a practical mode of determining that a case is deserving of review, the theory being that if four Justices find that a legal question of general importance is raised, that is ample proof that the question has such importance. This is a fair enough rule of thumb on the assumption that four Justices find such importance on an individualized screening of the cases sought to be reviewed" (*Ferguson v. Moore-McCormack Lines, Inc.* 1957, 529, dissenting opinion).[3]

Agenda Setting

The cert pool, discuss list, Conference procedures, and Rule of Four provide the contours of a process by which the roughly 1 percent of petitioned cases make it to a full hearing by the Supreme Court. These contours alone, however, do not provide much insight into why the Court (or at least four of its members) deems particular cases worthy of full review. What explains the selections justices make?

There is no categorical answer to this question. The Court does not have a checklist that identifies all the conditions necessary and sufficient for granting cert. Moreover, as the Rule of Four itself indicates, justices do not necessarily agree on whether cases warrant a full hearing. The Court does provide some general guidance on what it might take for cert to be granted. In addition, political scientists and legal scholars interested in understanding what shapes the Court's agenda have identified a number of factors that help explain why the Court chooses to hear some but not other cases.

"Splits Not Likely to Heal"

The Supreme Court adopts formal rules and guidance covering a wide array of topics, including the usage of the Court's library, the dates of the Court's term, the requirements for admission to practice before the Court, requirements for what must be included in a petition for a writ of certiorari, and much more. Among these is Rule 10, "Considerations Governing Review on Certiorari" (*Rules of the Supreme Court of the United States* 2019, 5–6).[4] Rule 10 notes the Court's discretionary authority, states that cert will be granted only for "compelling" reasons and identifies issues the Court takes into consideration. In particular, Rule 10 highlights conflicting decisions in the lower tribunals as a reason why the Supreme Court might take a case: namely, when "on the same important matter" divergent rulings have been reached by two federal appeals courts, a federal appeals court and a state supreme court, or two state supreme courts.

In 2003, Justice Ruth Bader Ginsburg described such conflict among lower courts as a chief motivator for providing review. "[W]e take cases primarily to keep federal law fairly uniform, to resolve strong disagreements—splits not likely to heal—among federal or state tribunals over the meaning of a federal statute or executive regulation, or constitutional provision. Currently, about 70 percent of the cases we agree to hear involve deep divisions of opinion among federal courts of appeals or state high courts" (Ginsburg 2003, 521).

Research on the Supreme Court also indicates that while conflicting rulings among the lower courts is not a necessary condition, it is one of the main factors that increases the likelihood of a grant of cert. According to one study, nearly 40 percent of the majority opinions written in the 1997–2001 terms cited lower court conflict as the reason for accepting a case, and according to another estimate, 80 percent of cert grants involve conflicts between federal appeals courts (Baum 2004, 97–98).

Significance

Rule 10 also states that cert might be granted when a U.S. court of appeals "has so far departed from the accepted and usual course of judicial proceedings, or sanctioned such a departure by a lower court, as to call for an exercise of this Court's supervisory power" or when a state court or federal appeals court "has decided an important question of federal law that has not been, but should be, settled by this Court, or has decided an important federal question in a way that conflicts with relevant decisions of this Court" (*Rules of the Supreme Court of the United States* 2019, 5–6). Both of these components of Rule 10 highlight that the importance of an issue matters to justices.

Determining what issues rise to the level of being significant enough to warrant Supreme Court intervention is hard to pin down. But as political scientist Lawrence Baum explains, if granting cert would only have an impact on the particular parties to the case, the Court is not likely to issue such a grant. "The justices look for cases in which a decision would have broad effects on courts, government, or society as a whole" (Baum 2004, 98).

Who Is Involved

One factor that may signal the significance of a case is who is in involved. In practice, the parties, lawyers, and "friends of the court" involved in cases can make a big difference in the chances of cert being granted.

In particular, the federal government and its solicitor general, the federal government's chief lawyer, have a notable advantage at gaining a hearing: 70–80 percent of cases petitioned to the Court by the federal government receive cert (Epstein and Walker 2018, 15). Because the United States is party to many lawsuits appealed to the Supreme Court, the solicitor general's office and staff have extensive experience handling such cases. The solicitor general routinely appears before the Court representing the federal government and is sometimes called upon by the Court to weigh in on cases in which the federal government has an interest but is not a party. Indeed, some refer to the solicitor general as the "tenth justice" (see, e.g., Caplan 1987). Moreover, the solicitor general's office does not bring every case to the Court. By selecting only a subset of cases, the solicitor general's office works to screen out cases that are not likely to be granted cert. Given this type of pre-screening and the routine involvement of the U.S. government in Supreme Court cases, it is not surprising that the solicitor general has a much higher rate of success in getting cert petitions granted.

Political scientists Lee Epstein and Thomas G. Walker also point to evidence showing the influence on cert grants of other "elite" attorneys (Epstein and Walker 2018, 15). A *Reuters* report published in 2014 and examining nine years of cases revealed that "66 of the 17,000 lawyers who petitioned the Supreme Court succeeded at getting their clients' appeals heard at a remarkable rate. Their appeals were at least six times more likely to be accepted by the court than were all others filed by private lawyers during that period" (Biskupic, Roberts and Shiffman 2014). Notable among this group of sixty-six is their prior experience: half of them worked for past or sitting Supreme Court justices.

Interest groups are also influential. Interest groups can make their voices heard in Supreme Court cases at the petition stage as "friends of the court" by way of filing amicus briefs. Cert-stage amicus briefs are not that common but are correlated with a higher rate of cert grants. In the 2014 term, for instance, friends of the court filed a total of 403 briefs prior to cert decisions in 177 out of 7,006 cases. Interestingly, almost 18 percent of these 177 cases were granted cert, as compared to the 1 percent rate of all filed petitions (Feldman 2016). In another noteworthy study of interest group influence, legal scholars Gregory Caldeira and John Wright found that for cases with a reasonable chance of acceptance in the first place, "amicus curiae briefs can mark the difference between success and failure. . . . When a case involves real conflict or when the federal government is petitioner, the addition of just one amicus curiae brief in support of certiorari increases the likelihood of plenary review by 40%–50%. Without question, then, interested parties can have a significant and positive impact on the Court's agenda by participating as amici curiae prior to the Court's decision on certiorari or jurisdiction" (Caldeira and Wright 1988, 1122).

Policy, Ideology, Strategy

Researchers also point to evidence suggesting that the political, policy, and ideological preferences of justices can make a difference to whether cert will be granted or denied. The findings of this line of research suggest not only that political leanings of justices are influential but that members of the bench make strategic choices in voting to grant cert. These choices are based on their predictions of how the case will likely be decided if cert is given. "Considerable evidence suggests that justices engage in this prediction process. One study demonstrated that justices are much more likely to vote to grant certiorari when the Court's decision could be expected to reflect their ideological leanings rather than to run contrary to those leanings" (Baum 2004, 99).

Importantly, research showing that the Court's cert decisions and agenda setting are influenced by the political views and preferences of justices suggests that this applies regardless of where justices fall along the liberal and conservative ideological spectrum. As Epstein and Walker summarize it, "Researchers tell us that the justices during the liberal period under Chief Justice Earl Warren (1953–1969) were more likely to grant review to cases in which the lower court reached a conservative decision so that they could reverse, while those of the moderately conservative Court during the years of Chief Justice Warren E. Burger (1969–1986) took liberal results to reverse" (Epstein and Walker 2018, 16).

CASE DISPOSITION: DENIALS, GRANTS, OPINION WRITING, AND DECISIONS

The disposition of the cases the Court receives varies notably, of course, by whether the petitions are selected or denied full review. The Court has a few other options as well for handling petitions.

Denial of Cert

As noted earlier, ninety-nine out of every hundred cert petitions submitted to the Court are denied. The disposition of these cases is, generally speaking, relatively simple. The Clerk of the Court enters the order and notifies "counsel of record and the court whose judgment was sought to be reviewed" (*Rules of the Supreme Court of the United States* 2019, 17). The order denying cert is also reported to the public.

A denial of cert leaves in place the decision of the lower court. Notably, though, a denial of cert does not set legal precedent or provide affirmation that the Supreme Court accepts the logic and legal analysis contained in the lower court ruling. In addition, while the lower court ruling remains in force, it only applies to the jurisdictions governed by that court.

Cert denials are rarely accompanied by an opinion or explanation. However, justices who disagree with a cert denial sometimes write a dissenting opinion. For example, in December 2018, the Supreme Court denied cert in two cases concerning a state's authority to refuse Medicaid reimbursements to Planned Parenthood, a non-profit that provides reproductive health services, including abortion. The cert denial left in place lower court rulings that permit recipients of Medicaid to challenge a state's determination of who is a "qualified" Medicaid provider. The refusal to hear the case elicited an admonishing dissent written by Justice Clarence Thomas and joined by Justices Samuel Alito and Neil Gorsuch: "So what explains the Court's refusal to do its job here? I suspect it has something to do with the fact that some respondents in these cases are named 'Planned Parenthood.' That makes the Court's decision particularly troubling, as the question presented has nothing to do with abortion. . . . Some tenuous connection to a politically fraught issue does not justify abdicating our judicial duty. If anything, neutrally applying the law is all the more important when political issues are in the background" (*Gee v. Planned Parenthood of Gulf Coast* 2018, 410).

Summary Consideration, GVR Orders, Cases Held Over

To a handful of cert petitions, the Court provides summary consideration. In some summary consideration cases, the Court arrives at a judgment on the merits of the case and issues a brief and unsigned *per curiam* (by the Court) opinion that explains its judgment. In others, the Court issues an order without oral argument. However, in most summary consideration cases, the Court does not produce a decision on the merits; instead, it sends the case back to the lower court for that court's further review. In these instances, the Court *grants cert, vacates* the lower court decision (effectively making that decision void), and *remands* the case back to the lower court. A common reason for issuing such a *GVR order* is that relevant circumstances changed after the lower court issued its ruling, and the Supreme Court asks the lower to reconsider the case in light of those changes.

The Court sometimes exercises the option to hold a case over—that is, to defer action on it until some future time. This has sometimes happened in the context of the Court requesting additional information or arguments. In other contexts, the Court holds a case over in order to await a decision in a similar case.

Full Review

When cert and full review are granted, the case is put on the Supreme Court's schedule, and the parties to the case file written legal briefs laying out their legal arguments. These briefs, which offer arguments as to how the Court should decide the merits of the case, differ from the briefs written at the cert stage, which present arguments explaining whether the Court should give the case full review. While the parties to the case have particular issues and arguments they want to present for consideration in their legal briefs, the Court has the authority to determine which issues to hear. Thus, the Court can restrict its grant of cert to a particular matter addressed in the original cert petition or expand its consideration beyond the scope of that original petition.

Additional legal briefs concerning the merits of the case may be submitted by others who are not direct parties to the litigation but who might nevertheless have an interest in its outcome. Just as "friends of the court" can submit briefs at the cert stage, such amicus curiae briefs can be filed on the merits after cert is granted. The U.S. government or government of states may file such a brief without requesting permission from the Court or the parties involved. Other groups and organizations that wish to submit an amicus brief may do so if the parties to the litigation consent or if the Court gives permission.

Oral Arguments

In full review cases, after the parties and "friends of the court" file written legal briefs, the Court hears oral arguments. Oral arguments are typically heard beginning at 10:00 a.m. on Monday, Tuesday, and Wednesday mornings (on two-week cycles from October to April), with two cases usually argued each of those days. Each party usually has thirty minutes to make their case, though the Court occasionally allots more time. If the U.S. government has an interest in the case, albeit not as a direct party, it may be given time at oral argument to present the government's view.

Supreme Court oral arguments are neither televised nor video recorded, but they are open to the public and audio recorded, with written and audio transcripts released later in the day and week, respectively. Attending or listening to oral arguments, one can quickly tell that they do not take the form of a lecture. Nor are they akin to closing arguments made by lawyers in trials. By contrast, they tend to be occasions where the justices pepper attorneys with questions, generating back-and-forth exchanges that are generally respectful even as the justices routinely interrupt attorneys midsentence.

Justices also sometimes use oral arguments not to gain clarity from the attorneys but to try to persuade other justices of how the case should be decided. They do this, for example, by asking questions that might expose a weakness or strength in the arguments of the attorneys. Sometimes justices jump in to help an attorney make a point. By contrast, some justices say little during oral arguments. Justice Clarence Thomas is so well known for his relative silence during oral argument that it makes the news when he speaks up. For example, as the *Washington Post* reported in 2016, "For first time in 10 years, Justice Clarence Thomas asks questions during an argument" (Barnes 2016).

Voting, Opinion Assignment, and Opinion Writing

At the next scheduled Conference after oral arguments, the justices consider the heard cases and take a preliminary vote. The chief justice discusses the case first, and accordingly, frames the discussion. The other justices weigh in, by order of seniority and with each offering a tentative vote on how to decide the case. That vote controls who will write the opinion for Court. According to Court norms, the senior justice who votes with the majority decides which justice writes the opinion for the Court. Thus, the chief justice assigns the writing of the Court's opinion whenever the chief votes with the majority; conversely, when the chief justice votes with the minority, the assignment is made by the senior (longest-serving) justice who voted with the majority.

Importantly, though, a case may result in the issuance of multiple opinions: the opinion of the Court (which may be either a "majority" or "plurality" opinion); concurring opinions; and dissenting opinions. Understanding the difference between these types of opinions and the authority they carry is critical. Even when the *vote on the outcome* of a case gains a majority, that does not mean that the opinion for the Court will be joined by a majority of justices. This is because judicial opinions contain not only the outcomes of the cases, but also the logic, reasoning, and legal tests that may become precedent, which are, in theory at least, binding on lower courts. For example, knowing that the Supreme Court found a ban on contraception unconstitutional in *Griswold v. Connecticut* (1965) tells us the outcome of that case; knowing that the Court arrived at that outcome by finding in the Constitution a general right to privacy gets us to the logic and reasoning of the ruling, and its potential implications for future conflicts.

As discussed in chapter 2, the doctrine of stare decisis holds that, in future cases, lower courts and future Supreme Courts are generally obligated to apply rules and principles established and settled by the Court of last resort. That is, they are generally obligated to follow precedent. Consider again the example of *Loving v. Virginia* (1967) discussed earlier. It matters not only *that* the Supreme Court ruled anti-miscegenation laws unconstitutional, but also *how* the Court arrived at and justified the ruling, and *whether* a majority of justices agreed with the justification. The opinion for the Court—in the case of *Loving*, a unanimous opinion joined by the nine justices—held that the Virginia law violated the Constitution because it conflicted with both the Equal Protection Clause and the Due Process Clause. "There can be no doubt that restricting the freedom to marry solely because of racial classifications violates the central meaning of the Equal Protection Clause," the Court opinion explained (12). In addition, the Court justified its holding by appealing to liberty protected by the

Due Process Clause of the Fourteenth Amendment. "The freedom to marry has long been recognized as one of the vital personal rights essential to the orderly pursuit of happiness by free men," and, quoting earlier Court rulings, stated that marriage "is one of the 'basic civil rights of man,' fundamental to our very existence and survival" (12). That majority-supported logic—identifying the freedom to marry as a personal right protected not only by equality but by liberty—has potential reverberations as precedent in future cases. So, the reasoning as well as the outcome of the case matters. Though the Court went to say that the "Fourteenth Amendment requires that the freedom of choice to marry not be restricted by invidious racial discriminations" (12), the language characterizing the freedom to marry as a basic civil right has implications not only for laws banning interracial marriage but also, as taken up in later cases, laws banning marriage between same-sex couples.

It therefore matters a great deal what the opinion for the Court says *and whether it is joined by a majority of justices.* An opinion of the Court is a majority opinion only if a majority of justices who heard the case are willing to join it; if, on the other hand, only a plurality of justices join, it is called a plurality opinion. If nine justices hear a case, at least five must join the opinion of the Court for it to be a majority and count as precedent; but if only four out of nine join, it amounts to a plurality opinion and does not count as precedent.[5]

In addition to the opinion of the Court, there may also be concurring and dissenting opinions issued by justices in a given case. Dissenting opinions disagree with both the outcome and rationale of the opinion of the Court. Though any justice who votes against the ruling of the Court can write a dissenting opinion, the primary dissent is assigned by the senior justice who voted with the minority.

Concurring opinions come in two different types. In one type, a justice accepts or joins the opinion of the Court, but writes a separate opinion to make a distinct point or amplify a point expressed in the Court's opinion. For example, Justice William Douglas joined the Court's opinion in *New York Times Co. v. United States*, but wrote a separate concurring opinion that began with these words: "While I join the opinion of the Court I believe it necessary to express my views more fully" (*New York Times Co. v. United States* 1971, 720, concurring opinion).

The other type of concurring opinion "concurs in judgment only." In this instance, the justice concurs with the outcome of the opinion of the Court but disagrees with the logic and reasoning used to arrive at that outcome. *Frontiero v. Richardson*, discussed in chapter 2, is illustrative. An opinion written by Justice Potter Stewart and another opinion written by Justice Lewis Powell (and joined by two other justices) concurred in the judgment of the Court's plurality ruling that the Air Force had violated the

Constitution, but disagreed with the logic. There was also a separate dissent in the case written by Justice William Rehnquist. Because the opinion of the Court, authored by Justice William Brennan, only garnered the signature and support of four justices, that opinion's call to view gender classifications as "inherently suspect" and subject to "strict judicial scrutiny" did not establish precedent (*Frontiero v. Richardson* 1973, 688). Justice Powell's separate concurrence explained his divergent rationale as follows:

> I agree that the challenged statutes constitute an unconstitutional discrimination against servicewomen in violation of the Due Process Clause of the Fifth Amendment, but I cannot join the opinion of MR. JUSTICE BRENNAN, which would hold that all classifications based upon sex, "like classifications based upon race, alienage, and national origin," are "inherently suspect, and must therefore be subjected to close judicial scrutiny." It is unnecessary for the Court in this case to characterize sex as a suspect classification, with all of the far-reaching implications of such a holding. *Reed v. Reed*, 404 U.S. 71 (1971), which abundantly supports our decision today, did not add sex to the narrowly limited group of classifications which are inherently suspect. In my view, we can and should decide this case on the authority of *Reed*, and reserve for the future any expansion of its rationale. (*Frontiero v. Richardson* 1973, 691–92, concurring in judgment)

An opinion for the Court might become a plurality if only eight justices participate in a case and split their vote four to four. (When a tie vote occurs, the ruling of the lower court stands.) But more common is that an opinion of the Court becomes a plurality rather than majority because the justices disagree on the logic even while agreeing on the outcome. This means that who writes the opinion for the Court matters, but also that the justice assigned to write the opinion for the Court does not have complete control over its content. Since a plurality opinion does not carry the weight of precedent, the justice assigned to write the Court's opinion in a given case will typically seek to make sure that a majority of the justices are willing to accept the written opinion, and the other justices who voted with the majority may try to shape the opinion to reflect the legal reasoning they find persuasive.

Thus, after Conference and the assignment of opinion writing in a given case, and before the announcement of a final decision in a case, the process of drafting and redrafting opinions unfolds. The justice charged with writing the opinion for the Court produces a draft, often with the assistance of law clerks, and circulates it to the other justices. Those justices who voted at Conference with the majority might accept the opinion as drafted or request amendments. Justices who voted with the minority might change their positions and join the majority or might ask for amendments to the opinion that would be sufficient enough to lead them to switch their votes. At the same time, other justices might be drafting opinions in the case that present different legal rationales and arguments, even if they agreed in Conference with the majority about the outcome of the case. Moreover, as this process unfolds, another drafted opinion might emerge as the one that garners a majority of votes and can become the opinion of the Court. It may even happen that a minority opinion emerges as a majority opinion. As Justice Ginsburg has commented, once or twice each term, a circulated dissent gains enough votes to become a majority opinion and thus the ruling of the Court (Ginsburg 2003, 526). Alternatively, if a majority of justices agree with the outcome of a case but the drafted opinion only earns a plurality vote, with others writing a separate "concurring in judgment only" opinion, then the opinion of the Court will end up as a "plurality" opinion.

In other words, the drafting and redrafting of what will eventually become the opinion of the Court can be a process of extensive negotiation, with justices conditioning their willingness to join an opinion on the language and legal arguments contained therein. Consider *District of Columbia v. Heller*, the 2008 holding that the Second Amendment protects an individual's right to own a gun for personal use. While arriving at that landmark decision, the majority opinion also states that Second Amendment rights, like most others, have limits, and "nothing in our opinion should be taken to cast doubt on longstanding prohibitions on the possession of firearms by felons and the mentally ill, or laws forbidding the carrying of firearms in sensitive places such as schools and government buildings, or laws imposing conditions and qualifications on the commercial sale of arms" (*District of Columbia v. Heller* 2008, 2816–17). Qualifying the Second Amendment right to bear arms by explicitly including examples of permissible gun regulations was, according to one insider's account, the result of negotiation by Justice Anthony Kennedy, so often the swing vote, who joined the five-vote majority in *Heller*. Justice John Paul Stevens, who vigorously dissented in *Heller*, "initially thought he might be able to persuade Justice Anthony Kennedy to vote with him and change the outcome of the case, but Kennedy did not change sides. Instead, Kennedy insisted—as the price of his vote—that the majority opinion, written by the late Justice Antonin Scalia, contain language that provided for reasonable gun regulations" (Totenberg 2019b).

Decision Day

Decisions in cases given full review are made public after the opinions in a case are written and the justices decide which opinions they will join. There is no rigid schedule about the timing of announcements. Sometimes decisions are released as early as December, but it is more common for decisions to be announced in spring and early summer. May and June are the most active months for the release of Supreme Court rulings, and in those months the Court meets at 10:00 a.m. every Monday to release its completed opinions. The month of June, just before the Court goes into summer recess, is primetime for decision announcements, and during the final week of the term, the Court sometimes designates additional days as "opinion days."

Announcements of Court opinions are made from the bench, with the author of the Court's opinion summarizing the ruling. Occasionally, dissenting justices will read from or summarize their opinions as well. In some high-profile cases, reporters are seen running from the Supreme Court with the decision in hand to communicate the outcome.

CONCLUSION

Among the notable things about the Court's structure and processes is just how much discretion justices have in case selection and decision making. Who the justices are, what approaches to jurisprudence they hold, which law clerks they select to serve as gatekeepers to the cert process, and so forth matter a great deal. In turn, how the justices are selected to the bench also matters. It is to the judicial selection process that the next chapter turns.

NOTES

1. The terms referenced here are those beginning in October 2008 and running through June 2018. See Chief Justice's Year-End Reports on the Federal Judiciary, available at https://www.supremecourt.gov/publicinfo/year-end/year-endreports .aspx.

2. However, for a catalog of several instances in which this precedent has not held, see Murphy et al. 2006, Chapter 6.

3. The Rule of Four is not without its critics because it gives considerable agenda-setting power to a minority of justices. It is "a device by which a minority of the Court can impose on the majority a question that the majority does not think it appropriate to address" (Kurland and Hutchinson 1983, 645).

4. The Court published the most recent version of these rules in 2019, but they date back to 1803 and have been revised multiple times over the Court's history. For the historical collection of these rules, see https://www.supremecourt.gov /ctrules/scannedrules.aspx.

5. Determining whether there is a majority or plurality depends on the total number of justices who heard the case in question, not the total of number of justices who serve on the Court. In some instances, fewer than nine justices hear a case. For example, a justice might be recused from a case owing to a conflict of interest.

4

The Justices and Judicial Selection

"The decision not to fill the Scalia vacancy. . . . I think that's the most consequential thing I've ever done."

—Senate Majority Leader Mitch McConnell,
New York Times Interview

"A Supreme Court confirmation process that calls for a nomination by the president (an elected official) and requires consent from the Senate (also composed of elected officials) is going to be a political process. It always has been, and always will be."

—Paul Collins and Lori Ringhand, "The Top Five
Supreme Court Nomination Myths"

On February 13, 2016, Justice Antonin Scalia died. Within a few hours of the announcement of his passing, Senate majority leader Mitch McConnell, a Republican representing Kentucky, declared that he would not hold confirmation hearings on any nominee appointed by Democratic President Barack Obama to fill the vacancy. That declaration, and McConnell's commitment to it, meant that the seat would remain empty until after the election of the next president.

Article II, Section 2, of the Constitution outlines in brief how justices will be appointed, stating that the president "shall nominate, and by and with the Advice and Consent of the Senate, shall appoint . . . Judges of the supreme Court." Because the Constitution requires the Senate's consent for appointments to the federal bench (except for temporary appointments the president might make when the Senate is in recess), McConnell acted within the scope of Congressional authority. But he broke with longstanding norms governing the selection of federal judges—norms that include giving a hearing to a Supreme Court nominee even if that nominee is ultimately not confirmed. McConnell reportedly pressured some reluctant Republican senators to fall in line by promising to support primary challenges against them if they did not (Totenberg 2019a). He also touted his decision this way: "One of my proudest moments was when I looked Barack Obama in the eye and I said, 'Mr. President, you will not fill the Supreme Court vacancy'" (Elving 2018). McConnell's public and aggressive rejection of established norms around the confirmation process advanced his political agenda. But in doing so, he also made it clear how much the Supreme Court had become politicized.

Politics in and politicization of the judicial selection process are not new. The intersection between politics and law is often laid bare around nominations and confirmations. This chapter will highlight such instances and explore a number of political factors manifest in the judicial selection process. Still, the rule of law relies on the perception that law and politics are not coterminous. Much of the discourse around judges and their selection is framed around the ideal that the courts are distinct from the political branches and that judges stand outside of and above the political fray. McConnell's stance made it plain that such ideals often can't survive the rough-and-tumble of American politics.

COMPOSITION OF THE COURT

Nine justices—a chief justice and eight associate justices—presently serve on the high bench. This number is not stipulated in the Constitution, but rather is designated by Congress. It has changed five times since it was first set at six justices by the Judiciary Act of 1789, and it has ranged from a low of six to a high of ten.[1] Though proposals have been made to increase the size of the Supreme Court over the years, including the famous court-packing plan suggested by President Franklin Delano Roosevelt in the mid-1930s, the number has not changed since just after the Civil War, when it was put at nine by the Judiciary Act of 1869.

The Constitution does not specify that justices who serve on the Supreme Court have any particular job qualifications or characteristics. Minimum age requirements exist for the president and members of Congress, but not for justices. No prior job experience or level of education—not even a law degree—is explicitly required. Nevertheless, all nominees to the Court have been lawyers (McMillion 2018, 9), though not all have earned law degrees. Indeed, since law schools did not become commonplace until the late 1800s, only seventeen of the fifty-seven justices confirmed to the bench prior to 1900 attended or graduated from law school. Since 1900, law school attendance has become almost universal for justices. Of the fifty-seven justices confirmed since the turn of the twentieth century, forty-six earned a law degree, and every justice since 1943 has graduated from law school (Epstein et al. 2019).

Brett Kavanaugh, confirmed in September 2018, became the 114th justice to serve on the Court. A white male from Washington, D.C., and a practicing Roman Catholic, he attended Yale College and Yale Law School, served as a law clerk for two U.S. Circuit Court judges and for Supreme Court Justice Anthony Kennedy. He worked in the Office of U.S. Solicitor General during Kenneth Starr's tenure as solicitor general. When Starr was later appointed as independent counsel to investigate President Bill Clinton, Kavanaugh worked for him again. After a brief stint in a private law firm, Kavanaugh served as counsel and then as staff secretary to President George W. Bush. Bush nominated Kavanaugh to the U.S. Court of Appeals for the D.C. Circuit in 2003. Though Republicans controlled the Senate at the time, they had only a two-vote margin. Democrats used the filibuster to block multiple nominations to the federal bench, including that of Kavanaugh. (The filibuster, when in use, requires a supermajority of sixty votes out of the one hundred members of the Senate to move forward with nominations.) President Bush nominated Kavanaugh for the D.C. Circuit again in 2006 after the Republicans gained seats in the Senate, and Kavanaugh was confirmed for that position on May 26, 2006.

In many respects, Justice Kavanaugh embodies the characteristics of those who have served on the high bench. According to the Pew Research Center's 2017 analysis of the 113 justices who served prior to Kavanaugh's appointment, many share similar education, training, and work experience. More than half were educated at Ivy League schools (and all members of the current bench studied law at Harvard or Yale, though Justice Ginsburg, who started at Harvard, transferred to and received her JD from Columbia). Kavanaugh joins all but 8 of the 113 who had worked in private practice, and at least 69 who had previous experience as judges, with 31 having served on the federal appeals bench. Like Kavanaugh, at least 24 had worked in the U.S. Department of Justice, but unlike Kavanaugh, a majority had been elected to public office (Bialik 2017).

Justice Kavanaugh also shares many demographic traits of other justices. All but 4 (Sandra Day O'Connor, Ruth Bader Ginsburg, Sonia Sotomayor, and Elena Kagan) of the 114 justices in American history have been men. There have been two African American justices (Thurgood Marshall and Clarence Thomas) and one Hispanic justice (Sonia Sotomayor); the rest have been white. While the Court has five sitting members as of early 2020 who are Catholic, Kavanaugh is among only thirteen Catholic justices who have served on the bench. There have been eight Jewish justices, three of whom are currently serving. The vast majority of justices have been Protestant (Yourish, Peçanha, and Griggs 2018).

When he was sworn in, Kavanaugh was 53 years old, the average age at which justices are confirmed (Bialik 2017). Since 1900, the age at which justices join the Court has trended slightly younger, dropping from an average of 55.4 to 52.2 (Khullar and Jena 2018). It is impossible to know how long Justice Kavanaugh will serve. If he stays for the average amount of time of all prior justices, he will serve for close to 17 years (Bialik 2017). More likely, though, his tenure on the Court will be considerably longer. The longest-serving justice was William O. Douglas, who retired in 1975 after a tenure of 36 years and 209 days. Kavanaugh replaced Justice Kennedy, who retired at the age of 82 after 30 years of service. As of 2020, Justices Ginsburg and Stephen Breyer, both in their 80s, have served 26 and 25 years respectively. Justice Thomas has been on the Court longer than Ginsburg and Breyer—for almost 28 years, having been nominated at age 43—and is comparatively young at 71. Consider, as well, that between 1789 and 1970 justices served an average of 14.9 years, while those who retired between 1970 and 2005 served much longer, averaging 26.1 years (Calabresi and Lindgren 2006, 770–71). Continuing this trend, the six departures from the bench since August 2005 occurred after an average of 28.53 years of service (Feldman 2019).

Justice Kavanaugh also shares the jurisprudential views of some, though certainly not all, of his fellow jurists. And while a number of the characteristics noted earlier figure into the judicial selection process, so too does the jurisprudence of the nominee. In recent years, judicial philosophy has become front and center of the nomination and confirmation process. As will be discussed, contests over alternative approaches to interpreting the Constitution have contributed to the politicization of the nomination and confirmation process.

THE PATH TO JOINING THE COURT

Entry to membership on the Court is shaped heavily by the path of departure from the bench. According to Article III, Section 1, of the Constitution, "The Judges, both of the supreme and inferior Courts, shall hold their Offices during good Behaviour," and Article II, Section 4, stipulates that "[t]he President, Vice President and all civil Officers of the United States, shall be removed from Office on Impeachment for, and Conviction of, Treason, Bribery, or other high Crimes and Misdemeanors." These two sections of the Constitution have been interpreted as meaning that Article III judges, including Supreme Court justices, can only be removed through impeachment proceedings.[2] In other words, Supreme Court justices have lifetime appointments, and openings on the bench occur only when a justice retires, resigns, dies, or is removed through impeachment. Thus, unlike selection of members of Congress and the president, which occur at regular intervals, changes of personnel on the bench happen intermittently and unpredictably.

Also, unlike the selection of members of Congress and the president, justices are not elected. Under the checks and balances system established by the Founders, who wanted to insulate the courts from the electoral process, the executive and legislative branches share the responsibility of selecting justices. The president nominates a candidate when a seat on the Court becomes available. Under the Constitution's delegation to the Senate of authority to give "advice and consent" to the president on various appointments, nominees only gain a seat on the bench if confirmed by a majority vote in the Senate.

Presidents and members of Congress will often claim during the selection process that they assess candidates solely on their merits. At the same time, they will often accuse the other party of politicizing the selection process. Whatever claims they make about their own motivations or those of others, there is widespread agreement among political science researchers, legal scholars, and court observers that the selection of justices is a political and politicized process. Because the average tenure of justices lasts far longer than the eight years a president can hold office, judicial nominations can leave a president's lasting mark on American governance and politics. This fact alone creates incentive for a president to select candidates who share a similar political ideology and are likely to advance the president's political and policy positions. But this is not all. The nomination and confirmation of justices can appeal to particular voting constituencies and interest groups, and thereby matter in electoral politics for both the president and his or her party. The nomination of a justice might meet with resistance in the Senate, a possibility that can influence a president's choice. Or a nomination might be a reward for someone who has served the president or political party. In short, while the number and combination of factors influencing a particular choice of nominee is complex, the process is undoubtedly infused with and shaped by politics.

Appointments

Potential appointees to the Court are identified often before a vacancy becomes available. Authority to select a nominee to fill a vacant seat lies with the president, but he or she receives assistance from several players in identifying and assessing the pool of potential candidates. In the executive branch, the White House counsel, the Department of Justice (especially the attorney general), and various White House aides play an important role in compiling a list of and screening prospective candidates. The president also often consults with party leaders and various elected officials, including members of Congress and governors. The president may also receive guidance from organized groups, as, for example, President Trump did from the Federalist Society, a conservative and libertarian legal organization that has become an influential player in judicial selection. Even sitting members of the Supreme Court have been known to identify and recommend candidates. It has even been reported that Justice Kennedy met privately with President Trump to suggest Brett Kavanaugh—one of Kennedy's former law clerks—as a possible candidate for the Court (Marcus 2019). The meeting reportedly followed the swearing-in ceremony over which Kennedy presided for newly confirmed Supreme Court Justice Neil Gorsuch—also a former law clerk to Kennedy (Barnes 2019a).

With so many voices and perspectives constructing the list of contenders, what explains how the pool is whittled down? Several factors influencing the ultimate selection of Supreme Court nominees are detailed here.

Professional Qualifications and Integrity

Despite constitutional silence on judicial qualifications, *credentials and experience* generally matter, and historical norms suggest that appointment to the federal bench is "different from run-of-the-mill patronage. Thus, although the political rules may allow a president to reward an old ally with a seat on the bench, even here tradition has created an expectation that the would-be judge have some reputation for professional competence, the more so as the judgeship in question goes from the trial court to the appeals court to the Supreme Court level" (Carp and Stidham 1996, 240–41).

Among those who evaluate the professional qualifications of nominees to the federal bench is the American Bar Association (ABA), the leading professional organization of lawyers in the United States. In 1952, the administration of President Dwight D. Eisenhower began what would become a longstanding practice of seeking the ABA's input on potential nominees to the Supreme Court and lower federal courts. Since 1952, most presidential administrations sent confidential lists of candidates under consideration for judicial appointments to the ABA's Standing Committee on the Federal Judiciary for evaluation. While the presidential administrations of George W. Bush and Donald Trump stopped the practice of seeking the ABA's input prior to nomination, the ABA continues to evaluate candidates once they have been nominated to the federal bench.

The goal of the Standing Committee on the Federal Judiciary, as described by the ABA, is "to support and encourage the selection of the best-qualified persons for the federal judiciary. It restricts its evaluation to issues bearing on professional qualifications and does not consider a nominee's philosophy or ideology. The Committee's peer-review process is structured to achieve impartial evaluations of the integrity, professional competence and judicial temperament of nominees for the federal judiciary" (ABA 2020a). Since 1981, for an announced nomination to the Supreme Court, the Standing Committee conducts interviews, relies on law professors and practicing lawyers with Supreme Court experience to examine the nominee's legal writings "for quality, clarity, knowledge of the law, and analytical ability," and then rates the nominee as either "Well Qualified," "Qualified," and "Not Qualified" (ABA 2020b). The reported ratings include whether the Standing Committee was unanimous or divided.

While the ABA has never issued a "not qualified" assessment for a nominee to the Court, nominations to the federal District and Circuit Courts have garnered negative ratings. Moreover, pre-nomination evaluations by the Standing Committee might influence a president's choice of nominee. And even when a majority of the Standing Committee deems a Supreme Court nominee "well qualified," a divided assessment can figure into how the Senate votes. Consider, for example, President Ronald Reagan's nomination of federal appeals court judge Robert Bork to the Supreme Court in 1987. While a number of factors led the Senate to vote against confirmation, the ABA's divided vote, and the assessment of some on the Committee who questioned Bork's "judicial temperament," arguably "provide ammunition" against his candidacy (Taylor 1987). As the *New York Times* reported, "Of the 15 members of the A.B.A.'s Standing Committee on Federal Judiciary, 10 gave Judge Bork the highest rating, 'well qualified,' four voted 'not qualified' and one 'not opposed,' one source said. The number of dissenters was highly unusual; in the view of Judge Bork's opponents, this could pose a problem for his nomination to the vacancy on the Supreme Court" (Taylor 1987).

The *integrity and ethical behavior* of prospective justices also come into play, and the ABA evaluates candidates for integrity. But, importantly, winnowing down the pool of prospective nominees usually involves personal background investigations conducted by the Federal Bureau of Investigation (FBI). These investigations go deeper as the list of potential nominees gets shorter, with the FBI looking into financial matters, conflicts of interest, and personal actions that might prove disqualifying. The public will not necessarily learn the results of such background checks when they are performed during the vetting process because they are, in that context, used to weed out potentially problematic candidates.

In some cases, ethical questions and misconduct allegations emerge only after a president has announced the appointment. Claims of sexual misconduct besieged—though ultimately did not overcome—the nominations of Clarence Thomas and Brett Kavanaugh. Both men denied the allegations made against them. In other instances, the disclosure of ethical concerns has doomed candidates, as it did to President Reagan's 1987 nomination of Douglas Ginsburg, a judge on the U.S. Court of Appeals for the D.C. Circuit. Questions were raised about Judge Ginsburg's truthfulness and handling of a prior case in which he might have had a conflict of interest. Of greater consequence, Judge Ginsburg admitted to smoking marijuana, a revelation that made his confirmation to the Supreme Court untenable given, among other things, that Reagan had declared a "War on Drugs" in 1982 and touted Judge Ginsburg's nomination as "vitally important to the fight against crime" (Roberts 1987). Moreover, public attitudes about recreational marijuana use during the 1980s were considerably different than they are today. Administration officials and conservative Republicans in Congress began to express misgivings about Reagan's choice. On November 8, 1987, nine days after his nomination, Ginsburg asked President Reagan to withdraw his nomination.

Political Considerations

While presidents and their advisors investigate the professional qualifications and personal integrity of prospective nominees, it is also beyond question that political factors play a role. Legal scholar David M. O'Brien puts it this way: "The Supreme Court is not a meritocracy. This is so for essentially two reasons: the difficulties of defining merit and the politics of judicial selection" (O'Brien 2014, 33). In calling out the "myth of merit," O'Brien does not deny that experience and ability figure into the selection process. Instead, he argues that "[m]erit competes with other political considerations" (33).

Among these considerations is the use of appointments as a form of *political patronage*, that is, as a reward for friends, allies, or party loyalists. There are several examples of presidents appointing "friends and confidantes," including, Franklin Delano Roosevelt's nomination of Felix Frankfurter, Harry S. Truman's appointment of Fred Vinson, John F. Kennedy's selection of friend Byron White, and Lyndon B. Johnson's choice of Abe Fortas (Epstein and Posner 2016, 402). "Some appointments to the Court were direct rewards for political help. Eisenhower selected Earl Warren to serve as chief justice in part because of Warren's crucial support of Eisenhower at the 1952 Republic convention. As governor of California and leader of that state's delegations, Warren had provided needed votes on a preliminary issue, and Eisenhower's success on that issue helped to secure his nomination" (Baum 2004, 40).

As a reward for past actions, patronage is a backward-looking political consideration. Selections are also influenced by forward-looking political and pragmatic factors. Presidents must be cognizant of how a nomination will fare with the electorate and how it will play politically in the Senate confirmation stage. Additionally, presidents view nominations as a way to advance their ideological agenda and shape future policy.

Senate influence on the Court's composition weighs heavily during the confirmation phase, as discussed later. But it can also be important at the nomination stage. Certain customs and longstanding practices have led presidents to consult with Senate leaders and members of the Senate Judiciary Committee prior to naming a candidate to the bench. One such custom is "senatorial courtesy." When the president names someone for federal office and the senator from nominee's home state opposes the nomination, the norm of senatorial courtesy calls on other senators to oppose confirmation. This norm does not typically apply to Supreme Court nominees but, rather, to other federal appointments, including lower court judges. Nevertheless, it appears to have been used in some past instances to block Supreme Court nominations.[3] Moving forward, though, it is unlikely to be used for Supreme Court nominations, and respect for the norm has begun to fade under the Republican-controlled Senate (see Hawkings 2018).

For the Supreme Court what is more influential than the norm of senatorial courtesy is whether the president anticipates resistance from the opposing political party in the Senate and what the magnitude of the resistance might be. "When confronted with a hostile Senate, [presidents] have modulated their appointments, moving to the right or left as necessary. Ford's nomination of the moderate John Paul Stevens rather than the conservative Robert Bork in light of an overwhelmingly Democratic Senate is a prime example of this kind of presidential pragmatism" (Epstein and Segal 2005, 78).

This type of modulation, which produces compromise candidates, is not necessary when the party of the president has a strong majority in the Senate. Instead it tends to operate when the party of the president does not control the Senate. Moreover, it has historically also operated when the president's party has only a slim majority control in the Senate because of the filibuster, which, as noted previously, requires a supermajority of sixty votes out of the one hundred members of the Senate to move forward with nominations. But the recent demise of the filibuster in Supreme Court confirmations means that presidents do not necessarily need to modulate their appointments when their party controls the Senate, even by only a slim margin.

Electoral considerations are another important political factor, and presidents are often moved by an interest in mobilizing certain voting blocks. In an effort to make electoral gains by appealing to certain constituencies and interest groups, presidents have made appointments based on such things as geography, religion, race, ethnicity, and gender. Geographic considerations were more important in the nineteenth century, when America was still growing across the continent and regional representation had greater influence. But President Richard Nixon was preoccupied with selecting jurists who would "help his 1972 reelection bid, and in particular . . . with enhancing the Republican party's appeal to southerners by appointing a justice from that region" (57). Religion has also been an important factor historically, though for much of the Court's history it mattered most in terms of homogeneity, with an overwhelming number of justices representing Protestant denominations. The same is true of race, ethnicity, and gender. Only recently has the Court become somewhat more diverse, and, only recently, have presidents begun to make a point of bringing diversity to the bench.

In June 1967, President Lyndon B. Johnson nominated the first African American to the bench. He did so after having first appointed Thurgood Marshall to be U.S. solicitor general, "a politically crafty plan that was years in the making to groom Marshall as the first African-American on the high court. It was part of a broader White House strategy to implement the president's civil rights agenda, something he openly hoped would cement his legacy and strengthen the Democrats' base" (Mears 2011).

As noted earlier, only one other African American has served on the Supreme Court, Justice Clarence Thomas, who was nominated by George H. W. Bush to fill the seat vacated when Marshall retired. That nomination is thought to have resulted in part from Bush's interest in ensuring some racial diversity on the Court. In May 2009, President Barack Obama nominated Sonia Sotomayor to replace departing Justice David Souter. That nomination resulted in the first Hispanic representation on the Court.

It was Reagan, a Republican president, who named the first women to serve on the Supreme Court, fulfilling a campaign promise to do so. Sandra Day O'Connor's appointment in 1981 came after many years of pressure by women's organizations and demands for gender representation. O'Connor remained the lone woman on the Court until President Bill Clinton appointed Ruth Bader Ginsburg in 1992. President Obama named two women to the Court: Sonia Sotomayor, followed shortly thereafter by Elena Kagan.

There are, of course, other types of electoral considerations that factor into a president's nomination. These include substantive considerations, such as appointing a justice who is thought to appeal ideologically to certain voting constituencies or interest groups. On the 2016 campaign trail, for example, then presidential candidate Donald Trump said he would name "pro-life judges" who would "have a conservative bent" (Blake 2016). He pledged as well to "appoint judges very much in the mold of Justice Scalia" (Adler 2017).

Substantive considerations are not only about appealing to voters. They are, as well, about advancing a *president's ideological and policy positions*. Presidents and their advisors review candidates' prior record to evaluate their judicial philosophies and their policy leanings. Judicial opinions, work experience, academic writings, speeches, and other public remarks can provide a trove of information, and individual interviews with prospective nominees can also prove illuminating.

Vetting candidates for ideological compatibility often, but certainly not always, produces the policy and ideological outcomes a president seeks. President Reagan's appointments to the Supreme Court provide a case in point. Reagan—a conservative Republican—appointed justices O'Connor, Scalia, and Kennedy to the bench and elevated Justice William Rehnquist to the position of chief justice when Warren Burger retired. In doing so, the Reagan administration was undoubtedly responsible for a marked shift toward a more conservative Court (and a more conservative federal judiciary in general). Among many other things, his appointment of Justice Scalia significantly contributed to the development and advancement of originalist jurisprudence, which has become a dominant judicial philosophy. But Reagan also sought and failed to constitute a Court that would overturn the right to abortion established by *Roe v. Wade*. Indeed, in 1992, two of his appointees—O'Connor and Kennedy—joined the pivotal and closely divided ruling in *Planned Parenthood of Southeastern Pennsylvania v. Casey* that reaffirmed the constitutional right to abortion (albeit with new limitations). In addition, although O'Connor and Kennedy joined more conservative rulings on a host of issues, they also aligned with more liberal positions on affirmative action and religious establishment cases. Perhaps most notable was Kennedy's position on LGBTQ rights. He not only joined but authored multiple Court rulings that extended rights to the LGBTQ community, including *Obergefell v. Hodges* (2015), the landmark Supreme Court decision granting same-sex couples the right to marry.

Using an appointment for patronage, electoral purposes, or policy advancement does not necessarily mean the selected candidate lacks merit. Appointments can be influenced by multiple factors at once, and a highly qualified and meritorious candidate can also appeal to key constituencies and align with a president's policy prerogatives.

The Confirmation Process

It is plain that the nomination process plays an important role in shaping the membership of Supreme Court. But the Senate's part should not be understated. The path to a seat on the Supreme Court runs directly through the Senate.

From the Court's establishment in 1789 through 2019, presidents have officially submitted to the Senate 163 nominations for the Court, including nominations for the position of chief justice. The Senate confirmed 126 of these nominations, 77 percent of the total.[4] The confirmation rate is actually better than that, given that a few named candidates were not confirmed when first put forward, but were later nominated again and confirmed. For instance, President George W. Bush named John Roberts to replace Justice O'Connor but, prior to Senate confirmation hearings, withdrew that nomination when Chief Justice Rehnquist died. President Bush then nominated, and the Senate confirmed, John Roberts for the chief justice position. Accounting for such things as repeated nominations and those withdrawn as a formality, twenty-six nominated individuals did not receive Senate confirmation.[5]

The rate of successful Supreme Court nominations, then, is closer to 80 percent. Moreover, most of what can be labeled as "failed" nominations occurred prior to 1900. Since then, out of sixty-seven nominations (not double-counting candidates nominated twice and later confirmed), there have been only seven failed nominations. The full Senate voted against President Herbert Hoover's nominee John Parker in 1930. Sitting Supreme Court Justice Abe Fortas, nominated in 1968 by President Lyndon B. Johnson for the position of chief justice, was withdrawn from consideration after failing to overcome a Senate filibuster. The full Senate rejected President Richard Nixon's nominations of Clement Haynsworth in 1969 and G. Harrold Carswell in 1970. In 1987, the Senate voted against President Reagan's nominee Robert Bork after contentious hearings in which Democratic Senators raised concerns about the candidate's conservative jurisprudence. Harriet Miers, nominated by President George W. Bush in 2005, was withdrawn from consideration owing in part to resistance from the president's own party. And, as alluded to at the outset of this chapter, the Senate refused to act upon President Obama's appointment of Merrick Garland in 2016.

Still, while the rate of failed nominations since 1900 is only at about 10 percent, the last eight presidents (from Nixon to Trump) have seen failures jump back up to 20 percent. This does not compare favorably to a much higher rate of successful confirmation of appointments to cabinet-level positions, which is at about 99 percent (see Whittington 2006). What's more, polarization and controversy over nominations in the past fifty years have been notable. Controversy over nominations has often been on public display in Senate confirmation hearings, even for candidates who ultimately earn confirmation. Votes in favor of nominated candidates have narrowed in the contemporary era, with unanimous or near unanimous support on the decline. And in recent years, as explained in the sections that follow, the polarization around appointments to the Court has led to rule changes governing how the Senate handles its advice and consent function.

Senate Judiciary Committee

Before the entire Senate takes up consideration of a judicial nominee, the nomination is generally referred to the Senate Judiciary Committee. The Committee is chaired by a member of the party that has majority control of the Senate, and the Committee's membership also reflects the party distribution in the Senate. Over the past sixty-five years, the typical practice has been for the Committee to review the detailed written record and convene public hearings. When hearings are complete, the Judiciary Committee votes on whether to recommend the nomination to the full Senate. The Committee can recommend to the full Senate that the nominee be granted or denied confirmation; or the Committee can send the nomination forward without a recommendation.

Confirmation Hearings

The Judiciary Committee is not required to hold confirmation hearings, and they have only become the norm in the modern era. Prior to 1925, all nominations, with three exceptions, were handled without a hearing. The exceptions were in 1873, 1916, and 1922, when the Judiciary Committee held hearings in the nominations, respectively, of George Williams, Louis Brandeis, and Pierce Butler. Only the hearing on the Brandeis nomination was public—marking the first public hearing for a Supreme Court nominee—and while witnesses were called to these sessions, in none did the nominee testify (Collins and Ringhand 2016a).

The 1925 nomination of Harlan Fiske Stone marked the first hearing at which the candidate testified before the Judiciary Committee. His testimony, in a closed session, was limited to answering questions about how, as attorney general, he pursued prosecutions in the Teapot Dome bribery scandal. That precedent-setting hearing did not routinize the practice of nominees testifying. Neither did the hearing for Felix Frankfurter who, in 1939,

became the first nominee to take unrestricted questions in an open, transcribed, public hearing. At the beginning of his hearings, numerous witnesses accused Frankfurter, a founder of the American Civil Liberties Union, with being a radical with ties to the Communist Party. Although Frankfurter did not plan on testifying, his advisors, reacting to the advice of members of the Committee, persuaded him to appear in person and refute these claims. Frankfurter's hearings became somewhat of a media circus, centered on allegations of his alleged sympathy to communist and socialist causes. When Frankfurter unequivocally and dramatically renounced any allegiance to communism or the Communist Party, the crowd reacted enthusiastically, reportedly standing on chairs, cheering, and rushing forward to shake his hand. (Collins and Ringhand 2013, 35)

Public hearings in which nominees testify became the norm beginning with the appointment of John Harlan in 1955, but even after that, nominee testimony was often perfunctory. Byron White was confirmed to the bench in 1962 after testimony before the Committee that lasted eleven minutes (Cohen 2012). Televised hearings started with the appointment of Sandra Day O'Connor in 1981, and over the last forty years, such hearings have become a highly publicized and anticipated step in the confirmation process. "Nominee testimony before the Committee frequently captures the national imagination, sparking intense debate about a nominee's fitness for the bench and the proper place of the Court and the Constitution in the US political system" (Collins and Ringhand 2016a, 126).

In its modern-day practice, the Committee hearings provide an opportunity to question the nominee and relevant witnesses. As such, they not only allow the senators and the public to learn about the candidates, they also offer a platform for senators to speak to the public and their constituents. This gives Judiciary Committee members a vehicle to stake out and communicate policy positions, and to gain media attention and increase their own visibility (Collins and Ringhand 2016a, 133). In other words, public hearings can have political benefits and consequences for members of the Senate as well as the president and his or her nominee.

Most confirmation hearings are rather routine, with Senate Judiciary Committee members asking candidates about their qualifications and jurisprudence, and the candidates commonly avoiding being too specific about particular issues that might come before them if confirmed to the bench. But some hearings have been political and dramatic spectacles.

Among the most contentious was the confirmation battle over the nomination of Robert Bork in 1987. Bork brought to his candidacy extensive experience as a Yale law professor, solicitor general, and federal judge, but he also had expressed clear and controversial jurisprudential positions on such hot-button issues as racial segregation, abortion, and the right to privacy.

Even before the hearings began, some Democrats—the party that held the majority in the Senate at the time—signaled their political and ideological opposition. Indeed, shortly after President Reagan announced Bork's nomination, Senator Edward Kennedy, a Democrat from Massachusetts, decried what he described as the candidate's "extremist view" of the Constitution: "Robert Bork's America is a land in which women would be forced into back-alley abortions, blacks would sit at segregated lunch counters, rogue police could break down citizens' doors in midnight raids, and schoolchildren could not be taught about evolution, writers and artists could be censored at the whim of government, and the doors of the federal courts would be shut on the fingers of millions of Americans" (Broder 2009).

This impassioned speech helped mobilize opposition to Bork, despite complaints from Bork supporters that Kennedy had "distort[ed] the record of a distinguished scholar and judge" (Toobin 2017). Though arguably an exaggerated and sensationalized portrayal of the constitutional consequences of adopting the type of jurisprudence advocated by Bork, Kennedy's characterization had a basis in Bork's explicit views about voting rights, privacy rights, women's rights, abortion rights, racial discrimination, equal protection, and the First Amendment. The confirmation hearings explored this basis at length:

> Contemporaneous news reports consistently identified the same issues as the ones that stymied Bork: a disavowal of any sort of constitutionally protected privacy right; a view of the Equal Protection Clause that did not give heightened scrutiny to state actions discriminating on the basis of gender; a skepticism of constitutional or congressional authority over voting rights issues; a restricted view of the speech rights contained in the First Amendment; and a rejection of almost all judicial protection of rights not specifically enumerated in the text of the Constitution. (Collins and Ringhand 2013, 201)

The Judiciary Committee, controlled by Democrats, voted 9–5 against confirming Bork. Two weeks later, the full Senate, also controlled by Democrats by a 54–46 margin, rejected his confirmation by a vote of 58–42.

The failed Bork nomination stands as a prime example of how politics, ideology, and jurisprudential views can shape the Court. The legacy of the Bork confirmation hearings resides not only in the creation of the verb "bork," a synonym for obstruct or thwart, but also in that Bork's nomination is often cited as having produced a long-lasting effect on how nominees and their advisors handle hearings. The common, though not universally-held, wisdom is that the lesson to be gleaned from the Bork hearings is that it taught "earnest nominees to say to the Senate Judiciary Committee nothing at all candid, specific, or profound about their judicial philosophies or views of the law" (Cohen 2012; for an alternative view, see Collins and Ringhand 2013).

There have been other contentious, dramatic, and, indeed, emotional confirmation hearings. Most salient, though atypical, were the hearings for Clarence Thomas in 1991 and Brett Kavanaugh in 2018, both of whom faced allegations of sexual misconduct. Anita Hill testified that Clarence Thomas had sexually harassed her while he served as her supervisor at the Equal Employment Opportunity Commission. Christine Blasey Ford accused Brett Kavanaugh of sexually assaulting her at a high school party when she was fifteen and he was seventeen. Thomas and Kavanaugh vehemently denied the allegations, and some of their defenders questioned the credibility of their accusers.

During the tense and lurid hearings, neither nominee backed down. To the contrary, the nominees staunchly defended themselves and aggressively criticized the process, the Judiciary Committee, and, especially, members of the opposition party.

After each of these hearings, the Judiciary Committees sent the nominations forward to the full Senate. In Thomas's case, the Committee voted 13–1 to send the nomination forward without a recommendation. The Committee reviewing Kavanaugh's candidacy sent the nomination to the full Senate with a favorable recommendation on a party line vote of 11–10. Thomas and Kavanaugh ultimately earned confirmation from the full Senate by close margins: 52–48 and 50–48, respectively.

Full Senate Vote

If the full Senate chooses to consider the nomination following receipt of the Judiciary Committee's recommendation, as it did for Thomas and Kavanaugh, it holds debate. At the conclusion of the debate, the Senate votes. A simple majority of those present and voting is needed for confirmation, though in the case of a tie, the vice president of the United States casts the deciding vote.

While a vote to confirm only requires the margin of a simple majority, between 1949 and 2017 Senate rules governing debate effectively required the support of three-fifths of the Senate membership for confirmation to move forward. This is because the Senate is governed by various rules and procedures, including *unanimous consent*, the *filibuster*, and *cloture*. Unanimous consent provides any member of the Senate the right to refuse to consent to holding a vote on an issue and demand that debate continue. A senator who invokes such a right engages in what is known as a filibuster, a tactic that delays and may ultimately block a vote. But Senate rules also include a mechanism to overcome a filibuster. The Senate may override a filibuster and proceed to a vote by first holding a cloture vote, that is, a vote to place a time limit on Senate debate. If three-fifths of the chamber—sixty senators—vote in favor of cloture, then debate will end and a vote on the merits of the matter under consideration can proceed.

Both political parties have used the filibuster to hold up and even block nominees to the federal bench. The utility of the filibuster derives from the power it gives to the party that does not hold a majority of seats in the Senate. If a simple majority vote is needed to confirm a nomination or pass legislation, then when members of the majority party vote as a bloc, the minority party has little leverage. However, the filibuster gives the minority party considerably more leverage because the party in power does not often hold sixty Senate seats. In fact, only thirteen of the sixty sessions of Congress dating from January 1901 through January 2021 have held "filibuster-proof" majorities.[6] Requiring a supermajority of sixty votes out of the one hundred members of the Senate to move forward with nominations or legislation means the majority party must often rely on some members of the minority to move forward.

Notably, however, the Senate can change the rules governing unanimous consent, the filibuster, and cloture *by a simple majority vote*. This means that the majority party can reduce or remove the filibuster leverage afforded to the minority party by altering Senate rules, and this, in fact, is exactly what has occurred after protracted and intensifying partisan battles over federal judicial nominations.

Going Nuclear

The escalating use of the filibuster in that past twenty years has contributed to increasing polarization around nominations to the federal bench. During the presidency of Republican George W. Bush and following the 2002 midterm elections, when Republicans took majority control of the Senate, Democrats used the filibuster to block multiple nominees to the federal bench, almost all to the U.S. Circuit Courts. So effective was the tactic that in early 2004 it led a frustrated President Bush to install two filibustered candidates to Circuit Court judgeships as "recess appointments," that is, appointments made when Congress is not in session. Article II, Section 2, of the Constitution gives the president the authority "to fill up all Vacancies that may happen during the Recess of the Senate, by granting Commissions which shall expire at the End of their next Session." President Bush defended the temporary appointment of these previously rejected candidates by saying that "a minority of Democratic Senators has been using unprecedented obstructionist tactics to prevent. . . qualified individuals from receiving up-or-down votes" (Chafetz 2017, 98). But recess appointments used to bypass the Senate are themselves outside the norm of political engagement, especially for appointments to the judiciary. As then-Democratic Senate minority leader Tom Daschle complained: "In spite of the Senate's judgment, the President has chosen to take the unprecedented step of using recess appointments to bypass the Senate on two occasions. . . . At no point has a President ever used a recess appointment to install a rejected nominee on to the Federal bench. . . . This White House is insisting on a radical departure from historic and constitutional practices" (99).

President Bush and Democratic senators made a deal shortly thereafter under which Bush agreed not to make additional recess appointments during that term and Democrats allowed several stalled judicial nominations to move forward. After Bush won reelection in 2004 and Republicans increased their margin of control in the Senate, majority leader Bill Frist demanded that Democrats reign in their use of the filibuster. If not, he threatened to change Senate rules to reduce the number of votes required for cloture from three-fifths to a simple majority, a threat that became colloquially referred to as the "nuclear option." Bush again nominated several candidates who had previously been blocked, bringing the confrontation over the use of the filibuster to a head.

The Republican Senate did not proceed with the nuclear option. Instead, a bipartisan coalition of senators—seven Republicans and seven Democrats, called the Gang of Fourteen—averted use of the option. The Democrats in the Gang agreed to support cloture votes on most of the nominees. In return, the Republican Gang members agreed to vote against any effort to change the Senate rules.

Threat of the nuclear option came back during the presidency of Democrat Barack Obama, after the 2010 midterm elections reduced the Democrat's margin of control in the Senate. This time around it was Republicans in the minority who used the filibuster to impede judicial nominees and other appointments to administrative agencies. In response, a frustrated President Obama used recess appointments in January 2012. He did not do so for the judiciary, however, but rather to install officers to open positions on the National Labor Relations Board and the Consumer Financial Protection Bureau. After Obama's reelection in November 2012, Republican efforts to stall his nominations continued.

President Obama had grounds for frustration. According to a PolitiFact analysis conducted in November 2013 (Jacobson 2013), which relied on reports by the Congressional Research Office, up to 2013 there had been a total 147 individual nominees blocked by cloture in the history of the Senate's use of cloture for nominations, which began in 1949.[7] A disproportionate number of these occurred during Obama's term in office. The analysis showed, in fact, that five years into the Obama presidency, 79 individual nominees were blocked by cloture (including both judicial and nonjudicial nominees). In other words, more than half of the 147 cloture blocks starting in 1949 were aimed at Obama nominations. With respect to individual judicial nominees, PolitiFact found that "cloture was filed on 36 judicial nominations during the first five years of Obama's presidency, the same total as the previous 40 years combined" (Graves 2017). Put slightly differently, "Less than one nominee per year was subject to a cloture filing in the 40 years before Obama took office. From 2009–13, the number of nominees subject to a cloture filing jumped to over seven per year" (Graves 2017).

It was in the context of this escalated use of the filibuster that then-Democratic majority leader Harry Reid partially deployed the nuclear option. In November 2013, by a vote of 52–48, the Senate ended the use of the filibuster for most, though not all, presidential nominees. The 2013 change applied to all nominations to the executive branch and to the judicial branch *except the Supreme Court*, and it allowed the Senate to end debate with a simple majority vote rather than sixty votes. It also left the filibuster available for debate and votes on legislation.

Republicans regained majority control of the Senate as a result of the 2014 midterm elections. It was during this Congressional term—the 114th Congress, which ran from 2015 to 2017—that Justice Scalia died and Republican Senate majority leader Mitch McConnell refused to hold confirmation hearings on Merrick Garland, President Obama's nominee to replace Scalia. The seat, which remained vacant from February 2016 until April 2017, was thus available to be filled when Republican Donald Trump took office after winning the 2016 presidential election.

On January 31, 2017, President Trump nominated Neil Gorsuch, then a judge on the U.S. Circuit Court of Appeals for the Tenth Circuit. Democrats, who viewed the vacant seat on the bench as a stolen seat, filibustered the nomination. Republicans held a slim majority in the Senate, at fifty-two seats, and could not override the filibuster. Faced with the prospect of a failed confirmation, Republican majority leader Mitch McConnell moved to extend the 2013 rule change on filibusters to Supreme Court nominees. That move succeeded by a party-line vote of 52–48, but it further poisoned relations between Democrats and Republicans in Congress. "The move, once unthinkable among senators, is a testament to the creeping partisan rancor in recent years, after decades of at least relative bipartisanship on Supreme Court matters," wrote *New York Times* reporter Matt Flegenheimer. "Both parties have warned of sweeping effects on the court itself, predicting the elevation of more ideologically extreme judges now that only a majority is required for confirmation" (Flegenheimer 2017).

Further expansion of the nuclear option took effect in April 2019, when the Republican-controlled Senate voted to cut the time for debate from thirty hours to two hours for some categories of presidential nominees. The change applies to U.S. District Court nominees and to lower-level nominees to the executive branch, but it does not affect debate over cabinet-level nominees, federal appeals judges, or the Supreme Court (Snell 2019).

Factors Influencing Confirmation

Political scientists and legal scholars have identified a variety of factors as potential influences of whether the Senate will confirm a Supreme Court nomination. The broad categories that influence the president's selection of candidates also influence the chances of confirmation. Thus, qualifications and integrity of the nominee matter. So too do ideology and politics.

Political scientist Henry J. Abraham identifies multiple factors that contribute to failed nominations. While a perceived lack of qualifications is among the factors, the others turn on politics. Abraham cites disapproval of a nominee's policy positions or jurisprudence, as well as concerns that a nominee might bolster the views of an unpopular Court, shift the Court's ideological balance, or fail to support the party in power. Abraham argues that interest groups or a senator of the nominee's home state can generate considerable resistance, or that opposition to the president, rather than the nominee, can prove decisive. These factors often combine rather than function alone (Abraham 1992, 39).

Political scientist Keith Whittington narrows (and in some ways combines) the factors into three main categories. According to Whittington, "failed Supreme Court nominations can be accounted for by three primary, and partly related, factors: divided government, the timing of vacancies relative to the electoral calendar, and the personal characteristics of the nominees themselves" (Whittington 2006, 410–11). Divided government occurs when different parties control the legislative and executive branches, or, more relevant for the confirmation process, when the Senate is controlled by a party that differs from the president. In his historical analysis of nominations and confirmations, Whittington highlights the influence of divided government, especially when combined with late-term appointments. It is this intersection, according to Whittington, that largely accounts for seventeen failed nominations (427). Notably, Whittington argues that while divided government explains most of the failures across Supreme Court history, it is only in the most recent era that nominations have failed "because the party that controlled the Senate was hostile to the jurisprudential goals of the president and was willing therefore to veto presidential choices for the Supreme Court" (435).

Of the other failed nominations, Whittington focuses on various personal characteristics of the candidates that have produced lack of support and resistance. He highlights the influence of patronage and infighting *within* a party that has led to failed confirmations, mostly prior to 1900. He also notes presidential missteps in selecting nominees. Worth emphasizing—and, perhaps, contrary to what we might expect—is that it is not always conflict across parties that explains unsuccessful confirmations. The failed nomination of Harriet Miers offers a telling example. That selection, by Republican President George W. Bush, generated considerable resistance from members of the Republican Party who expressed skepticism about her qualifications. It was that resistance that led Bush to withdraw the nomination.

Leaving the Court

Though debate remains about the degree to which politics influences the selection of justices, no one doubts its impact. Leaving the Court also appears to be shaped to some extent by politics, though arguably far less than the selection process.

As noted previously, lifetime appointment to the bench means that judicial departures are irregular and typically unpredictable. Though 50 of the 114 Supreme Court justices have died while in office, since 1954 only 3—Robert Jackson, William Rehnquist, and Antonin Scalia—have passed away while serving.

Justices can theoretically be removed against their will through the impeachment process, but this has yet to happen. Only Supreme Court Justice Samuel Chase faced formal impeachment proceedings. In 1804, with President Thomas Jefferson seeking to wrest away Federalist control of the judiciary, the House of Representatives voted along party lines to impeach Chase. The Senate, however, failed to convict, and Chase remained on the bench until his death in 1811.

No other justice has been impeached, but the threat has occasionally loomed over and pressured some jurists. A House committee considered but failed to approve a resolution to impeach Justice William O. Douglas in 1970. Justice Abe Fortas was under an impeachment cloud owing to allegations of financial misconduct and may well have faced actual impeachment had he not resigned from the Court in 1969.

In the modern era, voluntary departure has led to almost all of the vacancies on the Court. Justices can simply resign from the bench, but justices who meet certain eligibility requirements retire with considerable pension benefits, including the salary they received at the time of retirement for the rest of their life, as well as Court chambers, administrative support, and a law clerk.

Still, justices often continue their service well into their 70s and 80s, and occasionally into their 90s. Moreover, many justices remain on the Court even in the face of declining health. As Nina Totenberg describes, in 2005, "it was painfully clear for most of the court term that Chief Justice William Rehnquist, who had been operated on for thyroid cancer, was mortally ill. Throughout the term, Rehnquist released almost no information about his health, and, at the end of the term, he decided against retiring, only to die during the court's summer break" (Totenberg 2019b). In some cases, poor health directly interferes with a justice's ability to perform, as it did in the case of William O. Douglas who suffered a severe stroke but remained on the bench. So significant were concerns about Douglas's performance that all but one of his colleagues agreed that his vote should not count in cases where it would be the decisive vote in a 5–4 split. This prompted opposition from Justice Byron White who demanded, at least, that the public be notified of this decision. Shortly thereafter, Douglas retired (Totenberg 2019b).

Obviously, the timing of vacancies has direct consequence for replacements, and this is where politics may, in fact, figure into the calculus of departure. A retirement gives the sitting president an opportunity to nominate a new justice and the current Senate the opportunity to confirm or reject that nominee. Waiting to leave the bench until the next presidential election opens the door for the next president and the next Senate to shape the Court. To the extent that justices care about the future composition of the Court and which president or political party has the most control over that composition, they might choose to depart or to stick around. And to the extent that others care about the future composition of the Court, they might encourage or seek to pressure a justice to stay or go.

In recent years, Justice Ginsburg, who was eighty-six at the close of 2019 and has fought cancer multiple times, has been the object of such attention. Many wonder whether she will be able to remain on the Court until after the 2020 election. And given her liberal jurisprudence and policy views, many question why she did not step down during the Obama presidency. During an interview at an awards dinner in September 2019, Ginsburg was asked if she regretted not stepping down while Obama was president. Obviously aware of questions and concerns around her tenure, Ginsburg's reply was telling, "It has been suggested by more than one commentator, including some law professors, that I should've stepped down during President Obama's second term. When that suggestion is made I ask the question: Who do you think the president could nominate that could get through the Republican Senate that you would prefer to have on the court than me?" (Burack 2019).

Also telling is a comment Justice Thomas purportedly made about his plan to remain on the bench for forty-three years, a plan that, if fulfilled, would make him the longest-serving justice. Thomas was confirmed to the bench at age forty-three, after a tumultuous confirmation fight. A few years after joining the Court, Thomas is said to have told his law clerks this: "The liberals made my life miserable for 43 years, and I'm going to make their lives miserable for 43 years" (Lewis 1993).

CONCLUSION

Confirmations of justices in recent years have been won by relatively narrow margins, reflecting increasingly bitter partisan divides. Consider that, since 1975, the confirmations of Stevens, O'Connor, Scalia, Kennedy, Ginsburg, Souter, and Breyer all gained an overwhelming majority of votes. Of these, only Breyer won support from fewer than ninety senators (his confirmation vote was 87–9), and four of these justices received no negative votes. To be sure, conflict over the nominations of Robert Bork and

Clarence Thomas was stark, and William Rehnquist was elevated to the position of chief justice by a 65–33 vote. Still, between 1975 and 2004, as politicized as the appointment process was, there remained much room for senators to vote in favor of confirming a nomination made by the president of the opposing party.

By contrast, the largest margin of the six most recent justices to be confirmed was that enjoyed by Chief Justice Roberts, at 78–22. Alito, Gorsuch, and Kavanaugh—all appointed by a Republican president—were confirmed in sharply divided votes: 58–42, 54–45, and 50–48, respectively. Sotomayor and Kagan—nominated by a Democratic president—were confirmed with votes of 68–31 and 63–37. And nominee Merrick Garland was not afforded a chance at an up or down vote at all.

Whether the heightened politicization of the nomination and confirmation process affects the perceived legitimacy of the Supreme Court remains a question. There is no question, though, that it was on the mind of Chief Justice John Roberts, who bemoaned the politicized selection process even before the recent Garland, Gorsuch, and Kavanaugh nominations. According to Roberts, "When you have a sharply political, divisive hearing process, it increases the danger that whoever comes out of it will be viewed in those terms. You know, if the Democrats and Republicans have been fighting so fiercely about whether you're going to be confirmed, it's natural for some member of the public to think, well, you must be identified in a particular way as a result of that process" (Roberts 2016a).

NOTES

1. Congress set the number of justices at seven in 1807, nine in 1837, ten in 1863, seven in 1866, and nine in 1869 (Collins and Ringhand 2013, 18).

2. There are other federal judges, such as administrative law judges who adjudicate disputes involving federal administrative law and policies made by federal agencies, such as the Social Security Administration or the Veterans Affairs Department. These judges and their tribunals are established under Article I of the Constitution. Judges who serve on Article I courts, as they are called, do not have lifetime appointments and are thus distinct from judges who serve on Article III courts (i.e., the Supreme Court, the Circuit Courts, the U.S. District Courts, and the U.S. Court of International Trade).

3. Political scientist Henry J. Abraham, for example, cites Senator David B. Hill's successful use of senatorial courtesy to block President Grover Cleveland's nominations of William B. Hornblower in 1893 and Wheeler H. Peckham in 1894. See Abraham (1992, 27).

4. The 163 nominations only include those formally submitted to the Senate and not, for example, the nomination of Douglas Ginsburg, which was withdrawn before its formal submission. Of the 126 confirmed, 7 declined to serve. See Supreme Court Nominations (1789–Present) (2020).

5. The specifics of this accounting come from Hogue 2010, modified with additional information of nominations and confirmations that took place between August 2010 and January 2020.

6. The sixty sessions counted here run from the 57th Congress, which began in January 1901, to the 116th Congress, which commenced on January 3, 2019, and will conclude on January 2, 2021. The 95th Congress, in session from 1977 to 1979, was the last time either party held sixty or more seats. See U.S. Senate Statistics on Party Division 2020.

7. The history of the Senate's use of cloture and the filibuster dates back much further, to the early 1800s.

5

Influences on Supreme Court Decision Making

In 2005, the Senate Judiciary Committee held confirmation hearings to consider President George W. Bush's nomination of John Roberts to serve as chief justice to the Supreme Court. Roberts offered the following sports analogy in his opening remarks:

> Judges are like umpires. Umpires don't make the rules; they apply them. The role of an umpire and a judge is critical. They make sure everybody plays by the rules. But it is a limited role. Nobody ever went to a ball game to see the umpire. . . . Judges are not politicians who can promise to do certain things in exchange for votes. I have no agenda but I do have a commitment. If I am confirmed, I will confront every case with an open mind. I will fully and fairly analyze the legal arguments that are presented. I will be open to the considered views of my colleagues on the bench. And I will decide every case based on the record, according to the rule of law, without fear or favor, to the best of my ability. And I'll remember that it's my job to call balls and strikes and not to pitch or bat. (Roberts 2005)

The notion that judges are neutral and objective arbiters guided only by law—making decisions in a bubble insulated from both external pressures and their own internal ideologies, values, and desires—is a common characterization and aspiration. Unlike politicians who parade their party affiliations and partisan positions, judges are typically expected to set aside their personal, political, and policy preferences. However, researchers who study judicial decision making and the Supreme Court suggest that this expectation is unrealistic.

In particular, research into judicial behavior posits a number of "nonlegal" or "extralegal" factors thought to influence the decisions made by courts. Broadly speaking, these factors suggest that judicial behavior is human behavior, and, as such, subject to influences that are not merely or purely legalistic and rule-bound in nature. Even the most rule-bound judge who strives for impartiality and aims for the goal of "blind justice" cannot un-see all they have seen and experienced. Taken together, studies of judicial decision making call into question the image of a judge simply calling balls and strikes.

Here we take up some of the main sources of influence that research in political science and public law identifies as shaping judicial—and especially Supreme Court—decisions. These contrast with the view that judges make decisions guided solely by law, jurisprudence, and the specific methods of constitutional interpretation highlighted in chapter 2. The first part of this chapter provides an overview of three competing theories of judicial behavior. The second part of the chapter identifies some of the main external influences thought to pressure Supreme Court decision making.

THEORIES OF JUDICIAL BEHAVIOR

In 1992, the Supreme Court ruled that the inclusion of a religious prayer at a public school graduation violated the First Amendment's Establishment Clause. In 2008, the Court overturned a Washington, D.C. ban on handguns and held that the Second Amendment provides a right to individual gun ownership for personal use. In 2015, the Court ruled that the Fourteenth Amendment guarantees same-sex couples the right to marry. In each of these cases—and, of course, in many others—the Court's ruling came in a narrow 5–4 vote. How is it that the votes of justices diverge so much on such important matters? Do alternative jurisprudential approaches adopted by the justices alone explain the divergence? Or are there other explanations for how judges arrive at their decisions?

Attitudinal Model

According to one strand of research in political science, the answer to these questions can be found in the ideologies, policy preferences, and personal values of justices. In a pioneering work published in 1948, political scientist C. Herman Pritchett argued that the increasing number of dissents on the Supreme Court could be explained in terms of the individual preferences of justices. Pritchett's book, *The Roosevelt Court: A Study in*

Judicial Politics and Values, 1937–1947, and, more generally, the behavioral revolution that marked political science in the 1940s and 1950s, sparked a line of research emphasizing the study of judicial behavior. The behavioral turn in political science, which aimed toward a more scientific approach to the study of politics, began to include empirical testing of formulated hypotheses. Applying behavioralism to the study of judicial decision making and building upon the work of Pritchett and others, later researchers put forward statistical models to test and predict judicial decisions.

The "attitudinal model," as it has come to be called, argues that judicial attitudes are the primary explanatory factor for why justices rule as they do. The attitudinalist pays special attention to Supreme Court decision making. Justices face far fewer constraints on their decisions compared to judges in lower courts, who must answer to higher courts and who may aspire to appointment on a higher bench. Supreme Court justices are therefore freer to vote in accordance with their own preferences. Consequently, the attitudinal model tends to study Supreme Court decision making, classifying where justices fall on the liberal-conservative ideological spectrum and then explaining and predicting the votes of justices.

Consider, for example, a classic article by Jeffery A. Segal and Albert D. Cover (1989) titled "Ideological Values and the Votes of U.S. Supreme Court Justices." The authors begin by classifying the ideology of the eighteen justices who served on the Court from the time of Earl Warren to Anthony Kennedy. They do so by using a measure of ideology that rates justices on a scale of extremely conservative to extremely liberal, deriving that rating through an analysis of editorials from the *New York Times*, *Washington Post*, *Chicago Tribune*, and *Los Angeles Times*. Justice Antonin Scalia fell on the extremely conservative end of the spectrum, with Justice William Rehnquist near that end, and Justices William Brennan, Abe Fortas, and Thurgood Marshall fell on the extremely liberal end. Using this measure of ideology as the independent or explanatory variable, Segal and Cover then look at the votes of these eighteen justices in civil liberty cases (e.g., cases involving criminal procedure, civil rights, First Amendment, due process, and privacy) to see whether those votes correlate with the ideology of the justices. What the authors find is a high correlation: that is, justices rated as more liberal tended to vote in a liberal direction, and justices rated as more conservative tended to vote in a conservative direction. The results, they conclude, "provide exceptional support for the attitudinal model as applied to civil liberties cases" (Segal and Cover 1989, 562).

This example illustrates the methods used by attitudinal researchers: coding justices and their votes in terms of ideology, and using statistical analysis to determine the extent of the relationship between the two. It also illuminates the main line of argument put forward by proponents of the model: rather than being influenced by existing law and precedent, the

Supreme Court "decides disputes in light of the facts of the case vis-à-vis the ideological attitudes and values of the justices. Simply put, Rehnquist votes the way he does because he is extremely conservative; Marshall voted the way he did because he [was] extremely liberal" (Segal and Spaeth 1993, 65).

While political scientists who study the Supreme Court generally accept the view that ideology, preferences, and values influence judicial decisions, not all accept the attitudinal model. Some critics of the attitudinal approach argue that it overemphasizes judicial attitudes to the neglect of institutional contexts and constraints that influence judicial values, attitudes, and decisions. These critics point out that justices are not as unconstrained or free to act on their preferences as the attitudinal model assumes. On this view, judicial behavior, like political behavior or any human behavior, must be examined with reference to "the institutional arrangements and cultural contexts that give it shape, direction, and meaning" (Gillman and Clayton 1999, 3).

> This is just another way of saying that different contexts make it more or less possible for individuals to act on different sets of beliefs. When participants interpret the experience of freedom or constraint as a set of opportunities and risks they may find themselves engaging in a form of cost-benefit analysis in order to think through what course of conduct seems most rational in light of their goals. A less strategic conception of the constraints imposed by institutional contexts would suggest that certain settings hold a sense of appropriateness about what kinds of behaviors or motivations are considered acceptable under certain circumstances. Either way, whether one's orientation to context is accomplished via calculation or a sensitivity to propriety, it is still the case that our sense of what can be done flows out of our encounters with particular contexts, and thus an account of purposeful human behavior must always be attentive to the relationship between various courses of conduct and the settings within which they are embedded. (Gillman and Clayton 1999, 3–4)

Two main versions of approaches that emphasize institutions, contexts, and constraints are discussed the following sections. One approach provides a *strategic account* of the choices justices make in light of institutional contexts. These critics of the attitudinal model acknowledge that the individual ideology and policy preferences of justices matter, but insist that the strategic choices justices make in light of their institutional contexts and constraints are significant. A second approach, labeled *new institutionalism* or *historical institutionalism*, stresses how legal institutions, norms, and practices influence the attitudes and preferences of justices.

Strategic Account

Borrowing from rational choice theory in economics and political science, a strategic account of judicial decision making emphasizes strategic choice and behavior. Like the attitudinal approach, the strategic approach accepts that justices are influenced by ideology and policy preferences. The strategic model diverges from the attitudinal approach, though, in allowing that justices may also be influenced by legal and jurisprudential principles. But in a more significant divergence, this account argues that justices, whether influenced by ideology or law or both,

> are not unsophisticated characters who make choices based merely on their own political preferences. Instead, justices are strategic actors who realize that their ability to achieve their goals depends on a consideration of the preferences of others, of the choices they expect others to make, and of the institutional context in which they act. In other words, the choices of justices can best be explained as strategic behavior, not solely as responses to either personal ideology or apolitical jurisprudence. The implications of this claim . . . are many. Most important is that law, as it is generated by the Supreme Court, is the long-term product of short-term strategic decision making. (Epstein and Knight 1998, xiii)

Political scientists Lee Epstein and Jack Knight, among the most influential proponents of the strategic approach, emphasize the complex context of judicial decision making. They state that context is shaped by a justice's goals, interactions with other justices, and the institutions that shape those interactions. First, justices, like other individuals, act in ways that seek to achieve their goals. Their goals, according to Epstein and Knight, are predominantly oriented toward advancing the individual justice's policy and ideological preferences, though those are not necessarily the *only* goals that drive a justice. Second, acting to achieve one's goals requires strategic choices informed by how others will act. Because Supreme Court opinions only become precedent if they are accepted by a majority of justices, the justices understand that for their individual goals to prevail, they need the support of others. Thus, individual justices act strategically, that is, in ways that are cognizant of how other justices will act. As Epstein and Knight put it, "To say that a justice acts strategically is to say that she realizes that her success or failure depends on the preferences of other actors and the actions she expects them to take, not just on her own preferences and actions" (12). Third, acting to achieve one's goals is also shaped by institutions. Institutional rules and norms structure relationships and interactions, which, in turn, shape the choices of justices. For Supreme Court justices, internal rules—such as the Rule of Four and the way opinion writing is assigned—can influence and constrain the choices a justice makes to advance a particular policy preference. Likewise, external institutional contexts—including the relationship between the Supreme Court and the other branches of the federal government, and the Court's relationship to the American public—figure into the choices justices make. In short, "if the members of the Court wish to create efficacious policy, they not only must be attentive to institutions that govern their relations with their colleagues but also take account of the rules that structure their interactions with external actors" (138–39).

Unlike the attitudinalist who will tend to view Supreme Court justices as largely unconstrained actors when it comes to making decisions, those who advocate a strategic account emphasize that judicial choices are constrained, leading to bargaining, negotiation, and compromise. Some strategic choice scholars argue that when it comes to assigning opinions, writing opinions, and voting on the Court, the result is collegial and strategic coalition building; individual preferences factor into these choices, but "preferences alone do not dictate the choices justices make" (Maltzman, Spriggs, Wahlbeck 2000, 149).

New Institutionalism

The strategic account clearly takes institutions into consideration in seeking to explain and understand judicial decisions. But that account focuses squarely on the choices and cost-benefit analysis individual justices make when they act. The level of analysis remains on the individual justice, with institutions shaping and constraining individual choices. By contrast, and presenting an account that is less individualistic and strategic, the new institutionalist approach takes on a broader lens, seeking to explain constitutional decisions "as consequences of their political, historical, ideological, and institutional contexts" (Gillman, Graber, and Whittington 2013, 13).

New institutionalism is motivated not so much by the question of why individual justices make the choices that they make, but by the wider question of why certain issues and policies emerge and gain a foothold at particular moments. Thus, for example, "Rather than ask what particular Supreme Court justices thought about pornography or originalism, they ask why obscenity issues arose during the time period when those particular justices were on the Court" (Gillman, Graber, and Whittington 2013, 13). Because some emphasize the significant influence that historical factors have on constitutional decision making, a subset of new institutionalists are sometimes labeled and identified as "historical institutionalists."

The new institutionalist is also interested in understanding how the values and preferences of justices are themselves shaped by the Court, as an institution, and its political, historical, and cultural context. That is, while the attitudinal and strategic accounts assume that justices have and act on well-formed attitudes, preferences, and policy goals, the institutionalist explores "how judicial attitudes are themselves constituted and structured by the Court *as an institution* and by its relationship to other institutions in the political system at particular points in history" (Clayton and Gillman 1999, 2). Put slightly different, the attitudinal and strategic accounts focus on the individual justice's attitudes, preferences, and policy goals as the independent variable that explains how decisions are made and which policy outcomes the Court produces. The institutionalist flips the direction of the analysis, suggesting that legal and judicial institutions themselves help explain and form judicial attitudes, preferences, and goals.

In explaining the value of new institutionalism, political scientists Howard Gillman and Cornell Clayton argue that "there may be much to be gained by focusing less on the policy preferences of particular justices and more on the distinctive characteristics of the Court as an institution, its relationship to other institutions in the political system, and how both of these might shape judicial values and attitudes" (Gillman and Clayton 1999, 3). Legal scholar Ronald Kahn puts it this way: "[I]nstitutions both structure one's ability to act on a set of beliefs that are external to the institution and are a source of distinctive political purposes, goals, and preferences." This approach "assumes that the Court's institutional norms and commitments are important for the maintenance of constitutional principles and Court decision-making" (Kahn 1999, 176).

What institutional norms and commitments are important to the Court? New institutionalists explore a variety of institutional norms thought to influence judicial attitudes, preferences, and goals. Among these are the norms of following precedent, respecting the distinction between law and politics, and concern for the Court's institutional legitimacy (see Kahn 1999, 177).

Note, then, the different kind of analysis that a new institutionalist might provide as compared to the accounts of an attitidunalist or strategic choice theorist. On the issue of abortion, for example, an attitudinalist will look to see whether a conservative justice and a liberal justice diverge on their votes considering the constitutionality of abortion restrictions. A strategic choice approach might analyze how justices negotiated over how to adjudicate a legal challenge to abortion restrictions and whether those negotiations produced a compromise position on how the claim of an abortion right should be treated by the Court. By contrast, an historical institutionalist might seek to understand why the claim of a constitutional right to abortion emerged in the 1970s, and a new institutional might examine how the commitment to the institutional norm of stare decisis or concerns about the legitimacy of the Court shaped the attitudes of justices in a way that led to continued recognition of the right to abortion in *Planned Parenthood v. Casey* in 1992 and to the present.

EXTERNAL POLITICAL INFLUENCES AND RELATIONSHIPS

The attitudinal approach, strategic model, and new institutionalism situate the Court in context, identifying how things other than the law itself might shape judicial decision making. Here we take up some of the main external factors and political pressures that social scientists identify as influencing the Court and its decisions.

The President and Congress

We need not dwell here on all of the direct influences that the president and Congress have on the Supreme Court, since several have already been addressed in previous chapters. The nomination and confirmation process, taken up in chapter 4, directly shapes the high bench and, in that way, indirectly affects its decisions. Even the prospect that a sitting president will typically have the opportunity to nominate a replacement to the Court should a justice retire may influence whether a justice remains on or departs from the Court. Other direct influences addressed earlier include the role play by the solicitor general, discussed in chapter 3.

There are additional direct and indirect influences worth identifying and discussing, however. Congress has authority (subject to presidential veto power) to pass legislation structuring the federal courts, including modifying its jurisdiction, changing the number of federal courts and the number of judges, setting the budget of the judiciary, and even setting the pay of federal judges (though the Constitution prohibits pay reductions during a federal judge's time in office). This authority has been exercised by Congress at various points in the Supreme Court's history and can, at least indirectly, weigh on judicial decision making. Congress changed the number of Supreme Court justices in the 1860s to both increase (for Abraham Lincoln) and then decrease (for Andrew Johnson) the president's ability to shape the Court. And the threat of court packing during President Roosevelt's administration in the 1930s is often credited with producing the "switch in time that saved nine," that is, in generating an actual substantive change in Court interpretation (see Introduction).

Congressional influence is also consequential when it comes to the Court's exercise of statutory interpretation. Consider, for example, a case brought by Lilly Ledbetter and the resulting judicial interpretation of the Civil Rights Act of 1964, a sweeping federal statute governing civil rights in such areas as voter registration, public accommodations, and employment. Title VII of the Civil Rights Act prohibits sex-based (and other forms of) discrimination in the workplace and requires a plaintiff claiming a Title VII violation to file a lawsuit within 180 days "after the alleged unlawful employment practice occurred."[1] Lilly Ledbetter, who worked for Goodyear Tire, discovered as she neared retirement that she had received lower pay than her male counterparts. She subsequently sued the company, claiming gender-based discrimination under Title VII. But the Supreme Court, offering a particular reading of the language of Title VII that ran contrary to the interpretation of the Equal Employment Opportunity Commission (EEOC), ruled that Ledbetter had not filed her claim in a timely fashion. The 2007 ruling in *Ledbetter v. Goodyear Tire & Rubber Co.* found that plaintiffs must file a formal complaint within 180 days *after their pay was set*, which considerably limited the scope of time for filing as compared to what the EEOC and Ledbetter argued, namely that "each paycheck that reflects the initial discrimination is itself a discriminatory act that resets the clock on the 180-day period" (Greenhouse 2007). Justice Ginsburg, in a dissenting opinion joined by three other justices, not only criticized the majority's opinion as "a cramped interpretation of Title VII, incompatible with the statute's broad remedial purpose," but noted that earlier "cramped" Court interpretations resulted in Congress passing new legislation. She then issued what could be read as a call to action: "Once again, the ball is in Congress' court. As in 1991, the Legislature may act to correct this Court's parsimonious reading of Title VII" (*Ledbetter v. Goodyear Tire & Rubber Co.* 2007, 661, dissenting opinion).

A few years later, Congress took up Ginsburg's call and passed the Lilly Ledbetter Fair Pay Act of 2009. The new law, signed by President Barack Obama in January 2009, amended Title VII of the Civil Rights Act of 1964 by allowing the clock for filing a pay discrimination suit to restart with each new paycheck affected by that alleged discriminatory action (EEOC). In so doing, Congress directly nullified the majority ruling in *Ledbetter v. Goodyear Tire & Rubber Co.* by rewriting the statute.

This type of direct reversal of a Supreme Court ruling by Congressional legislation is possible because the Court is interpreting statutes passed by Congress in the first place. When the Court reads language in a Congressional statute in a manner contrary to how Congress wants the statute to be read, Congress can simply change the statute. Of course, it is not always as simple as that, because Congress must gather enough votes to rewrite the law and gain presidential support (or override a presidential veto with a greater number of Congressional votes, as the case may be). Still, reversing the Court's statutory interpretation by amending a law or creating a new law is far easier than reversing the Court's constitutional interpretation.

There are, though, two direct ways that Congress can reverse, or at least mitigate, the Court's constitutional interpretation. The first is by proposing a constitutional amendment. This method is rarely used, to be sure, and rarely effective. But the Eleventh Amendment is one such rare instance. The Eleventh Amendment, which limits the authority of the federal courts by restricting individuals from suing states in federal courts, was a direct reversal of an early Supreme Court decision, the 1793 ruling in *Chisholm v. Georgia.* There, the Court ruled against the state of Georgia's claim that, as a sovereign state, it was immune from a lawsuit to which it did not consent brought by a citizen in federal court. The Court relied on language of

Article III in the Constitution, which specifically assigned federal judicial authority to controversies "between a State and Citizens of another State." The states and Congress were, nevertheless, quite displeased with the Court's decision—one of the very early efforts the Court took to exert its nascent and untested authority. The ensuing response was swift and unfavorable; the Eleventh Amendment, which would undo *Chisholm v. Georgia*, was proposed by Congress in 1794 and enacted through state ratification in 1795.

Because successful ratification of a constitutional amendment requires the support of supermajorities (two-thirds of Congress, three-quarters of the states), this type of pressure on the Court is limited indeed. But in the context of constitutional interpretation, there are occasions when other forms of Congressional intervention are possible. Take, for instance, the decision in *Employment Division, Department of Human Resources of Oregon v. Smith* (1988). The case involved an Oregon policy that denied unemployment compensation to people who had been fired for work-related misconduct. When Oregon rejected Alfred Smith and Galen Black's claims for unemployment compensation on misconduct grounds—they had been fired for consuming the hallucinogenic drug peyote—they sued, arguing that Oregon violated their right to free exercise of religion under the First Amendment. Smith and Black, members of the Native American Church, raised the free exercise claim because they had consumed peyote as part of a religious ritual. The Supreme Court rejected the free exercise claim, holding that states need not create religious exceptions to religiously neutral and generally applicable criminal laws. In particular, the Court held that where a criminal law is religiously neutral, generally applicable, and within the constitutional authority of government to enact, the incidental burden the law imposes on religion does not necessarily violate the First Amendment. Importantly, and contrary to earlier precedent, the Court held that in such cases the government need not demonstrate that it has a "compelling interest" to enact such religiously neutral laws of general applicability.

The Court in *Employment Division v. Smith* thereby lowered the level of judicial scrutiny applied to laws of general applicability that incidentally burden religious practice. Prior to the ruling, when the government passed a law that had the incidental effect of making religion more difficult to exercise—even if that was not the intent of the law—the Court subjected such laws to a high degree of judicial scrutiny. It demanded that the government justify its burden on religion by showing a compelling interest and by making sure the law was narrowly tailored. With the *Smith* ruling, the Court's scrutiny of incidental burdens on religion imposed by criminal laws became much more deferential to government's authority to regulate.

The change in standard of scrutiny applied to free exercise cases elicited a significant and negative reaction from Congress that led to the enactment of the Religious Freedom Restoration Act (RFRA). This Act, passed in 1993, tried to rewrite the higher standard of judicial review test back into law. It pronounced that "[g]overnment shall not substantially burden a person's free exercise of religion even if the burden results from a rule of general applicability" except if it can demonstrate that it is using the least restrictive means to further a compelling government interest (Religious Freedom Restoration Act 1993, 42 U.S. Code § 2000bb–1). Congress thereby sought to "restore" increased protection to religious freedom through its statutory authority and in light of the Supreme Court's diminishment of the constitutional protection. Congress ended up being partly, but not completely, successful in this effort, because RFRA sought to enforce this higher standard upon both federal and state governments. The Court, in turn, had its own reaction to RFRA. In *City of Boerne v. Flores* (1997), the Supreme Court found applying RFRA to states was an unconstitutional overreach of Congressional authority. The law, though, still stands with respect to federal agencies. Moreover, Congress passed the Religious Land Use and Institutionalized Persons Act in 2000, a narrower bill later upheld by the Supreme Court. This law protects the religious freedom of persons in prisons and provides protections for religious organizations that are subject to state and local land-use regulations. In addition, many states have enacted laws that function as RFRA does at the federal level.

The Lilly Ledbetter Fair Pay Act, the Religious Freedom Restoration Act, and the Religious Land Use and Institutionalized Persons Act serve as reminders of a few things about the relationship between Supreme Court decision making and the other branches of the federal government. For one thing, the Court does not always have the "final word." To be sure, the Court's say over the meaning of the Constitution is more powerful than its say over the meaning of Congressional statutes, because the latter can be changed more easily than the Constitution. But even on constitutional interpretation, Congress (and even states) can under certain conditions mitigate the reach of the Court's interpretation through legislation. This is especially so in contexts like RFRA, where federal and state legislatures want to afford extra protections that go above what the Court interprets the Constitution to provide.

Public Opinion: Mass Public Opinion and Elite Opinion

"Do judges respond to public opinion?" This question, versions of which are asked and researched by generation after generation of legal scholars, was put to Chief Justice William Rehnquist. He rejected the notion that judges respond in simplistic ways to public opinion, such as by ruling on a particular constitutional interpretation simply because prevailing public opinion favors that interpretation. Instead, he re-stated the question by asking, "Are judges influenced by public opinion?" To this more subtle question, Rehnquist offered a realistic answer. Judges work in an insulated atmosphere, but

> these same judges go home at night and read the newspapers or watch the evening news on television; they talk to their family and friends about current events. Somewhere "out there"—beyond the walls of the courthouse— run currents and tides of public opinion which lap at the courthouse door. Just as the nineteenth century European astronomers discovered that the presence of the then unknown planet Neptune had an effect on the orbit of Uranus, if these tides of public opinion are sufficiently great and sufficiently sustained, they will very likely have an effect upon the decision of some of the cases decided within the courthouse. This is not a case of judges "knuckling under" to public opinion, and cravenly abandoning their oaths of office. Judges, so long as they are relatively normal human beings, can no more escape being influenced by public opinion in the long run than can people working at other jobs. (Rehnquist 1986, 768)

In these remarks, Rehnquist joined other jurists in acknowledging a connection between public opinion and the Court. As Justice Benjamin N. Cardozo observed, "The great tides and currents which engulf the rest of men, do not turn aside in their course, and pass the judges by" (Cardozo 1921, 168). But these admissions run counter to the often-repeated view that the Supreme Court's insulation from elections and politics mutes the influence of public opinion on their deliberations. Those who maintain that public opinion does not affect decision making on the Court typically highlight the institutional design that keeps justices free from electoral pressures. Recall from chapter 1 that part of the debate over whether the Court is a problematically counter-majoritarian institution emerges because unelected justices with life-time tenure do not face electoral accountability. An independent judiciary need not worry about public opinion. Some observers (and some justices) argue that this insulation keeps justices obliged to the laws and to the Constitution rather than to the ebb and flow of public views.

Recall as well from chapter 2 that certain methods of interpretation— especially originalism and textualism—reject the idea that justices should be permitted to take public opinion into consideration to discern the meaning of the Constitution. On these views, democratic processes and democratically elected institutions provide the venues for expression of public opinion; judicial interpretation does not and should not. As Justice Antonin Scalia lamented in an opinion addressing the constitutionality of abortion regulations, "In truth, I am as distressed as the Court is . . . about the 'political pressure' directed to the Court: the marches, the mail, the protests aimed at inducing us to change our opinions. How upsetting it is, that so many of our citizens (good people, not lawless ones, on both sides of this abortion issue, and on various sides of other issues as well) think that we Justices should properly take into account their views, as though we were engaged not in ascertaining an objective law but in determining some kind of social consensus" (*Planned Parenthood v. Casey* 1992, 999–1000, concurring in the judgment in part and dissenting in part).

Other justices, by contrast, identify not only the influence of public opinion but its value in Supreme Court decision making. Take, for example, this argument put forward by Justice Sandra Day O'Connor: "We don't have standing armies to enforce opinions, we rely on the confidence of the public in the correctness of those decisions. That's why we have to be aware of public opinions and of attitudes toward our system of justice, and it is why we must try to keep and build that trust" (quoted in Greenhouse 2012, 72).

Among political scientists and legal scholars who study the influence of public opinion on the Supreme Court, there is debate over the mechanisms of influence. "A vast literature documents an empirical association between public opinion and judicial decisions. But, scholars continue to debate whether the justices, and thus the Court's outputs, actually respond to the public's preferences" (Casillas, Enns, and Wohlfarth 2011, 74).

There are a number of explanations for why Court decisions correspond with public opinion. First, public opinion and judicial decision making may be indirectly linked through the judicial selection process. This linkage was noted by political scientist Robert Dahl, who in 1957 famously argued that "policy views dominant on the Court are never for long out of line with the policy views dominant among the lawmaking majorities of the United States" (Dahl 1957, 285). The tethering of the Court to prevailing views owes to the judicial selection process, which happens frequently enough for the Court's substantive decisions to align with the policy preferences of those who put the justices on the bench. It is not that individual justices change their views directly in response to public opinion once justices are on the bench. Rather, the justices who are put onto the Court are put there because they hold views that coincide with prevailing opinion.

There may also be an indirect tie between public and judicial opinions as reflected by the "public mood." Those who identify this connection assert that justices do not directly respond to public opinion; instead, the views of justices tend to correspond with the views of the public because justices are shaped by many of the same social, political, cultural, and economic forces that sway public opinion. This explanation might suggest, for example, that changes in prevailing attitudes about sexism, gender roles, and gender discrimination that emerged prominently in the 1960s and 1970s implicated not only the public at large but those who would serve on the bench.

Another theory is that judges directly respond to public opinion in making decisions. There are several reasons why justices might respond directly, including Justice O'Connor's observation about the Court's interest in retaining public trust. Institutional legitimacy may matter to those who occupy the bench, as the plurality ruling in *Planned Parenthood v. Casey* explained. "As Americans of each succeeding generation are rightly told, the Court cannot buy support for its decisions by spending money and, except to a minor degree, it cannot independently coerce obedience to its decrees. The Court's power lies, rather, in its legitimacy, a product of substance and perception that shows itself in the people's acceptance of the Judiciary as fit to determine what the Nation's law means and to declare what it demands" (*Planned Parenthood v. Casey* 1992, 865).

If the Court's power rests in its perceived legitimacy and its acceptance by the public, it would not be too surprising if justices were reticent to risk too much harm to the Court's legitimacy by stepping too far away from prevailing public sentiment. Relatedly, if the Court's long-run institutional effectiveness in securing legal policy hinges on public opinion and acceptance, justices might be more inclined to hew to prevailing public views. Insofar as these things matter, public opinion could directly influence judicial decisions.

Another reason why justices might respond directly to public opinion derives from social psychology. Justices, like other human beings, generally care what others think of them and might be motivated to act accordingly. "The desire to be liked and respected by other people is a fundamental psychological motivation, and self-esteem depends heavily on the esteem in which one is held by others. We would hardly expect Supreme Court Justices to be immune to this motivation. Indeed, it is likely to be especially salient to them" (Baum and Devins 2010, 1532). If the desire to be liked does carry weight, then broad public sentiment might sway a justice.

A social psychological argument might point, though, away from the mass public as the audience from which justices seek approval. Political science and legal scholars Lawrence Baum and Neal Devins argue, for example, that "[j]ustices seek both to advance favored policies and to win approval from audiences they care about. These audiences may include the public but are more likely to include elites—individuals and groups that have high socioeconomic status and political influence. The primary reason is that Supreme Court Justices themselves are social and economic elites. As such, they are likely to care a great deal about their reputations among other elites, including academics, journalists, other judges, fellow lawyers, members of other interest groups, and their friends and neighbors" (Baum and Devins 2010, 1516–17).

So, "Are judges influenced by public opinion?" The answer given by political scientists Lee Epstein and Andrew D. Martin is illuminating, even as it admits of uncertainty: "Possibly Yes: (But We're Not Sure Why)" (Epstein and Martin 2010).

CONCLUSION

The preceding discussion highlights a range of potential influences on judicial behavior and decision making. Note that the proposed explanations reviewed in this chapter treat judicial decision making as the thing to be explained. In other words, the broad question explored here has been "What causes justices to rule the way they do?"

Two related inquiries are also of interest to students, scholars, and observers of the Supreme Court. These inquiries reverse the direction of explanation and analysis by looking to see how the Court is perceived and received by the public and whether the Supreme Court can produce social change. It is to these inquiries that chapters 6 and 7 turn.

NOTE

1. The Act stipulates that this filing deadline extends to three hundred days if the charge also is covered by a state or local antidiscrimination law.

6

The Court, the Media, and the Public

A documentary film titled *RBG*, released in 2018, earned a nomination for best documentary and was a smash hit (as documentaries go). It was followed in 2019 by a feature-length film called *On the Basis of Sex*. Both films focus on the life of Supreme Court Justice Ruth Bader Ginsburg. On Saturday Night Live, the long-running sketch comedy that often engages in political satire, the talented comedian Kate McKinnon impersonates Justice Ginsburg. McKinnon as Ginsburg offers acerbic and critical commentary, and delivers her punchline, "that's a 'Gins-burn,'" followed by a suggestive and hilarious dance. The *RBG* documentary shows footage of the real Ginsburg watching and cheerfully laughing at Kate McKinnon's sendup. Showing her own sense of humor about the Saturday Night Live parody, in an interview at the Sundance Film Festival where *RBG* had its world premiere, Justice Ginsburg said, "I would like to say 'Gins-burn!' sometimes to my colleagues" (Withers 2018).

Ginsburg has become a surprising icon, and her level of celebrity—which includes people sporting tattoos of her image—is not typical of most justices. To be sure, many justices have become well known. Many have been well studied, with biographies and other scholarly and journalistic analyses written about them. But public awareness of the Supreme Court remains, by most accounts, relatively limited. At the same time, public perception of the Court appears to be trending negative.

Chapter 5 addressed one part of the relationship between the Court and the public, exploring public opinion's influence on the Court. This chapter turns to the other direction of that relationship. How does the public perceive the Court? To what extent does the public know about and pay attention to Supreme Court decisions and the institution itself? What role does the media play in shaping public attitudes about and approval of the Court? And how does public perception of the Court relate to the legitimacy of the institution?

PUBLIC KNOWLEDGE

"Most research on the public's knowledge of the Supreme Court concludes that the public knows little about the Court or its workings" (Kritzer 2001, 34). Knowledge can change at least temporarily and modestly after high profile Court decisions, as a study conducted by political scientist Herbert M. Kritzer found in the immediate aftermath of the 2000 Supreme Court decision in *Bush v. Gore.* That ruling determined the outcome of the presidential election and was about as high profile as it gets, with a decision that was "dramatic, subject to unprecedented media coverage, controversial, and to many very surprising (the decision by the Court to get involved as well as the decision itself)" (38). Still, the effects of the case and its coverage showed only a modest impact on public evaluation and knowledge of the Court.

Other surveys of public knowledge of the Supreme Court show limited familiarity with the institution. According to an August 2018 C-Span poll of likely U.S. voters, while 48 percent were able to name a sitting Supreme Court justice, 52 percent could not do so or named a justice no longer on the Court ("Supreme Court Survey" 2018). Of those who correctly named a sitting justice, 14 percent selected the chief justice, and another 14 percent mentioned Clarence Thomas. Justice Ginsburg, perhaps not surprisingly, received the most mentions, at 25 percent.

Polls conducted by the PEW Research Center show similar results. The PEW surveys in 2010 and 2012 asked respondents if they could identify the chief justice from a list of four names. In 2010, the listed names were John Roberts, John Paul Stevens, Thurgood Marshall, and Harry Reid, who served as the Senate majority leader from 2007 to 2015. Only 28 percent of respondents gave the correct answer. In 2012, immediately following the highly-covered Supreme Court decision upholding the Affordable Care Act—a decision in which Chief Justice Roberts joined the liberal wing of the Court to cast the deciding vote—only 34 percent picked Roberts from a list that also included Stephen Breyer, William Rehnquist, and Harry Reid. In both 2010 and 2012, over half of respondents did not know or refused to answer, while the rest selected one of the other names (Dost 2015).

Additional surveys by PEW confirm limited public knowledge of who serves on the Court. Only 33 percent gave the correct answer to a 2015 question asking how many justices are women (which, at the time, was three: Justices Ruth Bader Ginsburg, Elena Kagan, and Sonya Sotomayor). A 2013 survey presented the names and photos of Justices Ginsburg, Antonin Scalia, Anthony Kennedy, and Clarence Thomas and asked respondents to identify who in recent years had most often been the Court's "swing vote." Only 28 percent of respondents selected the correct answer: Justice Kennedy (Dost 2015).

A somewhat older, though nevertheless revealing, poll produced by Zogby in 2006 found greater familiarity with Snow White's Seven Dwarfs than the justices on the bench. Among Americans asked to name two of each, 77 percent correctly named the former, compared to 24 percent naming the latter. To be fair to the Supreme Court, public lack of knowledge ranges across political institutions and across other subject matters, including literature and science. The Zogby poll, for example, found that considerably more people could name the Three Stooges than the three branches of the federal government. It also found only 37 percent of respondents correctly knowing which planet is closest to the sun, whereas 60 percent named Krypton as Superman's home planet. As one headline reporting the poll results summarized, "More Americans Know Snow White's Dwarfs Than Supreme Court Judges, Homer Simpson Than Homer's Odyssey, and Harry Potter Than Tony Blair" (Business Wire 2006).

Being able to name a sitting justice is not a perfect proxy for awareness of the judiciary. Political scientists James L. Gibson and Gregory A. Caldeira argue, for example, that using open-ended recall questions (e.g., name a justice on the Supreme Court) is not a useful measure of political knowledge. They also present countervailing evidence that shows some greater knowledge. In surveys they conducted in 2001 asking close-ended questions, they found about 75 percent of respondents knew that justices are appointed, and 66 percent knew justices serve life terms. Gibson and Caldeira found similar levels of knowledge in 2005, with 65 percent and 60 percent, respectively, answering questions about judicial appointment and life tenure correctly (Gibson and Caldeira 2009, 433).

Other research finds somewhat better knowledge of the Court among the public, at least in some contexts. Political scientist Valerie Hoekstra, for instance, studied public knowledge and attitudes about Supreme Court rulings by examining the effects of four cases in the local communities where the disputes originated. Relying on evidence drawn not from national public opinion polls but from surveys of local communities, Hoekstra concludes that court decisions matter.

> When the issue is perceived as important and is covered by the media, the public exhibits rather surprisingly high levels of awareness. In addition to geographic proximity, awareness is affected by education, gender, attention to the media, and the frequency of political discussions. At the very least,

we ought to be skeptical about research suggesting that Court decisions go unnoticed by the public. Most people may not know about most, or even many, of the rulings, but they do hear about those that have some relevance to their community. Furthermore, there is evidence that satisfaction with those decisions influences subsequent evaluations of the Court. (Hoekstra 2000, 97)

Even national surveys of prominent cases sometimes find substantial knowledge. Following the 2013 Supreme Court ruling in *United States v. Windsor* that married gay couples are entitled to federal marriage benefits, a PEW poll found that 66 percent of respondents correctly identified that the decision favored supporters of same-sex marriage. On the other hand, in 2012, "fewer Americans correctly answered a basic question about the court's ruling on the Affordable Care Act. Despite a lengthy buildup to the court's ruling and high public interest in the case, just 55% knew that the court had upheld most provisions of the ACA; 15% said the court had rejected most parts of the law, while 30% said they didn't know" (Dost 2015).

PUBLIC ATTITUDES

Asking the public to name justices or to identify other information about the institution or its decisions is one approach used to gain a sense of how the public perceives the Court. Another approach explores public attitudes about the Court's performance. Does the public think the Court is doing a good job? Does the public have confidence in the Court? Does the public view the Court as political? Do attitudes about the Court vary notably among subsets of the population and over time, and, if so, how and why?

The short answers to these questions run roughly as follows. Compared to the other branches of government, the Court's approval rating tends to be notably higher. So do ratings of public confidence in the Court, though polls have tracked a general decline in trust in the judiciary since the early 2000s. The public's perception that the Court as a political institution seems to be growing, and attitudes about the Court do vary across such things as party affiliation and ideological views. Also noteworthy is that surveys have found that people with greater knowledge about the judiciary are more likely to have faith in the institution.

An October 2019 Gallup poll, conducted after Justice Brett Kavanaugh's first year on the Supreme Court, provides a number of details about public approval of the Court. The poll reports that 54 percent of respondents approve of the way the Court is handling its job, while 42 percent disapprove. Consider how this compares to approval and disapproval over the past two decades. In 2000, approval was at 62 percent, and for the first few years of the early 2000s approval remained near or above 60 percent. But approval vacillated between 42 and 61 percent from 2005 to 2009, then fell to the mid to high 40's from 2011 to 2017, only returning above 50 percent in 2018 (Gallup 2019c).

Approval and disapproval of the Court's performance of its duties form one metric for gauging public attitudes. Gallup also asks survey respondents the following question: "How much trust and confidence do you have at this time in the judicial branch headed by the U.S. Supreme Court—a great deal, a fair amount, not very much or none at all?" A clear majority of 2019 respondents expressed either a fair amount (53 percent) or great deal (16 percent) of trust in the Court (Gallup 2019c). Compared to levels of trust in Congress and the president, the Supreme Court rates quite well. For the "executive branch headed by the president," 21 percent indicated a fair amount trust, while 24 percent expressed a great deal of trust (Gallup 2019b). The legislative branch fares the worst, with only 34 percent registering a fair amount of trust and a meager 4 percent reporting a great deal of trust (Gallup 2019a).

Other polls show a similar degree of confidence in the Court. An Annenberg survey in October 2019 found that 68 percent trust the Court to operate in the best interests of the American people, while 70 percent say the Court has "about the right amount of power" (Barnes 2019b). A poll conducted by Marquette Law School found that when asking which of the three branches of government do you trust the most, the Court far outpaced the other two branches, with 57 percent for the judiciary, 22 for Congress, and 21 for the executive (Barnes 2019b).

Still, public confidence in the Court appears to have taken a hit in the last two decades. In addition to the trust question about the federal judiciary, Gallup also queries the public about their level of confidence in the Court. From 1981 to 2006 those who responded by expressing either a great deal or quite a lot of confidence ranged from 39 percent to 56 percent, but only once dipped to 39. By contrast, between 2007 and 2019, the percent ranged from 30 to 40, but only once reached as high as 40 (Gallup 2019c).

"It's possible, of course, that the decline in support for the court is just a symptom of the country's growing distrust of institutions overall" (Thomson-DeVeaux and Roeder 2018). But increasing polarization and politicization around the Court may be manifest in polling data. For example, the 2019 Annenberg poll that found high levels of trust in the Court also "identified troubling signs in how the Supreme Court and the justices are perceived by the public, suggesting that the distinction between judges and elected politicians is becoming blurred. More 'than half of Americans (57%) agree with the statement that the court 'gets too mixed up in politics.' And just half of the respondents (49%) hold the view that Supreme Court justices set aside their personal and political views and make rulings based on the Constitution, the law, and the facts of the case" (Annenberg 2019).

Moreover, it is telling that confidence in and approval of the Court are often linked to ideology and party identification. In the 2019 Marquette survey, conducted at a time when conservatives held a majority on the Court, 52 percent of "very conservative" respondents reported high confidence in the Court, compared to only 31 percent of "very liberal" respondents. In addition, 36 percent of "very liberal" respondents expressed low confidence (Franklin 2019, 20). Furthermore, the Marquette survey found that "[a]mong those who perceive the Court as either very conservative or conservative, there is a sharp relationship between the respondent's degree of conservatism and confidence in the Court" (20).

With respect to approval of the job the Court is doing, the 2019 Gallup poll found not only sharp divergence by party affiliation, but also considerable recent changes in attitudes based on that affiliation:

> 73% of Republicans approve and 38% of Democrats approve, with independents falling squarely between at 54%. Republicans' approval of the court increased sharply spanning the transition from Barack Obama's presidency to Trump's, rising from 26% in 2016 to 65% in 2017. The September 2017 rating was recorded after Trump saw his first Supreme Court nominee, Justice Neil Gorsuch, confirmed. Since then, GOP approval of the court has only inched higher, making today's rating the highest since 2006 when 74% approved. That reading was Gallup's first measure after Chief Justice John Roberts and Justice Samuel Alito, both George W. Bush nominees, joined the court in late 2005/early 2006. Democrats' approval of the court, on the other hand, has been below 40% the last two years, roughly tying the low level previously seen toward the end of Bush's presidency in 2008. (Saad 2019)

Approval of the Court has also been tied to gender at times. According to a Gallup poll conducted in September 2018, in the midst of the Kavanaugh confirmation hearings but before the sexual assault allegations against him became public, the gender gap in Court approval was wide: 60 percent of men expressed approval compared to 43 percent of women. That divergence was a departure from 2017, when the approval of men and women was virtually the same (McCarthy 2018).

These gauges of public attitudes suggest a somewhat mixed bag. On the one hand, as political scientist Lawrence Baum put it in reacting to the October 2019 polls by Gallup, Annenberg, and Marquette, the findings suggest "a fairly deep reservoir of support for the court" (quoted in Barnes 2019b). Approval of the job the Court is doing remains strong, both in absolute and relative terms. This reservoir of support has a long history, suggesting that the Court can ride waves of fluctuating approval. On the other hand, given the party-line variations in attitudes and growing indications that many sectors of the American public see the Court as a political institution, "Some see other trouble ahead for the court" (Barnes 2019b). As one observer put it, "That a majority of Americans do not believe the justices make impartial decisions is striking. . . . This may explain, in part, a remarkable finding from the Marquette data: nontrivial public support for measures to reform the Supreme Court" (Golde 2019).

The reform measures surveyed by Marquette include proposals to expand the number of justices on the Supreme Court and to impose terms limits on justices. Calls for such reforms have gained more currency of late, even while chances of making the changes are quite remote. Regardless of the low prospects for actually achieving those changes, the "remarkable" findings in recent polling include a whopping 72 percent in favor of term limits for justices (Franklin 2019, 21). The findings also show considerably less but still surprising support for court-packing proposals, with 43 percent indicating support for increasing the number of justices on the Supreme Court (21). Interestingly, support for assigning justices fixed terms is similar among those who identify as Republicans, Democrats, or Independents. On court-packing, though, party identification matters, with Democrats and Independents showing more support for increasing the number of justices than Republicans (22–23).

Whether these sentiments forebode a crisis of legitimacy is up for debate. But the question of whether the Supreme Court—and even the entire judicial system—is at risk of a legitimacy crisis appeared to be on the mind of Chief Justice Roberts when he issued his annual end-of-the-year report on the federal judiciary in 2019:

> I ask my judicial colleagues to continue their efforts to promote public confidence in the judiciary, both through their rulings and through civic outreach. We should celebrate our strong and independent judiciary, a key source of national unity and stability. But we should also remember that justice is not inevitable. We should reflect on our duty to judge without fear or favor, deciding each matter with humility, integrity, and dispatch. As the New Year begins, and we turn to the tasks before us, we should each resolve to do our best to maintain the public's trust that we are faithfully discharging our solemn obligation to equal justice under law. (Roberts 2019, 4)

MEDIATING PUBLIC OPINION

The Supreme Court issues its rulings in the form of lengthy and detailed written opinions that are available to the public. The Supreme Court also delivers shortened versions of its rulings in oral form from the bench, but it allows no cameras in the courtroom. Oral arguments are open to the pubic—at least those who can fit into the Court chamber—and audio recordings of those arguments are released, but not on the same day as the arguments are heard. Supreme Court justices often give public speeches at various venues where somewhat more direct communication to the public occurs. But by and large, public information about and perceptions of the Court are mediated through the media. Given the limited way in which the Court communicates with the public, some argue that the media's role as intermediary is more consequential (see, e.g., Hoekstra 2003; Slotnick and Segal 1998). As one recent study put it, the "media is the single most important channel through which the American public receives its information about the Supreme Court" (Denison, Wedeking, Zilis 2020, 121).

Media outlets, of course, frame and filter the public's consumption of other areas of government and political activity. But because the Supreme Court and its personnel do not typically engage in familiar forms of media and communications outreach (e.g., press conferences and appearances on news programs), the media's interaction with the Court is notably different. Consider this characterization of how the press covers the Supreme Court, offered by journalist Dahlia Lithwick:

> In my almost two decades of covering the high court, I have become accustomed to a press policy that affords access to only a handful of reporters, only to oral arguments, which I must cover with a pen and a notepad, having been robbed—by way of a magnetometer at the entrance—of any recording devices, photographic equipment, and Apple watches. Audio recordings of these oral arguments are offered to the public only on Friday evenings, when the press cannot find any use for them (thus the advent of the Amicus podcast!), and video or even still photos of public sessions of the court are made available to the press only, well, never. Not ever. The justices do not give press conferences; the press officers do not give press conferences; a single, weird, *Brady Bunch*–style photo of the robed justices serves as the lone photographic image of the court all year, and the answer to most truly interesting inquiries directed at the public information officers is a resounding "no comment." (Lithwick 2017)

Furthermore, as veteran Supreme Court reporter Linda Greenhouse observed, "Sources, leaks, casual contact with newsmakers—none of these hallmarks of Washington journalism exists on the Court beat" (quoted in O'Brien 2014, 319).

All of that said, it is worth emphasizing that members of the press have no shortage of material to cover. "No other institution explains itself at such length, such frightening length," *Washington Post* reporter Fred Barbash observed (quoted in O'Brien 2014, 319). The cases themselves and the opinions issued by the justices provide the main material for media coverage. As Greenhouse described it, "[F]ollowing the docket and doing the best I could to understand the cases they were deciding and the implications— that was how the Court interacted with the public and how the Court was to be evaluated both immediately and in history" (quoted in Palleschi 2018).

What do we know about how the media covers the cases themselves? Research shows that only a relatively small number of reporters cover the

Court for primary print, television, and radio outlets. Such research also routinely finds selective reporting of Court decisions. That is, traditional media outlets do not cover the entire Court docket; far from it, most rulings issued by the Court generate little or no media attention.

Those cases and decisions that do generate media attention tend to address hotly contested issues. Publicly salient cases and those that lead to closely divided rulings are typically the ones deemed newsworthy. Notably, though, research suggests that what counts as salient is, itself, influenced by the media coverage, and the tone of media coverage can influence public attitudes about the issues covered. It is not simply that media attention is given because the public cares about or holds views on a particular topic. Media coverage also shapes and drives public opinion, including what topics are of concern to the public and how those topics are framed.

A study of the Supreme Court's 2003 ruling in *Lawrence v. Texas* suggests some of these dynamics. The case, which overturned a 1986 Court decision, found that constitutional protections for privacy extend to decisions by same-sex couples to engage in private, consensual sexual activity. In particular, a majority of the Court deemed that privacy, protected under the Fourteenth Amendment Due Process Clause, precludes states from criminalizing sodomy between consenting adults. Studying that case, researchers found that the tone of the media coverage—including a pattern of increasingly negative coverage—"was associated with a dramatic shift in public opinion on gay rights issues. . . . [D]ata suggests that public opinion did change as a result of the Court's decision, and this was likely enhanced by the media's increasing negative coverage of the case" (Allen and Haider-Markel 2006, 226).

Interestingly, this study also points to the "scathing" dissent in *Lawrence*, authored by Justice Scalia, as having encouraged negative media coverage. "Because conflict often draws media coverage, conflict within the Court, manifested through dissenting opinions, can serve to intensify societal disputes and encourage negative coverage of the decision" (224). A more recent study of a thousand news articles covering rulings from the Court's 2014 term bolsters the idea that the wording of Court rulings can contribute to negative news coverage, though with findings that are more complicated and subtle. "While the negativity in an opinion can increase coverage of the Court's decisions, this is also conditional upon the interaction of three other factors (size of majority coalition, ideology of decision, and whether the coalition is strictly organized along ideological lines) that may result in the amount of negative media coverage decreasing or staying the same" (Denison, Wedeking, and Zilis 2020, 122). In other words, even where Court opinions contain strongly negative language, the less divided the Court is—and in particular the less divided it is along clear ideological lines—the less likely it is that negative media treatment will follow.

If the preceding findings are representative of broader trends, they suggest that heightened concerns about judicial polarization and legitimacy may be grounded in not just the fact that the Court is sometimes divided, but in how (and how negatively) the Court presents itself in divided and divisive decisions. Moreover, the Court has some ability to mitigate negative media portrayals by emphasizing consensus, downplaying ideological splits, and writing opinions that are less caustic (Denison, Wedeking, and Zilis 2020).

In many ways, these findings about how the media might pick up on and replicate negativity emanating from Court decisions are not surprising. Indeed, one might respond by saying that if the Court is issuing opinions that contain strongly negative language, it is the responsibility of the media to report this. However, if the media is selective in which Court decisions are covered *and* the selected cases are those characterized by the most conflict, then it may well be that the media portrayal of the Court overemphasizes controversy and skews public perception by giving heightened attention to polarization.

Media coverage of the Court has also evidenced another commonly used framing trait associated with media treatment of other institutions, namely an approach that frames issues in terms of a game. "Game framing" treats news coverage like a game, presenting subject matter in terms of a competition highlighting who is in the lead and who is behind, who wins and who loses. Within a game frame, policy, substance, and principle tend to be downplayed in favor of strategy and tactics. Research on media coverage of politics in general has found game framing to be dominant. Of note here, research by political scientists Matthew P. Hitt and Kathleen Searles published in 2018 has found it to be increasingly common in television broadcast reporting of the Court.

Covering the Court using a game frame may be particularly easy. With respect to the cases themselves, there are, indeed, identifiable opposing parties. After all, as discussed in chapter 3, one of the justiciability rules is that suits contain an adverse relationship. There are other rules of the game that govern legal disputes. There is a timeline. There are even chief justices who use sports metaphors saying they serve as umpires calling balls and strikes. With respect to the Court as an institution, a game framing approach also fits. Nomination and confirmation processes can be easily framed in terms of partisan winners and losers, as can talk of judicial retirements.

While game framing may be an easy fit for the Court, its impact may be problematic in terms of how it affects public attitudes of the judiciary. According to Hitt and Searles, "Presenting the Court in terms of partisan wins, losses, and competition may rob it of its veneer of sincerity and principle" (Hitt and Searles 2018, 580). Indeed, not only do Hitt and Searles find an increase in game framing in their analysis of television broadcast coverage from 1990 to 2010, they also use a survey experiment to demonstrate that this type of coverage of a Court ruling "lessens specific support for that decision" (580). Arguing that game framing in media coverage of the Court is partially responsible for recent declines in support for the institution, they suggest that "one likely mechanism for declining (although still robust relative to other branches) public support for the Court: increasingly politicized news coverage diminishes the perception that the Court is especially principled or apolitical. As such, citizens become more realist in their view of the Court, and their specific support for the Court declines" (580).

CONCLUSION

Americans harbor a complicated mix of public knowledge and attitudes about the Court. While knowledge of the Court is limited, public approval of and confidence in the Court tend to be notably higher compared to the public support for other branches of government. At the same time, declining confidence in the Court is a mark of the last fifteen years.

Media portrayals, including limited and selective coverage focusing on contentious cases, almost certainly influence public awareness. Certain types of media framing may shape attitudes about the Court, possibly contributing to declining confidence. Future research exploring possible links between media coverage and decreasing trust in the judiciary may become more complicated given the twenty-four-hour news cycle, cable news, talk radio, as well as the explosion of Twitter, Facebook, YouTube, blogs, podcasts, and other online news and politics sources. These platforms have expanded coverage of and access to information about the Court, though it is unclear whether they are enhancing the public's knowledge of the institution and understanding of its rulings.

With continued polarization in American politics in general, there may be reason to expect that trust in the Court will continue to dampen and, with it, perceptions of legitimacy. Though polarization and politicization may chip away at the perceived legitimacy of the Supreme Court, getting to the level of a legitimacy "crisis" is another matter. Still, it remains to be seen how deep the reservoir of support for the Court is in times of heightened and protracted political divisiveness.

7

Consequences, Impact, and Implementation

"In the hands of [Supreme Court justices] rest unceasingly the peace, prosperity, the very existence of the Union. Without them, the Constitution is a dead letter. . . . Their power is immense; but it is a power of opinion. They are omnipotent as long as the people consent to obey the law; they can do nothing once the people scorn the law."
                              —Alexis de Tocqueville, *Democracy in America*

The Supreme Court is undeniably a powerful and prestigious institution. It also faces constraints. At once influential and limited, this combination should not be too surprising given that the original formation of the federal system by America's Founding Fathers emphasized checks and balances, limited government, and skepticism of central governing authority.

What is, perhaps, somewhat surprising is the perennial debate over just how influential and impactful the Supreme Court really is. This enduring question is epitomized by President Andrew Jackson's purported reaction to *Worcester v. Georgia* (1832) and what he viewed as an unwanted Supreme Court ruling written by Chief Justice John Marshall. The Court ruled that the federal government has exclusive authority to regulate Native American territories, and that the seizure of Cherokee Nation lands by the state of Georgia violated federal law and treaties. President Jackson—who supported Georgia's seizures and was notorious for the forced removal of Native Americans from their ancestral lands—reportedly remarked, "John Marshall has made his decision, now let him enforce it."[1] Of course, John Marshall was not in a position to compel the state of Georgia to abide by the Supreme Court's ruling or to make President Jackson put the Court's decision into effect. As Alexander Hamilton put it years earlier in *Federalist Paper No. 78*, without "sword or purse" to compel compliance, the Supreme Court must regularly rely on other actors to give force to its rulings (Hamilton 2009, 392).

Still, because the Supreme Court sits at the apex of the judiciary in a system that ostensibly values the rule of law, some hold that Court decisions have special and multi-faceted influence. According to one commonly held view, the Supreme Court's insulation from electoral processes makes it uniquely situated to bring about direct change in contexts where legislative and executive avenues resist change. According to others, even though the reach of knowledge about the Court among the public at large is limited, Supreme Court decisions have the potential to confer legitimacy, raise awareness, mobilize activists, or change minds. Yet others argue that the Court's influence rests more in shaping and structuring the terms of debate on the most important issues of the day.

These more promising takes on the Court's influence do not assuage skeptics. To the contrary, some skeptics suggest that heightened but unwarranted expectations about judicial power do little more than lure people to a constrained institution.

This chapter surveys, though does not seek to resolve, ongoing debates about the Court's influence and impact. It does by using the 1954 decision in *Brown v. Board of Education* as a case study to illuminate alternative perspectives on whether the Court plays a significant role in bringing about social change. *Brown* serves as an illustrative case study to highlight three competing perspectives on the Court: one that evokes the Court's promise, a second suggestive of the Court's constraints, and a third that views both the opportunities and constraints as essential components of understanding the politics of the Court.

BROWN V. BOARD OF EDUCATION

On May 17, 1954, in *Brown v. Board of Education of Topeka (Brown I)*, the Supreme Court declared state-sanctioned segregation based on race in public schools to be unconstitutional. In the unanimous opinion written by Chief Justice Earl Warren, the Court held that the policy of segregating students by race violates the Fourteenth Amendment guarantee of equal protection regardless of whether the segregated schools are tangibly equal.

The Court explained that in the context of elementary and secondary education, separating students "solely because of their race generates a feeling of inferiority as to their status in the community that may affect their hearts and minds in a way unlikely ever to be undone" (*Brown I* 1954, 494). Because feelings of inferiority can affect motivation to learn, racial segregation impedes educational and mental development, and educational opportunity. Finding that comparable physical facilities, financial resources, and teacher and staff training across segregated schools do not mitigate these problems, the Court concluded that "[s]eparate educational facilities are inherently unequal," and "in the field of public education the doctrine of 'separate but equal' has no place" (495).

While declaring state-sanctioned racial segregation in public schools to be impermissible, the Court did not provide a remedy to the existing state of affairs or explain how its declaration would be put into effect. The Court did not, for example, demand an immediate end to racial segregation in public schools. Neither did the Court return the case to the district court for additional proceedings to determine how to desegregate or for entry of a decree that would bar the enforcement of statutes requiring racial segregation. Instead, the Court ordered that additional arguments be presented in the following term specifically addressing how to remedy the constitutional violation. The Court returned the case to its own docket and invited the U.S. Attorney General, as well as the attorneys general from all the states that required or permitted segregated schools, to join the parties in *Brown* to present arguments addressing the question of "the manner in which relief is to be accorded" (*Brown II* 1955, 298).

Those arguments were presented to the Supreme Court over several days in April 1955. On May 31, 1955, the Court handed down a second ruling, referred to as *Brown II*. In another brief and unanimous opinion authored by Chief Justice Warren, the Court reaffirmed its holding in *Brown I* and issued a decree requiring school districts to make "a prompt and reasonable start" at "the earliest practicable date" to admit students into public schools on a nondiscriminatory basis (300). The Court also allowed that implementation of *Brown I* might need different measures based on varying local needs and contexts, and identified local school authorities as having primary responsibility for implementation. But the opinion reminded those authorities that they must act consistently with *Brown I*, whether they agreed with the ruling or not. Importantly, the Court remanded the cases back to the U.S. District Courts for their oversight, explicitly charging those courts with the responsibility of ensuring compliance by considering whether school authority actions constitute "good faith implementation of the governing constitutional principles" (299). The ruling set no specific timeline or deadline, and acknowledged that lower courts may determine that school districts may need additional time to effectively and equitably comply with the principles set forth in *Brown I*, but the Court also insisted that implementation proceed "with all deliberate speed" (301).

LAW'S PROMISE: USING THE COURT TO ADVANCE JUSTICE

Among the most consequential aspects of the Court's historic 1954 ruling in *Brown I* was the repudiation, at least with respect to public education, of the "separate but equal" doctrine. That doctrine, established nearly sixty years earlier in *Plessy v. Ferguson* (1896), authorized the "Jim Crow" regime of racial discrimination that dominated the South. *Plessy* perpetuated a racial caste system long after the end of the Civil War and the passage of the Civil War Amendments. The term "Jim Crow" derives from an 1828 minstrel song called "Jump Jim Crow," and its associated racist dance routine, performed by a white man dressed in blackface, that caricatured African American men. By the late 1800s, the term "Jim Crow" came to signify the set of laws that perpetuated racial segregation even after inclusion of equal protection in the Constitution. Not only were schools segregated, so too were many public accommodations, including hotels, restaurants, and theaters. Separate bathrooms and water fountains were common features in the Southern landscape, as was segregation in railway cars, on buses, in housing, and in jails. Jim Crow laws separated the races at beaches, swimming pools, and other public amusements, and they governed marriage as well, as a majority of states prohibited interracial marriage during the first half of the twentieth century.

Efforts to reverse Jim Crow through electoral and political processes faced significant barriers, in part because legally sanctioned discrimination also limited the ability of African Americans to vote. At the turn of the twentieth century, many Southern states instituted poll taxes and literacy tests as conditions for voting, and, at the same time, used so-called grandfather clauses to remove these conditions for those who voted, or whose ancestors had voted, before the Civil War. The intent and effect of grandfather clauses were to suppress the African American vote. Another strategy that disenfranchised Black voters was the all-white primary election, deployed by the Democratic Party and many Southern states beginning in the late 1800s. Rules governing Democratic Party primaries—elections increasingly used at the turn of the twentieth century to nominate the party's candidates who would run for office—prohibited Blacks from voting. In some instances, these rules were adopted by Democratic Party organizations; in other instances, they were passed by state legislatures. Because the Democratic Party dominated Southern politics during this era, the exclusion of African Americans from participation in primary elections amounted to a sweeping electoral disenfranchisement.

In short, African American political representation and influence through elections and "democratic" processes were substantially curtailed, making efforts to seek racial justice through legislative avenues ineffectual. By contrast, pursuing change through the judiciary was seen as a pathway with at least some promise. The National Organization for the Advancement of Colored People (NAACP), founded in 1909, established a legal arm that gained some early legal victories from the Supreme Court. The 1926 Annual Report of the NAACP highlighted the value of pressing forward through the judiciary, and especially the federal courts, "where the atmosphere of sectional prejudice is notably absent" (Tushnet 1987, 1). The relatively low cost of pursuing litigation and the victories they might produce led the NAACP to develop a plan for coordinating litigation. The NAACP modified that "plan" frequently, with the litigation campaign "conducted on a terrain that repeatedly required changes in maneuvers" (146).

It was not lost on the lawyers and advocates pursuing this litigation campaign that the judiciary was itself significantly implicated in Jim Crow. As Thurgood Marshall, one of the chief architects of the NAACP's legal strategy (and future Supreme Court Justice), observed, it had been the Supreme Court that had limited the reach and scope of the Civil War Amendments in the first place. Writing in 1951 about the Court's early interpretation of the Fourteenth Amendment, Marshall said, "That many of the vestiges of slavery remain and that racial discrimination still is practiced in all sections of the United States is to a considerable extent the responsibility of the United States Supreme Court which spelled out the meaning of this new constitutional provision. The Court's narrow, cautious, and often rigid interpretation of the amendment's reach and thrust in the past gave constitutional sanction to practices of racial discrimination and prejudice" (Marshall 1951, 101).

Still, the NAACP won multiple Supreme Court victories in the decade prior to *Brown*. Among the important legal wins, for example, was a declaration that all-white primaries violated the Constitution. That pronouncement, handed down in *Smith v. Allwright* (1944), held that the Fourteenth and Fifteenth Amendments prohibit racial discrimination in voting. In *McClaurin v. Oklahoma* and *Sweatt v. Painter*, two key cases handed down on the same day in 1950, the Court ruled, respectively, that segregation based on race in graduate school education and law school violates equal protection guarantees. In *McClaurin*, the Black plaintiff had been admitted to University of Oklahoma graduate school of education, but was required to sit at separate tables and desks in (and sometimes outside) classrooms, libraries, and dining facilities. In *Sweatt*, Texas refused to admit the Black plaintiff to the University of Texas School of Law and set up a separate law school for African Americans. In both cases, the Supreme Court ruled that the differential treatment harmed the education of Blacks based solely on their race and thereby violated equal protection guarantees contained in the Constitution's Civil War Amendments.

This line of cases did not directly produce the reversal of *Plessy*'s "separate but equal" precedent. However, it certainly challenged that precedent, and by the time *Brown* arrived at the Supreme Court, a legal path had been paved, along with optimism that the judiciary would provide the avenue for change. Three years prior to the *Brown* decision, Thurgood Marshall offered the following appraisal of the federal judicial path: "The Supreme Court of the United States, far removed from the stresses which keep racial animosity alive, is best able to determine whether the state in fact provides equal protection of the laws as required by the Constitution" (Marshall 1951, 102). Furthermore,

> Any fair assessment of the Court's role in the past decade compels the conclusion that it has done considerably more than any other arm of the federal government to secure, preserve, and extend civil rights. Although its approach has been undeniably cautious, the Court seems to be making a real effort to deal effectively with our most disturbing problem with practical wisdom and insight. If it continues along the path blazed by its recent decisions, the Constitution's mandate of equal protection of the laws will eventually accomplish the objective its framers intended—that of prohibiting all forms of community discriminatory action based upon race or color. (110)

Thus, when the Supreme Court pronounced in *Brown I* the momentous constitutional end to the "separate but equal" doctrine in public education, it (a) upheld the rights of a political and marginalized minority, (b) in a context where electoral and legislative avenues for change were heavily constrained, and (c) in the face of what would be certain resistance by committed, ardent, and politically powerful racial segregationists. It's no wonder, then, that the decision lent support to—and, indeed, became the paradigm case for—the view of the judiciary as protector of minority and individual rights.

Other progressive social movements followed suit by literally filing suit, looking to the courts as an avenue to effectuate change. The women's rights movement began bringing cases to challenge gender-based discrimination, and movements advocating on behalf of the criminally accused, anti-war protesters, the environment, animal rights, and more turned their attention towards the Courts. The seeming success embodied in *Brown* was viewed as an opening to the halls of justice.

LAW'S FAILURE: THE ILLUSION OF JUSTICE

Political scientist Gerald N. Rosenberg published a seminal book in 1991 (and updated in 2008) examining the use of litigation by several different social movements in the United States. The subtitle of the book presents his research question: *Can Courts Bring About Social Change?* At least a third of the book is devoted to analysis of the civil rights movement, focusing on *Brown v. Board of Education* and its aftermath. Rosenberg's answer to his research question is captured rather pessimistically in the book's main title: *The Hollow Hope.*

According to Rosenberg's analysis of *Brown* and, more generally, the use of litigation by the civil rights movement, court rulings favorable to civil rights were met with widespread avoidance, resistance, and defiance. In particular, in the first decade after *Brown*, schools remained racially segregated, with political leadership at the local, state, and national levels at best unamenable to change—and quite often actively opposed to it. Southern segregationist views prevailed and proved resistant to court orders. Similarly, in areas beyond public school segregation, including segregation in transportation, housing, and public accommodations, Rosenberg finds that judicial action did not produce substantial reform, at least not until Congress and the executive branch stepped in. Whether it was President Eisenhower's decision to send federal troops to Little Rock, Arkansas, to enforce desegregation of Little Rock Central High School, or the passage of the Civil Rights Act of 1964 and the Voting Rights Act of 1965, it was only when the other branches supported civil rights and public sentiment began to shift that change occurred. With respect to civil rights, Rosenberg summarizes his findings this way:

> The use of the courts in the civil rights movement is considered the paradigm of a successful strategy for social change. . . . Yet, a closer examination reveals that before Congress and the executive branch acted, courts had virtually *no direct effect* on ending discrimination in the key fields of education, voting, transportation, accommodations and public places, and housing. Courageous and praiseworthy decisions were rendered, and nothing changed. Only when Congress and the executive branch acted in tandem with the courts did change occur in these fields. In terms of judicial effects, then, *Brown* and its progeny stand for the proposition that courts are impotent to produce significant social reform. *Brown* is a paradigm, but for precisely the opposite view. (Rosenberg 2008, 70–71)

Can this be correct? Were the courts impotent rather than important? And, if so, how is it that one of the most historic and momentous decisions by the Supreme Court had virtually *no direct effect* ahead of action by the other branches of the federal government?

With respect to *Brown*, it is widely accepted that the Court's direct impact on desegregating schools was severely limited. Desegregation occurred in states that bordered the South, and a number of Southern politicians who generally supported segregation took a restrained position in the immediate aftermath of the Court's ruling (see Klarman 2007, 246).

However, "massive resistance" soon came to characterize Southern states' responses to *Brown*. For example, in 1954 Georgia Governor Herman Talmadge announced that "Georgia is going to resist mixing the races in the schools if it is the sole state of the nation to do so" and "no amount of force whatever can compel desegregation of white and Negro schools" (quoted in Klarman 2007, 247). Similarly, Senator James Eastland of Mississippi declared in 1954 that "the South will not abide by or obey this legislative decision by a political court" (quoted in Klarman 2007, 247). In February 1956, Virginia Senator Harry Flood Byrd called for "massive resistance" to the Supreme Court's decision: "If we can organize the Southern States for massive resistance to this order I think that in time the rest of the country will realize that racial integration is not going to be accepted in the South" (quoted in Gates 2011, 117).

And organize they did. In March 1956, 101 Southern members of Congress signed a "Declaration of Constitutional Principles" that has come to be called "The Southern Manifesto." Introduced in the House of Representatives on March 12, 1956, and read into the Congressional Record in the Senate, the Manifesto stated that its signatories "regard the decisions of the Supreme Court in the school cases as a clear abuse of judicial power" and "pledge ourselves to use all lawful means to bring about a reversal of this decision which is contrary to the Constitution and to prevent the use of force in its implementation" (Declaration of Constitutional Principles 1956, 4459–60). Senator Strom Thurmond, one of the Manifesto's drafters, said this in his speech on the floor of the Senate: "The people and the States must find ways and means of preserving segregation in the schools" (quoted in Aucoin 1996, 175).

The ways and means of preserving racial segregation in public schools were many. Public schools were shuttered as some legislatures in Southern states authorized their closing in order to avoid complying with desegregation. Funding for public schools was stopped and diverted to allow students to attend private, racially segregated schools. And in an act of defiance that gained widespread media coverage, Arkansas Governor Orval Faubus ordered his state's National Guard to prevent integration of the all-white Central High School in Little Rock.

In the face of massive resistance and more subtle acts of delay and avoidance, it is not surprising that the promise of *Brown* proved elusive. The numbers are quite revealing: "On *Brown's* sixth anniversary in 1960, 98 of Arkansas's 104,000 black students attended desegregated schools; 34 of North Carolina's 302,000; 169 of Tennessee's 146,000; and 103 of Virginia's 203,000. In the five Deep South states, not one of the 1.4 million black school children attended a racially mixed school until the fall of 1960" (Klarman 2007, 178). While desegregation increased in the early 1960s, "Ten years after *Brown* only 1.2 percent of black schoolchildren in the South attended school with whites. Excluding Texas and Tennessee, the percent drops to less than one-half of one percent. . . . After ten years of Court-ordered desegregation, in eleven Southern states barely 1 out of every 100 black children attended school with whites" (Rosenberg 2008, 52).

During the original set of oral arguments in *Brown I*, Justice Felix Frankfurter foreshadowed these bleak results. "I think that nothing would be worse than for this Court—I am expressing my own opinion—nothing would be worse, from my point of view, than for this Court to make an abstract declaration that segregation is bad and then have it evaded by tricks" (*Brown*, Transcript of Oral Arguments 1952, 14). But the lack of success should not come as a surprise given the structure and nature of the judiciary.

The structure of the American political system places noteworthy constraints on the judiciary's ability to produce change. These constraints include (a) the limited nature of constitutional rights, which narrows the types of claims on which the courts are willing and able to act; (b) the judiciary's lack of insulation and independence, which leads courts to be generally deferential to other branches of government and to follow public opinion, rather than stray from it; and (c) the courts' limited power and capacity to implement its decisions (Rosenberg 2008, 9–21). According to Rosenberg, only when certain conditions are met that overcome these constraints can the courts, and the Supreme Court in particular, effectively generate change. However, those conditions include not only the availability of legal precedent upon which to ground rights, but also considerable support for change from outside the judiciary and some kind of mechanism to put court decisions into effect. In other words, Rosenberg argues that for the judiciary to be an effective producer of change, the change must be supported by the other branches of government, and the public either has to be on board with the change—or at least not be terribly resistant to it. Moreover, if those conditions are required for the judiciary to produce change, it seems hardly accurate to identify the judiciary as the producer of change. "A court's contribution, then, is akin to officially recognizing the evolving state of affairs, more like the cutting of the ribbon on a new project than its construction" (Rosenberg 2008, 422).

Stuart A. Scheingold's *The Politics of Rights* (1974) asserted that a "myth of rights" ideology prevails in the United States, leading to a naïve but alluring optimism in the law. Scheingold characterizes the myth of rights ideology as one that *"rests on a faith in the political efficacy and ethical sufficiency of law as a principle of government"* (17). Those who subscribe to this ideology are inclined to view the judiciary as legitimate and its declarations of rights as effective for securing a justice. The myth of rights encourages a romanticized view that the political order in America actually functions in a manner consistent with the patterns of rights and obligations specified in the Constitution. The ethical connotations of this rule of law system are based on a willingness to identify constitutional values with social justice. It encourages us to break down social problems into the responsibilities and entitlements established under law in the same way that lawyers and judges deal with disputes among individuals. Once the problem is analyzed, the myth, moreover, suggests that it is well on the way to resolution, since these obligations and rights are not only legally enforceable but ethically persuasive, because they are rooted in constitutional values. (17)

The problem, according to Scheingold, is that this view is a myth that both lures social reformers to the courthouse and misleads them into thinking that judicial rulings will directly translate into real change. The seductive power of this faith in law creates false hope, may siphon energy and resources away from other forms of political activism, and risks producing complacency. Moreover, what appears to be a judicial victory may turn out to be largely symbolic, with real effects that reinforce and maintain prevailing arrangements of power. As Scheingold asserts, a "sober assessment of the status of rights in American politics raises serious doubts about the capabilities of legal and constitutional processes for neutralizing power relationships. The authoritative declaration of a right is perhaps best viewed as the beginning of a political process in which power relationships loom large and immediate" (85).

Applied to *Brown v. Board of Education* and civil rights litigation, Scheingold's concept of the myth of rights serves as a cautionary counterpoint to the promise of law. And the symbolic draw of the myth, as Rosenberg also warns, lures activists to litigation like flies to flypaper (Rosenberg 2008, 427). It can further have the detrimental effect of producing intense backlash, of the sort seen following *Brown*, that might not have occurred if reform efforts had proceeded through legislative and electoral avenues rather than through litigation.

Perhaps *Brown* is an outlier. If this were so, then claims about the myth of rights and the limited impact of the Supreme Court would be less persuasive. However, legal scholars have exposed many notable instances beyond *Brown* of the wide gap between what Court rulings promise and what actually happens in the world. In one classic "gap study," for example, researchers found rural courts in Kentucky refusing to conform with a landmark Supreme Court decision that granted juvenile criminal defendants the right to legal counsel (Canon and Kolson 1971). In another, researchers revealed extensive refusal by public schools to comply with Supreme Court rulings that prohibited prayer in school (Dolbeare and Hammond 1971). Another analysis of Supreme Court rulings that grant pregnant minors a constitutional right to abortion found multiple impediments to the protection of those rights, including widespread ignorance of the law among the courts responsible for implementation, as well as outright resistance by judges to the idea that minors have a constitutional right to abortion (Silverstein 2007).

LEGAL MOBILIZATION: THE POLITICS OF RIGHTS

While *Brown* is certainly not an isolated or rare instance of the challenges associated with implementing Supreme Court decisions, *The Hollow Hope* and other assessments of the limited capacity of the Court to produce change are not without their critics. And the persuasiveness of an analysis like Rosenberg's turns, at least in part, on whether there are other ways for the Court to have an impact beyond its direct effects. Note that one of the main arguments Rosenberg puts forward is that *Brown* had little to no "direct effect" for at least a decade and that progress did not occur until the executive and legislative branches were moved to act. But if *Brown* produced "indirect effects" that contributed to change by, for example, pressuring Congress and presidents to act, then perhaps placing hope in litigation is not as hollow as it might sometimes seem.

Several scholars urge such an analysis of the Court's impact and influence. They argue that an understanding of whether the Court plays a significant role in bringing about social change requires attention to more than its direct effects. Legal scholar Joel F. Handler, for example, notes that litigation may be part of a broader campaign to produce reform and may generate several types of indirect benefits. Litigation might generate media attention and publicity, foster fund raising and movement mobilization, lend legitimacy to a particular cause, and increase leverage and bargaining power (Handler 1978). Other researchers highlight how these indirect effects might spur action by legislators and executives by bringing an issue to the forefront and placing pressure on a president or members of Congress or by mobilizing public opinion in a way that produces electoral change. In short, some argue that even when Court decisions produce limited direct effects, they can indirectly serve as the catalyst for broader political reform.

Rosenberg recognizes and addresses this possibility, but does not find evidence to support it. In addition to looking at *Brown's* direct effects, he examines whether it may have sparked and inspired other forms of political action by generating press coverage, influencing political leaders and elites, and shifting public opinion. He also explores whether *Brown* may have served as a catalyst that helped propel the civil rights movement by inspiring activists to protest, demonstrate, and become members of movement organizations. However, Rosenberg concludes that there is little empirical evidence to support that claim that *Brown* indirectly promoted the civil rights changes that began to take effect in the 1960s.

By contrast, other political and social science researchers question the evidence Rosenberg cites. For example, Rosenberg's analysis has been criticized for using data about the effect of *Brown* on African Americans that may not reflect the changing perspective of that community. Bradley C. Canon thus argues that the press coverage Rosenberg examined focused on those publications aimed at white audiences, not African American audiences (Canon 1998). Other researchers counter Rosenberg's finding by presenting evidence of the existence of indirect effects. In one notable counterpoint to Rosenberg's analysis, Michael Paris and Kevin J. McMahon find several important links not identified by Rosenberg between *Brown* and the 1965 Montgomery bus boycott (Paris and McMahon 1998). In another counterpoint, Michael W. McCann cites several civil rights leaders who claimed to be influenced by the ruling in *Brown*, whereas Rosenberg finds little evidence for such influence (McCann 1992). And in yet another, Aldon Morris argues that *Brown* had an important mobilizing effect for African Americans: "The winning of the 1954 decision was the kind of victory the organization needed to rally the black masses behind its program; by appealing to blacks' widespread desire to enroll their children in the better-equipped white schools it reached into black homes and had meaning for people's personal lives" (Morris 1984, 34).

Those who point out that Court rulings may produce indirect effects as well as direct ones do not argue that such effects will always occur or always be beneficial. Instead, the point these scholars make is that a more complete assessment of the judiciary's role in society and, in particular, the consequences of the Supreme Court, must attend to the multitude of ways in which the courts might, and sometime do, matter.

One main proponent of such a broader view is political scientist and public law scholar Michael W. McCann. McCann puts forward a model of legal mobilization attentive not only to tangible, albeit harder to measure, indirect effects like publicity and fundraising, but to more complex, subtle, and indeterminate ways in which law and legal rulings permeate and shape perceptions, attitudes, understandings, and expectations. Expanding on the works of other sociolegal scholars, McCann argues for a decentered view of law and litigation that "emphasizes that judicially articulated legal norms take a life of their own as they are deployed in practical social action. This points to what many analysts refer to as the *constitutive* capacity of law: Legal knowledge prefigures in part the symbolic terms of material relations *and* becomes a potential resource in ongoing struggles to refigure those relations" (McCann 1992, 733). Legal mobilization understood and analyzed in these terms pays attention to the direct and indirect effects, as well as to the constitutive character of law. On this view, law is "the agglomeration of cultural beliefs, norms, languages, and practices that reflects and constructs social relationships, regulates social interaction, and establishes and maintains order. . . . Although the official state institutions remain important to analyses of the legal system, it is by exploring the broader, unofficial realm of social interaction that we can develop a more subtle, complex, and expansive understanding of law" (Silverstein 1996, 4).

The legal mobilization model does not draw a simple equation between a litigation victory like *Brown* and the advancement of justice. Indeed, the model acknowledges the existence of the types of constraints addressed by *The Hollow Hope* and other critical legal scholarship, recognizing among other things the gap between a judicial order and its translation in practice. At the same time, the legal mobilization model notes that the turn to the judiciary may be far less the result of naïve optimism and illusions, and much more about the limited access to other avenues of influence. As Justice Thurgood Marshall said in 1992, a year after his retirement from the bench, the African American plaintiffs who litigated to end Jim Crow were essentially forced to turn to the courts. They used "the only weapon they had—their right to a day in court to gain the rights to which they were constitutionally entitled" (Marshall 1992). Moreover, the legal mobilization model does not see the law as so straitjacketed that it will inevitably reinforce the status quo. Instead, the framework envisions law as "neither just a resource nor just a constraint" but "encourages us to focus on how, when, and to what degree legal practices tend to be both at the same time" (McCann 1994, 12).

In arguing for this perspective, the legal mobilization model brings us back to Stuart Scheingold and the myth of rights. Scheingold's work identifies not only the allure of the myth of rights ideology but also what he calls "the politics of rights," which serves as the title of his influential book. According to Scheingold, because the power of rights discourse is founded, in part, on its symbolic and mythic value, rights can be reconfigured in a political way that has mobilizing possibilities: "It is possible to capitalize on the perceptions of entitlement associated with rights to initiate and to nurture political mobilization—a dual process of *activating* a quiescent citizenry and *organizing* groups into effective political units. Political mobilization can in this fashion build support for interests that have been excluded from existing allocations of values and thus promote a *realignment* of political forces" (Scheingold 1974, 131).

Many barriers impede effective deployment of the law, and Scheingold cautions that rights, like the law itself, cut both ways, "serving at some times and under some circumstances to reinforce privilege and at other times to provide the cutting edge of change. This ambivalence means that rights in the abstract cannot be thought of as either allies or enemies of progressive tendencies but rather as an arena for struggle" (Scheingold 1989, 76).

CONCLUSION: THE COURT AS AN ARENA OF STRUGGLE

On May 17, 1954, NAACP leaders met with the press to answer questions about the Court's ruling in *Brown*, handed down earlier that day. Asked to predict how long it would take to end public school segregation, Thurgood Marshall said it might take up to five years for the whole country. He further predicted that all forms of racial segregation would be eradicated by 1963—the hundredth anniversary of the Emancipation Proclamation ("N.A.A.C.P. Sets Advanced Goals" 1954).

As legal scholar Derrick Bell explains, however, "Marshall privately harbored less optimistic predictions; wandering through NAACP headquarters during a gleeful, post-*Brown* party, Marshall warned, 'You fools go ahead and have your fun, but we ain't begun to work yet'" (Bell 1985, 10). And while Marshall kept up that work for racial equality both as a civil rights attorney and a Supreme Court justice, his reflections on the judiciary presented in a speech he gave on July 4, 1992—a year after his departure from the bench and forty years after the first set of oral arguments in *Brown*—were not particularly sanguine:

> [H]ad I thought in the wake of Smith V. Allwright and Shelley V. Kraemer and Brown V. Board of Education that I would be giving a talk now on the anniversary of our Nation's independence, I would have predicted that I would have spoken with much pride and optimism of the enormous progress this Nation has made. . . . I wish I could say that racism and prejudice were only distant memories. I wish I could say that this Nation had traveled far along the road to social justice and that liberty and equality were just around the bend. I wish I could say that America has come to appreciate diversity and to see and accept similarity. But as I look around, I see not a Nation of unity but of division—Afro and White, indigenous and immigrant, rich and poor, educated and illiterate. . . . The legal system can force open doors and sometimes even knock down walls. But it cannot build bridges. That job belongs to you and me. Afro and White, rich and poor, educated and illiterate, our fates are bound together. (Marshall 1992)

As Marshall's comments to reporters in 1954 suggest, *Brown v. Board of Education* is sometimes held up as a model of the Supreme Court's role and influence: affording protection of fundamental constitutional guarantees that safeguard individual and minority rights against sometimes tyrannical majorities. But Marshall was not naïve about the Court's power. He, along with other lawyers, took a strategic approach to litigation. And, after serving on the other side of the bench for twenty-four years, he departed the Court dubious of its transformative potential: it can open doors, but opening doors is just the beginning.

The debate about the influence and impact of the Court will no doubt continue. But at least as important as examining *whether* the Court brings about social change, is looking at *how* the Court structures conflict.

Appealing to the Supreme Court is often done in an effort to seek change and gain consensus by settling conflicts over fundamental constitutional guarantees of equality and liberty. But, as legal scholar Reva Seigel argues, Americans should also attend to the Court's important role in structuring conflicts that it cannot settle and in continuing debate over constitutional meaning by channeling that debate into new forms (Siegel 2016, 4). "Judicial review does serve crucial conflict resolution goals. But . . . conflict resolution is not judicial review's sole function. When courts—and other government officials interpreting the constitution—lack power to impose particular constitutional settlements, they may still shape political conflict in ways that advance constitutional values. Law and politics help constitute one another, in many ways, by changing meanings and by altering the legitimacy conditions of political and legal argument. Advocates appreciate this. They advocate to win, and to shape debate when they cannot" (Siegel 2016, 4).

Siegel presents this argument by away of analyzing the more recent constitutional litigation over same-sex marriage, which resulted in the Court's momentous 2015 ruling in *Obergefell v. Hodges* recognizing the right of same-sex couples to marry. Comparing *Obergefell* and *Brown*, Siegel finds reason to view the Court as an important institution not because it ends discussion—because it does not. Instead, she highlights how the Court shapes ongoing discourse, debate, conflict, and engagement: "Just as *Brown* did not end debate over racial segregation, *Obergefell* has not ended debate over marriage but instead has channeled it into new forms. Public support for gay marriage has risen dramatically over the last decade, but many Americans remain passionately opposed, especially when one attends to differences in age, region, religion, and political party. These Americans are mobilizing to continue the fight over marriage, under the banner of conscience and religious liberty, in the courts and in campaigns for the presidency" (Siegel 2016, 4).

Siegel is not alone in emphasizing this aspect of the Court's role. The legal mobilization model and the politics of rights urge an analysis that considers conceptualizing rights and the Court itself as "an arena of struggle" (Scheingold 1989, 76). Viewing the Court in this way certainly continues to recognize its signature importance, as the highest judicial body in the country. But it also situates the Court in ongoing and iterative political conflicts and struggles. And, as Siegel concludes, "Looking at the conflict over same-sex marriage through the lens of constitutional culture, we can see how Americans—acting in courts, legislatures, and civil society—argued in ways that created *Obergefell's* conditions of plausibility. Using many of these same resources, Americans are continuing to argue in the decision's wake as they try to shape *Obergefell's* meaning for the next phase of conflict" (Siegel 2016, 7).

NOTE

1. It is not clear whether President Jackson said these words, and his actual comments may have been different. See Rosen (2017). Whether or not Jackson uttered this phrase, it is nevertheless telling that this quote is so frequently cited as evidence of the limits on the Court's power.

Conclusion: The Future of the Supreme Court

"Supreme Court decision making is shaped by social and political forces. . . . [T]he opinions and writings of the Justices make clear that the Court is product of its times."

—Lawrence Baum and Neal Devins, "Why the Supreme Court Cares about Elites, Not the American People"

"Presidents come and go, but the Supreme Court goes on forever."

—President and Chief Justice William Howard Taft

The future of the Supreme Court seems at once clear and elusive. Because those who serve on the bench often stay for extended periods, there is less turnover and more stability. Because the Court's annual docket of cases is small, the reach of its influence is attenuated. Because the institution has been guided by precedent, norms, and rules, there is a good amount of continuity. At the same time, with only nine justices on the bench, the departure of one or two, especially when being replaced by a president from the opposite party of the one who selected the departing justices, can seem and, in some instances is, seismic. Though the Court accepts a limited number of cases, those cases tend to have outsized significance, weeded down from a vast pool to a small set of often meaningful matters. And while precedent, norms, and rules serve as constraints to change, they do not straitjacket the Court. Rules can be modified, norms ignored, and precedent overturned.

What, then, can we expect of and from of the Supreme Court going forward?

CONSERVATIVE CONSOLIDATION

At the time of this writing, four justices (Sotomayor, Ginsburg, Kagan, and Breyer) fall clearly on the liberal side of the spectrum of sitting justices, while the other five (Thomas, Kavanaugh, Alito, Gorsuch, and Roberts) fall squarely on the conservative side of the spectrum (Epstein, Martin, and Quinn 2018). Justices Neil Gorsuch and Brett Kavanaugh are early in their tenures on the Court and, as such, have thinner track records on which to predict their future positions and votes. Still, according to one commonly used measure of judicial ideology, called the Martin-Quinn score,[1] Kavanaugh and Gorsuch fall within the conservative bloc, and the consensus view is that they are likely to be generally reliable members of the conservative coalition.

When Kavanaugh joined the Court in 2018 after the retirement of Anthony Kennedy, all accounts predicted a notably conservative shift on the Court. This is because Kennedy, as we have seen, had been the swing justice, voting most often with the conservative bloc of the Court, but sometimes joining and thereby creating a majority for the liberal bloc in key cases, like those addressing abortion rights and gay rights. Relatedly, "For much of his tenure, Justice Kennedy has been the median justice, falling in the court's ideological center, according to a measure based on voting patterns" (Parlapiano and Patel 2018). What's more, the power Kennedy had as median justice in forming majority opinions was particularly strong "because the distance between him and the justices on either side of him ideologically was so large in most of the years in which he had that role" (Parlapiano and Patel 2018).

While Kavanaugh was confirmed to the seat vacated by Kennedy, that does not mean Kavanaugh necessarily becomes the median justice or the swing justice. Before serving his first year on the bench, his stated positions, jurisprudence, and voting patterns on lower courts suggested that Kavanaugh might be to the ideological right of not just Kennedy, but also to the right of Chief Justice Roberts. If that early prognostication bears out, then Roberts may become the median justice.

But after Kavanaugh's one full term of service on the bench and Gorsuch's two full terms, there is early reason to think that they might each play a swing role, along with Roberts. In the 2018 term, Roberts and Kavanaugh voted the same in almost all the cases (94 percent of the time), and their Martin-Quinn scores for the term showed them closely related on judicial ideology, with Gorsuch to their right, and Alito and Thomas to their right further still (see Thomson-DeVeaux 2019). The 2018 term saw Gorsuch playing the swing role at times, joining the four liberal justices in a few cases concerning the rights of criminal defendants.

Whether Roberts, Kavanaugh, or Gorsuch becomes the ideological median on the bench, or whether one takes over (or all three share) the role of swing justice, it is more likely than not that we are witnessing a notable conservative shift on the Court. How long-lasting this will be, how it will affect the Court's direction and decisions, and how it might impact the Court's perceived legitimacy are interesting questions. The answers are somewhat speculative and depend, among other things, on electoral outcomes.

COURT COMPOSITION AND THE 2020 ELECTION

At the time of this writing, two of the Court's liberal justices—Ruth Bader Ginsburg and Stephen Breyer—are over the age of eighty. Also at the time of this writing, the 2020 presidential election lies ahead. If the Republican party wins the 2020 presidential election and maintains control of the Senate, the Court will almost certainly further consolidate what has already been a conservative shift. If the Democrats win the presidential election and take over control of the Senate, Ginsburg and Breyer would, if they depart, likely be replaced by justices that would stem the tide of a rightward shift. But it would take the departure of one of the conservative justices for Democrats to make inroads into what is presently a conservative bench. Whether those justices, especially the somewhat older Alito or Thomas, would retire from the Court during a Democratic presidential administration is unclear, but we should not expect that to happen.

If the party that wins the 2020 presidential election is different from the party that controls the Senate, we will almost certainly witness at least a continuation, if not escalation, of partisan acrimony over judicial selection. Given the precedent set by the Senate's refusal to even consider President Obama's nomination of Merrick Garland, if we face divided government, there is a real question as to whether the Senate will block all Supreme Court appointments made by a president from the opposing party.

There is also a question, as discussed in chapter 6, about whether the composition of the Court will change by way of court-packing efforts. Such a change does not require a constitutional amendment, but would require an act of Congress supported by the president or passed by enough votes to overcome a presidential veto. The prospect of court packing has garnered enough momentum from liberals that the *Washington Post* surveyed candidates for the Democratic presidential primary to gauge their support for it. Ten of the twenty-six candidates reported their openness to the proposal and one favors the idea. And of the eleven candidates who remained in the race prior to the Iowa primary, four expressed openness to the idea and one indicated support for it ("Supreme Court Packing" 2020). Still, though court-packing proposals are not unprecedented, changing the number of justices would be quite a dramatic move, and most prognosticators think it is rather improbable.

The safe bet, then, is that the current conservative shift on the Court (and the federal judiciary) will remain in place for some time, even if Democrats win control of the executive and Senate in 2020. If Republicans retain control, we will likely see the Court move even further to the right, in a shift that could last for at least a generation.

FUTURE DECISION MAKING

As past appointments demonstrate, justices do not always rule in ways that one might predict in advance. Earl Warren and William Brennan were both appointed by Republican President Dwight D. Eisenhower but pushed the Court in a decidedly liberal direction. And it would have been quite hard to imagine in 1987 when Republican President Ronald Reagan nominated Anthony Kennedy to the bench that the justice would become a pivotal voice to retain a constitutional right to abortion and support a constitutional right to same-sex marriage.

On the other hand, when Reagan nominated Robert Bork in 1987, it was relatively easy to predict his views on abortion, same-sex marriage, and a host of other issues because he had been quite clear about his positions. Similarly, when Democrat Bill Clinton selected Ruth Bader Ginsburg, her general views about the constitutional protection for gender equality were transparent. In some instances, then, particular positions of would-be justices can be discerned. Moreover, even where specific positions are not evident, jurisprudential approaches often are. So, while predictions on particular cases or particular subject matters might be challenging, there are plenty of jurists about whom much is known, and predictions about general tendencies and directions have a greater chance of being correct.

So, what might happen if the conservative consolidation on the Court persists or grows? There are key issue areas about which some educated guesses can be made. Three such issues—abortion rights, gun rights, and LGBTQ rights— will be briefly sampled here to preview the kinds of changes that may well be on the horizon.

Abortion Rights

It would be reasonable to expect the Court to allow additional and more significant curtailing of the right to abortion, a pattern that has been ongoing since President Reagan's administration. Just how far the Court will allow this curtailing to go is more difficult to predict. It is certainly possible that the Court will continue to take an incremental approach, chipping away at abortion rights by permitting states to increasingly regulate the procedure on the grounds that the restrictions do not unduly burden women. The Court might also make it harder to bring lawsuits challenging abortion regulations by modifying prior precedents about whether physicians have standing to sue in such cases. Such approaches, while not altogether overturning *Roe v. Wade* (1973), would widen state's authority to limit access to abortion.

Alternatively, and quite arguably more likely, is that the Court will directly overturn *Roe*. On June 27, 2018, Jeffrey Toobin, legal analyst for CNN and *The New Yorker*, tweeted, "Anthony Kennedy is retiring. Abortion will be illegal in twenty states in 18 months." Toobin's prediction has already been proven wrong, but perhaps only in its timeline. Eighteen months is lightspeed in Supreme Court time! And the Supreme Court is hearing an abortion case this term (*June Medical Services LLC v. Russo* 2020) in which some briefs have been submitted asking for a reversal of *Roe*. Many earlier cases have requested reversal without success, and the Court might not use this case as the avenue to upend the precedent, in part because this is an election year and the justices have an avenue to uphold the abortion restriction without directly considering or overturning *Roe*. Still, even if the Court does not take this opportunity to reject *Roe*, it will certainly be offered others as opponents of abortion are rapidly laying the groundwork to bring cases that, if granted cert, would require the Court to take the *Roe* decision head on. Reversal of *Roe* would likely mean that states would have near free reign to regulate and even ban abortion, which would lead to a wide mix of laws across states, with many outlawing abortions except where the mother's life is in jeopardy, and many others protecting a women's right to abortion.

Gun Rights

The Court's 2008 decision in *District of Columbia v. Heller* (2008) held that the Second Amendment of the Constitution protects an individual right to bear arms and thereby limits the federal government's ability to impose gun control. Two years later in *McDonald v. The City of Chicago* (2010), the Court extended that holding by finding that states must respect Second Amendment rights as well. But neither case delineated just how far those rights go or to what extent government—federal, state, or local—may regulate them. And, as discussed in chapter 3, *Heller* included language indicating that some restrictions on firearms might well be permissible. In the aftermath of *Heller* and *McDonald*, lower courts have seized upon that language to sustain numerous gun control policies.

The Supreme Court will without doubt have multiple occasions in the coming terms to further contemplate gun control laws. This term, the Court is considering one such case involving a restrictive New York law, though the Court may not reach a decision on the merits of the case because New York changed the law after the Supreme Court agreed to hear the complaint, possibly rendering the case moot. Still, the fact the Supreme Court took the case in the first place shows its interest in reviewing and clarifying gun rights.

As discussed in chapter 3, Justice Kennedy was not only the swing vote in *Heller*, but also reportedly responsible for its qualifying language about the permissibility of some gun control. Without Kennedy on the Court, there may be less inclination among the five conservative justices to qualify gun rights. Indeed, when Justice Kavanaugh, Kennedy's replacement, served on the Court of Appeals for the D.C. Circuit, he dissented in a case that upheld D.C.'s assault weapons ban (*Heller v. District of Columbia* 2011). According to legal scholar Adam Winkler, Kavanaugh's views on gun rights are "extreme and well-articulated," and "[g]iven what we know about the other justices, it seems clear that Kavanaugh's confirmation has reinvigorated the justices' appetite on the Second Amendment question" (quoted in Moon 2019).

Perhaps the magnitude of gun violence, the rise in casualties resulting from mass shootings, and polls demonstrating increasing public support for gun control will lead the Court to a less vociferous defense of the Second Amendment. Perhaps not. In any event, it is quite improbable that the Court would, in the near term, backtrack from its holdings in *Heller* and *McDonald*. Far more likely, though not certain, is that the current composition of the Court would favor increased protection for gun owners and resist strong gun control efforts.

LGBTQ Rights

Will the Court backtrack from its 2015 holding on marriage equality and gay rights? Justice Kennedy's 5–4 majority opinion in *Obergefell v. Hodges*—the landmark ruling finding that the Fourteenth Amendment prohibits states from denying marriage licenses to same-sex couples—cast marriage as a fundamental liberty and spoke of gay couples' interest in marrying as a quest for "equal dignity in the eyes of the law" (*Obergefell v. Hodges* 2015, 2608). But as sweeping and historic as *Obergefell* was, it did not, of course, settle every conflict around marriage rights, nor did it address entrenched discrimination against the LGBTQ community in multiple other realms, including employment and military service. Additionally, Chief Justice Roberts and Justices Scalia, Thomas, and Alito disagreed with the *Obergefell* holding, and each authored a dissenting opinion.

Even with Gorsuch and Kavanaugh replacing Scalia and Kennedy, a direct reversal of *Obergefell*, though not out of the question, seems unlikely in the near term. More likely is that there will be considerable resistance to extending equality rights to the LGBTQ community, and that we will see the type of undermining and chipping away similar to what has transpired in the area of abortion rights.

Tests of the reach of *Obergefell* and the Supreme Court's willingness to enforce it are ongoing. For example, are states required to list the names of married same-sex parents on their child's birth certificate? The state of Arkansas said no and the Arkansas Supreme Court agreed. In 2017 and with Kennedy still on the bench, the U.S. Supreme Court reversed that ruling in *Pavan v. Smith* (2017), holding that under *Obergefell* states must respect same-sex marriage rights and the benefits that attach to marriage. But perhaps in a sign of what might come, Gorsuch, Alito, and Thomas dissented.

Other cases asserting rights to treat same-sex couples differently from opposite-sex couples may garner more support from the current conservative bloc on the Court. Consider *Masterpiece Cakeshop v. Colorado Civil Rights Commission*, a 2018 case that pitted the owner of a bakery against a gay couple. After the owner of the bakery refused on free speech and religious freedom grounds to make a wedding cake for the soon-to-be-married couple, Colorado concluded that the owner violated the state's antidiscrimination policies. The U.S. Supreme Court granted cert in the case, but skirted a direct ruling on whether rights to free speech and free exercise of religion protected by the First and Fourteenth Amendments allow individuals to refuse service to gay couples. The Court did so in a very narrow ruling, finding in favor of the bakery owner that the Colorado Civil Rights Commission had failed to exercise religious neutrality in handling the case and showed hostility toward religion. Because the Court did not consider how to adjudicate conflicts between one individual's assertion of First Amendment rights and another's assertion of marriage equality rights, that battle lingers.

Masterpiece Cakeshop represents a type of case on the rise, pressed by opponents of gay marriage and LGBTQ rights. Whether it is Arlene's Flowers in Washington state, Aloha Bed & Breakfast in Hawaii, or Elane Photography in New Mexico, proprietors are claiming religious rights, free expression, and freedom of conscience to carve out exceptions to equal treatment of members of the LGBTQ community. Some lower courts are rejecting these claims for exceptions, as the Washington State Supreme

Court did when holding that the state's anti-discrimination laws require equal treatment in public accommodations and ruling that this "is no more about access to flowers than civil rights cases in the 1960s were about access to sandwiches" (Holson 2019). Whether the U.S. Supreme Court will reject these claims is another matter, but it would hardly be surprising to see the currently composed Court grant such First Amendment exceptions and thereby allow discrimination on the basis of LGBTQ status.

Beyond marriage rights and the related exercise of those rights, discrimination against members of the LGBTQ community continues to be legal in employment, except where states or cities have legislated otherwise. Rulings in two important cases being considered by the Court this term will likely impact whether discrimination against gays, lesbians, bisexuals, and transgender employees will remain legal. Both cases involve Title VII of the Civil Rights Act of 1964, discussed in chapter 5, and the prohibition against "sex" discrimination in the workplace. One of the cases was brought by two people who claim they were fired for being gay, and the other brought a claim of wrongful dismissal because of transgender status. The Court heard oral arguments on these claims in October 2019, and while rulings are not expected until later this term, the arguments offered some clues on how the justices might vote. In particular, questions posed by Gorsuch telegraphed that he may be on the fence: "[H]e repeatedly suggested that the words of Title VII may well bar employment discrimination based on sexual orientation and transgender status. The question was, he said, "really close, really close." But he added that he was worried about "the massive social upheaval" that would follow from a Supreme Court ruling saying so. Such a significant change, he mused, might be more appropriate coming from Congress rather than the courts" (Liptak and Peters 2019).

Another key dispute making its way through the federal courts concerns whether the executive branch may bar transgender people from serving in the military. Starting in 2016, under President Barack Obama, transgender members of the military were permitted to serve openly. President Donald Trump changed this policy by prohibiting, with some exceptions, most transgender service members (exceptions include, for example, some who are already serving and those willing to serve "in their biological sex"). Challenges to the Trump administration prohibition are making their way through the lower federal courts, and the Supreme Court has yet to directly consider whether the policy violates due process guarantees. But the Court did permit the restrictions to take effect while the lower courts are considering the matter. Doing so by a 5–4 vote, the Court removed two lower court injunctions that had previously stopped the restrictions from taking effect (Liptak 2019). Given both the composition of the Court and its general inclination to defer the executive branch on matters governing the military, it is likely that the discriminatory policy will be affirmed.

JUDICIAL PARTISANSHIP, POLITICIZATION, AND LEGITIMACY

We have seen in previous chapters that criticism of the Court is not new, and questions about the institution's legitimacy have emerged in previous eras. We have seen as well that the Court is shaped by a political and sometimes polarized selection process and that many justices, by their own accounts, pay attention to public opinion. But we have also seen that the current era is a period of intensifying politicization and polarization, marked by declining confidence in the Court and changing public approval linked to respondents' party identification. What does the future hold with respect to politicization of the bench and perceptions of the Court's legitimacy?

There may well be something new afoot. Political scientist Lee Epstein and law professor Eric Posner argue that the Court has entered a new era of partisan division characterized by a trend they describe as "extreme" and "alarming" (Epstein and Posner 2018). What is new and of concern is not that the Court is *ideological*, but rather that Court is *partisan*.

The difference between ideology and partisanship on the Court is of concern because it may matter to perceptions about the Court's politicization and legitimacy. It is one thing for the Court to be perceived as ideological and another for it to be viewed as partisan. An ideological Court with ideological justices might still be viewed as acting in accordance with principle. There might certainly be ideological divides on the Court—even very deep ones—and, in turn, justices acting according to divergent principles (e.g., originalism v. living constitutionalism). But it is possible to act both ideologically and in line with the principles of that ideology. By contrast, when justices are perceived as acting as partisans, they are taken to be voting not on principle but in order to advance the goals of a particular political party. It is that perception that may contribute to decreasing confidence in the Court and may raise the specter of a legitimacy crisis.

The empirical evidence that Epstein and Posner cite to support their argument that this is an unprecedented era of partisan division on the Court is this:

> In the 1950s and 1960s, the ideological biases of Republican appointees and Democratic appointees were relatively modest. The gap between them has steadily grown, but even as late as the early 1990s, it was possible for justices to vote in ideologically unpredictable ways. In the closely divided cases in the 1991 term, for example, the single Democratic appointee on the court, Byron White, voted more conservatively than all but two of the Republican appointees, Antonin Scalia and William Rehnquist. This was a time when many Republican appointees—like Sandra Day O'Connor, Harry Blackmun, John Paul Stevens and David Souter—frequently cast liberal votes.

In the past 10 years, however, justices have hardly ever voted against the ideology of the president who appointed them. Only Justice Kennedy, named to the court by Ronald Reagan, did so with any regularity. That is why with his replacement on the court an ideologically committed Republican justice, it will become impossible to regard the court as anything but a partisan institution. (Epstein and Posner 2018)

Epstein and Posner go on to explain that even in prior historical eras of strong ideological division on the Court, those divisions were not partisan. The Warren Court was liberal, for sure, but as Epstein and Posner argue not partisan, led by a chief justice and another liberal justice appointed by a Republican president. Similarly, the Lochner Era Court that rejected various components of New Deal legislation was conservative, but again, as Epstein and Posner argue, not partisan. Among the justices who opposed New Deal legislation was one appointed by a Democratic president and another who was, himself, a Democrat. On the flip side, two of the justices who supported New Deal legislation were Republican appointees. By contrast, Epstein and Posner note that given recent appointments and the way current justices vote in general partisan alignment and partisan division, if the pattern continues, "For the first time in living memory, the court will be seen by the public as a party-dominated institution, one whose votes on controversial issues are essentially determined by the party affiliation of recent presidents" (Epstein and Posner 2018).

Others are echoing Epstein and Posner's warnings of partisan divide and partisan capture. For example, law professor Kate Shaw remarked in a panel discussion in 2019 that while there have always been questions about the intermingling of politics and the Court,

> there is something different about the moment that we're in today. And that is that for the first time really in history, you have this perfect alignment in most high profile and high salience cases . . . of the policy preferences of the appointing president and the likely votes of the justices appointed by that president. So you have five Republican appointees who are likely to vote in favor of the Trump administration's policy initiatives and four Democratic appointees who are likely going to vote against it. And when that happens and when the public believes it's going to happen, you do have this potential erosion of the legitimacy of the Court. (Shaw 2019)

In addition, the demise of the filibuster for confirming judicial nominees is likely to have the effect of further reducing compromise and, in turn, selecting candidates with more extreme views. If it takes only a majority of the Senate to confirm a nomination to the Supreme Court, then the president faces less pressure to nominate someone who will appeal to at least some senators from the opposing party. Moreover, not having to worry about appealing to the opposition party, a president is freed up to select nominees who might mobilize the party base, which has the added effect of appointing and confirming nominees who appeal to the more extreme ends of the political and partisan spectrum.

CONCLUSION

It is certainly the case that there have been many moments in U.S. history when the future of the Supreme Court—and the country—have been especially uncertain. During the Founding era and the Civil War, the future of the Court and the country were precarious, indeed. Following the *Dred Scott* decision (1857), the Court's legitimacy was under assault. The Lochner Era and its culmination in FDR's court-packing threat marked a moment of intense scrutiny and questioning of the federal judiciary. *Brown v. Board of Education* (1954) led to a remarkable and fierce backlash against the Court. The Court weathered those moments and has, more often than not, been a generally steady and stable pillar of the federal government.

But this is presently a moment of high political polarization in American politics, manifest in multiple institutions: divided government, attacks on the media, and a sharply and closely divided electorate, not to mention an impeached president. The robes worn by justices that symbolize, among other things, judicial independence are not magical. They do not offer superhero protections against politicization and partisanship. And the insulation afforded by life tenure does not immunize the Supreme Court from heightened polarization, at the very least because that polarization implicates the selection of those who serve and do not serve on the bench.

The past suggests and observers routinely note that there is a deep reservoir of support for the Supreme Court (see Barnes 2019b). Studies suggest, as well, a faith in the rule of law and judicial institutions that typically outstrips confidence in elected officials and the other branches of federal government. But there are many signs that this moment is uniquely precarious and that past precedent may not predict what is to come.

NOTE

1. For information on Martin-Quinn scores, see http://mqscores.lsa.umich .edu.

Bibliography

ABA. 2020a. "About the Committee." ABA Standing Committee on the Federal Judiciary. https://www.americanbar.org/groups/committees /federal_judiciary/

ABA. 2020b. "Evaluations of Nominees to the Supreme Court of the United States." ABA Standing Committee on the Federal Judiciary. https:// www.americanbar.org/content/dam/aba/uncategorized/GAO /fjcscotusprocess.pdf

Abraham, Henry J. 1992. *Justices and Presidents: A Political History of Appointments to the Supreme Court.* 3rd Edition. New York: Oxford University Press.

Abumrad, Jad, and Suzie Lechtenberg. 2016. "The Political Thicket." *Radiolab Presents: More Perfect.* Podcast, episode June 10, 2016. https:// www.wnycstudios.org/podcasts/radiolab/articles/the_political _thicket

Adler, Jonathan H. 2017. "How Scalia-esque Will Donald Trump's Supreme Court Nominee Be?" *Washington Post*, January 26, 2017.

Administrative Office of the Court. 2018. "Table A-1—Supreme Court of the United States—Cases on Docket, Disposed of, and Remaining on Docket at Conclusion of October Terms, 2012 Through 2017." https://www.uscourts.gov/statistics-reports/caseload-statistics -data-tables?tn=&pn=All&t=547&m%5Bvalue%5D%5Bmonth%5D =&y%5Bvalue%5D%5Byear%5D=

Allen, Mahalley D., and Donald P. Haider-Markel. 2006. "Connecting Supreme Court Decisions, Media Coverage, and Public Opinion: The Case of *Lawrence v. Texas.*" *American Review of Politics*, 27: 209–230.

Aucoin, Brent. 1996. "The Southern Manifesto and Southern Opposition to Desegregation." *Arkansas Historical Quarterly*, 55, no. 2 (Summer): 173–193.

Balkin, Jack M. 2011. *Living Originalism.* Cambridge, MA: The Belknap Press of Harvard University Press.

Barnes, Robert. 2016. "For First Time in 10 Years, Justice Clarence Thomas Asks Questions during an Argument." *Washington Post*, February 29, 2016.

Barnes, Robert. 2019a. "Justice Kennedy Asked Trump to Put Kavanaugh on Supreme Court List, Book Says." *Washington Post*, November 21, 2019.

Barnes, Robert. 2019b. "Polls Show Trust in Supreme Court, But There Is Growing Interest in Fixed Terms and Other Changes." *Washington Post*, October 24, 2019.

Barzun, Charles L. 2018. "Three Forms of Legal Pragmatism." *Washington University Law Review*, 95, no. 5: 1003–1034.

Baum, Lawrence. 2004. *The Supreme Court.* 8th Edition. Washington, D.C.: CQ Press.

Baum, Lawrence, and Neal Devins. 2010. "Why the Supreme Court Cares about Elites, Not the American People." *Georgetown Law Journal*, 98: 1515–1581.

Bell, Derrick. 1985. "The Supreme Court, 1984 Term-Foreword: The Civil Rights Chronicles." *Harvard Law Review*, 99, no. 1: 4–83.

Berke, Richard L. 1991. "Thomas Accuser Tells Hearing of Obscene Talk; Judge Complains of 'Lynching.'" *New York Times*, October 12, 1991.

Bialik, Kristen. 2017. "What Backgrounds Do U.S. Supreme Court Justices Have?" Pew Research Center, March 20, 2017. https://www.pewresearch.org/fact-tank/2017/03/20/what-backgrounds-do-u-s-supreme-court-justices-have/

Bickel, Alexander M. 1961. "Foreword: The Passive Virtues." *Harvard Law Review*, 75: 40–79.

Bickel, Alexander M. 1962. *The Least Dangerous Branch: The Supreme Court at the Bar of Politics.* Indianapolis, IN: Bobbs-Merrill.

Biskupic, Joan, Janet Roberts, and John Shiffman. 2014. "The Echo Chamber." *Reuters*, December 8, 2014.

Blake, Aaron. 2016. "The Final Trump-Clinton Debate Transcript, Annotated." *Washington Post*, October 19, 2016.

Bobbitt, Philip. 1984. *Constitutional Fate: Theory of the Constitution.* New York: Oxford University Press.

Bork, Robert. 1985. "The Great Debate." Speech Presented at the University of San Diego Law School on November 18, 1985. https://fedsoc.org/commentary/publications/the-great-debate-judge-robert-h-bork-november-18-1985

Brennan, William. (1985) 2003. "The Constitution of the United States: Contemporary Ratification." In *Judges on Judging: Views from the Bench.* 2nd Edition, edited by David O'Brien. Washington, D.C.: CQ Press.

Broder, John M. 2009. "Edward M. Kennedy, Senate Stalwart, Is Dead at 77." *New York Times*, August 26, 2009.

Burack, Emily. 2019. "Ruth Bader Ginsburg on Why She Did Not Retire during Obama's term." *Jewish Telegraph Agency*, September 19, 2019. https://www.jta.org/2019/09/19/united-states/ruth-bader-ginsburg -on-why-she-didnt-retire-during-obamas-term

Business Wire. 2006. "New National Poll Finds: More Americans Know Snow White's Dwarfs Than Supreme Court Judges, Homer Simpson Than Homer's Odyssey, and Harry Potter Than Tony Blair." *Business Wire*, August 14, 2006.

Calabresi, Steven G., and James Lindgren. 2006. "Term Limits for the Supreme Court: Life Tenure Reconsidered." *Harvard Journal of Law and Public Policy*, 29, no. 3: 769–878.

Caldeira, Gregory A., and John R. Wright. 1988. "Organized Interests and Agenda Setting in the U.S. Supreme Court." *American Political Science Review*, 82, no. 4: 1109–1127.

Canon, Bradley C. 1998. "The Supreme Court and Policy Reform: The Hollow Hope Revisited." In *Leveraging the Law: Using the Courts to Achieve Social Change*, edited by David A. Schultz. New York: Peter Lang.

Canon, Bradley C., and Charles A. Johnson. 1999. *Judicial Policies: Implementation and Impact*. 2nd Edition. Washington, D.C.: CQ Press.

Canon, Bradley C., and Kenneth Kolson. 1971. "Rural Compliance with Gault: Kentucky, A Case Study." *Journal of Family Law*, 10, no. 2: 300–326.

Caplan, Lincoln. 1987. *The Tenth Justice: The Solicitor General and the Rule of Law*. New York: Vintage Books.

Cardozo, Benjamin N. 1921. *The Nature of the Judicial Process*. New Haven, CT: Yale University Press.

Carp, Robert A., and Ronald A. Stidham. 1996. *Judicial Process in America*. 3rd Edition. Washington, D.C.: CQ Press.

Casillas, Christopher J., Peter K. Enns, and Patrick C. Wohlfarth. 2011. "How Public Opinion Constrains the U.S. Supreme Court." *American Journal of Political Science*, 55, no. 1: 74–88.

Chafetz, Josh. 2017. "Unprecedented? Judicial Confirmation Battles and the Search for a Usable Past." *Harvard Law Review*, 131: 96–132.

Chemerinsky, Erwin. 2012. "Online Alexander Bickel symposium: It's Alexander Bickel's fault." Blog. *SCOTUSblog*, 2012. https://www .scotusblog.com/2012/08/online-alexander-bickel-symposium-its -alexander-bickels-fault/

Chief Justice's Year-End Reports on the Federal Judiciary. https://www .supremecourt.gov/publicinfo/year-end/year-endreports.aspx

Clayton, Cornell, and Howard Gillman. 1999. "Introduction: Beyond Judicial Decision Making." In *The Supreme Court in American Politics: New Institutionalist Interpretations*, edited by Howard Gillman and Cornell Clayton. Lawrence: University Press of Kansas.

Cohen, Andrew. 2012. "The Sad Legacy of Bork." *The Atlantic*, December 19, 2012.

Collins, Paul M., Jr., and Lori A. Ringhand. 2013. *Supreme Court Confirmation Hearings and Constitutional Change*. New York: Cambridge University Press.

Collins, Paul M., Jr., and Lori A. Ringhand. 2016a. "The Institutionalization of Supreme Court Confirmation Hearings." *Law & Social Inquiry*, 41: 126–151.

Collins, Paul M., Jr., and Lori A. Ringhand. 2016b. "The Top Five Supreme Court Nomination Myths." *Slate*. March 24, 2016. https://slate.com/news-and-politics/2016/03/the-top-five-supreme-court-nomination-myths.html

Courts Statistics Project. "Total Incoming Cases in State Courts, 2007–2016." http://www.courtstatistics.org/NCSC-Analysis/~/media//7F3DA5FEF1BF4BE1BE2BDE6BA0E86C60.ashx

Cushman, Clare, ed. 2013. *The Supreme Court Justices: Illustrated Biographies, 1789–1995*. 3rd Edition. Washington, D.C.: CQ Press.

Dahl, Robert A. 1957. "Decision-Making in a Democracy: The Supreme Court as a National Policymaker." *Journal of Public Law*, 6: 279–295.

Declaration of Constitutional Principles. 1956. *Congressional Record, 84th Congress Second Session*. Vol. 102, part 4, March 12, 1956, 4459–4460. Washington, D.C.: Governmental Printing Office.

Denison, Alexander, Justin Wedeking, and Michael A. Zilis. 2020. "Negative Media Coverage of the Supreme Court: The Interactive Role of Opinion Language, Coalition Size, and Ideological Signals." *Social Science Quarterly*, 101, no. 1: 121–143.

Devins, Neal, and Laurence Baum. 2017. "Split Definitive: How Party Polarization Turned the Supreme Court into a Partisan Court." *Supreme Court Review*, 2016, no. 1: 301–365.

Dolbeare, Kenneth M., and Phillip E. Hammond. 1971. *The School Prayer Decisions: From Court Policy to Local Practice*. Chicago, IL: University of Chicago Press.

Dost, Meredith. 2015. "Dim Public Awareness of Supreme Court as Major Rulings Loom." Pew Research Center, May 14, 2015. https://www.pewresearch.org/fact-tank/2015/05/14/dim-public-awareness-of-supreme-court-as-major-rulings-loom/

Dworkin, Ronald. 1996. *Freedom's Law: The Moral Reading of the American Constitution*. Cambridge, MA: Harvard University Press.

EEOC. "Notice Concerning the Lilly Ledbetter Fair Pay Act of 2009."
    https://www.eeoc.gov/laws/statutes/epa_ledbetter.cfm

Eig, Larry M. 2014. *Statutory Interpretation: General Principles and Recent
    Trends* (CRS Report No. 97-589). Congressional Research Service.
    https://fas.org/sgp/crs/misc/97-589.pdf

Elving, Ron. 2018. "What Happened with Merrick Garland in 2016 and
    Why It Matters Now." National Public Radio, June 29, 2018. https://
    www.npr.org/2018/06/29/624467256/what-happened-with-merrick
    -garland-in-2016-and-why-it-matters-now

Epstein, Lee, and Jack Knight. 1998. *The Choices Justices Make.* Washing-
    ton, D.C.: CQ Press.

Epstein, Lee, and Andrew D. Martin. 2010. "Does Public Opinion Influ-
    ence the Supreme Court? Possibly Yes (But We're Not Sure Why)."
    University of Pennsylvania Journal of Constitutional Law, 13, no. 2:
    263–282.

Epstein, Lee, Andrew D. Martin, and Kevin Quinn. 2018. "Replacing Jus-
    tice Kennedy." http://epstein.wustl.edu/research/ReplacingJustice
    Kennedy.pdf

Epstein, Lee, and Eric A. Posner. 2016. "Supreme Court Justices' Loyalty to
    the President." *Journal of Legal Studies,* 45: 401–436.

Epstein, Lee, and Eric Posner. 2018. "If the Supreme Court Is Nakedly
    Political, Can It Be Just?" *New York Times,* July 9, 2018.

Epstein, Lee, and Jeffrey A. Segal. 2005. *Advice and Consent: The Politics of
    Judicial Appointments.* New York: Oxford University Press.

Epstein, Lee, and Thomas G. Walker. 2018. *Constitutional Law for a
    Changing America. Rights, Liberties, and Justice.* 10th Edition.
    Washington, D.C.: CQ Press.

Epstein, Lee, Thomas G. Walker, Nancy Staudt, Scott Hendrickson, and
    Jason Roberts. 2019. "The U.S. Supreme Court Justices Database."
    http://epstein.wustl.edu/research/justicesdata.html.

Federal Judicial Center. "Jurisdiction: Original, Supreme Court." https://
    www.fjc.gov/history/courts/jurisdiction-original-supreme-court

Federalist Society. "Our Background." https://fedsoc.org/our-background

Feldman, Adam. 2016. "Successful Cert Amici 2014." Blog. *Empirical SCO-
    TUS,* March 15, 2016. https://empiricalscotus.com/2016/03/15
    /certamici-2014/

Feldman, Adam. 2019. "Justice Stevens, the Longest-Living Supreme Court
    Justices, and Other Age Milestones." Blog. *SCOTUSblog,* July 17,
    2019. https://www.scotusblog.com/2019/07/empirical-scotus-justice
    -stevens-the-longest-living-supreme-court-justices-and
    -other-age-milestones/

Flegenheimer, Matt. 2017. "Senate Republicans Deploy 'Nuclear Option' to
    Clear Path for Gorsuch." *New York Times,* April 6, 2017.

Fleming, James E. 2016. "Fidelity to Our Imperfect Constitution: A Response to Six Views." *Constitutional Commentary*, 31: 489–501.

Franklin, Charles H. 2019. "Public Views of the Supreme Court." Marquette Law School Poll: Complete Report. https://law.marquette.edu/poll/wp-content/uploads/2019/10/MULawPollSupremeCourt ReportOct2019.pdf

Gallup. 2019a. "Congress and the Public: Historical Trends." October 2019. https://news.gallup.com/poll/1600/congress-public.aspx

Gallup. 2019b. "The Presidency: Historical Trends." October 2019. https://news.gallup.com/poll/4729/presidency.aspx

Gallup. 2019c. "Supreme Court: Historical Trends." October 2019. https://news.gallup.com/poll/4732/supreme-court.aspx

Gates, Robbins L. 2011. *The Making of Massive Resistance: Virginia's Politics of Public School Desegregation, 1954–1956.* Chapel Hill: University of North Carolina Press.

Gibson, James L., and Gregory A. Caldeira. 2009. "Knowing the Supreme Court? A Reconsideration of Public Ignorance of the High Court." *Journal of Politics*, 71, no. 2: 429–441.

Gillman, Howard, and Cornell W. Clayton. 1999. "Beyond Judicial Attitudes: Institutional Approaches to Supreme Court Decision Making." In *Supreme Court Decision-Making: New Institutionalist Approaches*, edited by Cornell W. Clayton and Howard Gillman. Chicago, IL: University of Chicago Press.

Gillman, Howard, Mark Graber, and Keith Whittington. 2013. *American Constitutionalism: Volume II: Rights & Liberties.* 1st Edition. New York: Oxford University Press.

Ginsburg, Ruth Bader. 2003. "Workways of the Supreme Court." *Thomas Jefferson Law Review*, 25, no. 3 (Summer): 517–528.

Golde, Kalvis. 2019. "Recent Polls Show Confidence in Supreme Court, With Caveats." Blog. *SCOTUSBlog*, October 22, 2019. https://www.scotusblog.com/2019/10/recent-polls-show-confidence-in-supreme-court-with-caveats/

Graham, David A. 2018. "Kavanaugh Goes Nuclear: The Supreme Court Nominee Furiously Attacked Democrats and the Senate Confirmation Process in His Opening Statement Thursday." *The Atlantic*, September 27, 2018.

Graves, Allison. 2017. "Did Senate Republicans Filibuster Obama Court Nominees More Than All Others Combined?" *PolitiFact*, April 9, 2017. https://www.politifact.com/truth-o-meter/statements/2017/apr/09/ben-cardin/did-senate-republicans-filibuster-obama-court-nomi/

Greenhouse, Linda. 2007. "Justices Limit Discrimination Suits over Pay." *New York Times*, May 29, 2007.

Greenhouse, Linda. 2012. *U.S. Supreme Court: A Very Short Introduction.* New York: Oxford University Press.

Hamilton, Alexander. 2009. "The Federalist No. 78." In *The Federalist Papers*, edited by Ian Shapiro, 391–397. New Haven, CT: Yale University Press.

Handler, Joel F. 1978. *Social Movements and the Legal System.* New York: Academic Press.

Hawkings, David. 2018. "GOP Slips Past Another Senate Custom, and Democrats Turn Blue." *Roll Call*, May 30, 2018.

Hitt, Matthew P., and Kathleen Searles. 2018. "Media Coverage and Public Approval of the U.S. Supreme Court." *Political Communication*, 35, no. 4: 566–586.

Hoekstra, Valerie J. 2000. "The Supreme Court and Local Public Opinion." *American Political Science Review*, 94, no. 1: 89–100.

Hoekstra, Valerie J. 2003. *Public Reaction to Supreme Court Decisions.* New York: Cambridge University Press.

Hogue, Henry B. 2010. *Supreme Court Nominations Not Confirmed, 1789–2009* (CRS Report No. RL31171). Congressional Research Service. https://fas.org/sgp/crs/misc/RL31171.pdf

Holson, Laura M. 2019. "How Battles Over Serving Same-Sex Couples Play Out in Court." *New York Times*, June 17, 2019.

Homans, Charles. 2020. "Mitch McConnell Got Everything He Wanted, But at What Cost?" *New York Times Magazine*, January 22, 2020.

Jacobs, Julia. 2018. "Anita Hill's Testimony and Other Key Moments from the Clarence Thomas Hearings." *New York Times*, September 20, 2018.

Jacobson, Louis. 2013. "Harry Reid Says 82 Presidential Nominees Have Been Blocked under President Barack Obama, 86 Blocked under All Other Presidents." *PolitiFact*, November 22, 2013. https://www.politifact.com/truth-o-meter/statements/2013/nov/22/harry-reid/harry-reid-says-82-presidential-nominees-have-been/

Jefferson, Thomas. 1823. "From Thomas Jefferson to William Johnson, 12 June 1823." National Archives, Founders Online. https://founders.archives.gov/documents/Jefferson/98-01-02-3562

Kahn, Ronald. 1999. "Institutional Norms and Supreme Court Decision-Making: The Rehnquist Court on Privacy and Religion." In *Supreme Court Decision-Making: New Institutionalist Approaches*, edited by Cornell W. Clayton and Howard Gillman. Chicago, IL: University of Chicago Press.

Kay, Stanley. 2018. "The Highest Court in the Land." *Sports Illustrated*, July 25, 2018. https://www.si.com/nba/2018/07/25/supreme-court-building-basketball-court

Kersch, Ken I. 2016. "Originalism's Curiously Triumphant Death: The Interpenetration of Aspirationalism and Historicism in U.S.

Constitutional Development." *Constitutional Commentary*, 31: 423–439.

Khullar, Dhruv, and Anupam B. Jena. 2018. "How Modern Medicine Has Changed the Supreme Court." *New York Times*, August 31, 2018.

Klarman, Michael J. 2007. *Brown v. Board of Education and the Civil Rights Movement: The Supreme Court and the Struggle for Racial Equality*. Abridged Edition. New York: Oxford University Press.

Kritzer, Herbert M. 2001. "The Impact of *Bush v. Gore* on Public Perceptions and Knowledge of Supreme Court." *Judicature*, 85, no. 1: 32–38.

Kurland, Philip B., and Dennis J. Hutchinson. 1983. "The Business of the Supreme Court, O.T. 1982." *University of Chicago Law Review*, 50: 628–651.

Lewis, Neil A. 1993. "2 Years After His Bruising Hearing, Justice Thomas Can Rarely Be Heard." *New York Times*, November 27, 1993.

Lilly Ledbetter Fair Pay Act of 2009 (Public Law No: 111-2, S. 181).

Liptak, Adam. 2019. "Supreme Court Revives Transgender Ban for Military Service." *New York Times*, January 22, 2019.

Liptak, Adam, and Jeremy W. Peters. 2019. "Supreme Court Considers Whether Civil Rights Act Protects L.G.B.T. Workers." *New York Times*, October 8, 2019.

Lithwick, Dahlia. 2017. "Unsolicited Advice for the White House Press Corps: Film the Press Briefings, Ignore the Spin, and Revel in Your Nerdom." *Slate*, June 30, 2017. https://slate.com/news-and-politics/2017/06/advice-for-white-house-reporters-from-the-supreme-court-press-corps.html

Maltzman, Forrest, James F. Spriggs II, and Paul J. Wahlbeck. 2000. *Crafting Law on the Supreme Court: The Collegial Game*. New York: Cambridge University Press.

Marcus, Ruth. 2019. *Supreme Ambition: Brett Kavanaugh and the Conservative Takeover*. New York: Simon & Schuster.

Marshall, Thurgood. 1951. "The Supreme Court as Protector of Civil Rights: Equal Protection of the Laws." *The Annals of the American Academy of Political and Social Science*, 275: 101–110.

Marshall, Thurgood. 1992. "Liberty Medal Acceptance Speech." https://constitutioncenter.org/liberty-medal/recipients/thurgood-marshall

McCann, Michael W. 1992. "Reform Litigation on Trial." *Law & Social Inquiry*, 17, no. 4: 715–743.

McCann, Michael W. 1994. *Rights at Work: Pay Equity Reform and the Politics of Legal Mobilization*. Chicago, IL: University of Chicago Press.

McCarthy, Justin. 2018. "Women's Approval of SCOTUS Matches 13-Year Low Point." *Gallup*, September 28, 2018.

McMillion, Barry J. 2018. *Supreme Court Appointment Process: President's Selection of a Nominee* (CRS Report No. R44235). Congressional Research Service. https://fas.org/sgp/crs/misc/R44235.pdf

McMillion, Barry J., and Denis Steven Rutkus. 2018. *Supreme Court Nominations, 1789 to 2017: Actions by the Senate, the Judiciary Committee, and the President* (CRS Report No. RL33225). Congressional Research Service. https://fas.org/sgp/crs/misc/RL33225.pdf

Mears, Bill. 2011. "Tapes Reveal Thurgood Marshall's Rocky Road to the Supreme Court." CNN, February 24, 2011. https://www.cnn.com/2011/POLITICS/02/24/thurgood.marshall.court/index.html

Mill, John Stuart. 1985. *On Liberty.* London: Penguin Books.

Montgomery, David. 2019. "Conquerors of the Courts." *Washington Post Magazine*, January 2, 2019.

Moon, Emily. 2019. "Brett Kavanaugh Has Already Had an Impact on the Supreme Court, Starting with Gun Rights." *Pacific Standard*, January 24, 2019. https://psmag.com/news/brett-kavanaugh-has-already-had-an-impact-on-the-supreme-court-starting-with-gun-rights

Morris, Aldon. 1984. *The Origins of the Civil Rights Movement.* New York: Free Press.

"Most Americans Trust the Supreme Court, but Think It Is 'Too Mixed Up in Politics.'" 2019. *Annenberg Public Policy Center*, October 16, 2019. https://www.annenbergpublicpolicycenter.org/most-americans-trust-the-supreme-court-but-think-it-is-too-mixed-up-in-politics/

Murphy, Walter F., C. Herman Pritchett, Lee Epstein, and Jack Knight. 2006. *Courts, Judges, and Politics.* New York: McGraw-Hill.

Murrill, Brandon J. 2018. *Modes of Constitutional Interpretation* (CRS Report No. R45129). Congressional Research Service. https://fas.org/sgp/crs/misc/R45129.pdf

"N.A.A.C.P. Sets Advanced Goals: Officials Say They Will Drive for End of Residential and Job Discrimination." 1954. *New York Times*, May 18, 1954.

Nichol, Gene R., Jr. 1987. "Ripeness and the Constitution." *University of Chicago Law Review*, 54: 153–183.

O'Brien, David. 2003. *Judges on Judging: Views from the Bench.* 2nd Edition. Washington, D.C.: CQ Press.

O'Brien, David. 2014. *Storm Center: The Supreme Court in American Politics.* 10th Edition. New York: W.W. Norton & Company.

O'Brien, David. 2017. *Constitutional Law and Politics: Volume Two, Civil Rights and Civil Liberties.* 10th Edition. New York: W.W. Norton & Company.

Palleschi, Amanda. 2018. "The SCOTUS Beat: Reading the Tea Leaves of the Supreme Court." *Columbia Journalism Review*, July 9, 2018. https://www.cjr.org/politics/supreme-court-kennedy.php

Paris, Michael, and Kevin J. McMahon. 1998. "The Politics of Rights Revisited: Rosenberg, McCann, and the New Institutionalism." In *Leveraging the Law: Using the Courts to Achieve Social Change*, edited by David A. Schultz. New York: Peter Lang.

Parlapiano, Alicia, and Jugal K. Patel. 2018. "With Kennedy's Retirement, the Supreme Court Loses Its Center." *New York Times*, June 27, 2018.

Posner, Richard. 1990. "What Has Pragmatism to Offer Law?" *Southern California Law Review*, 63: 1653–1670.

Prakash, Saikrishna B., and John C. Yoo. 2003. The Origins of Judicial Review. *University of Chicago Law Review*, 70, no. 3 (Summer): 887–982.

Pritchett, C. Herman. 1948. *The Roosevelt Court: A Study in Judicial Politics and Values, 1937–1947.* New York: Macmillan Publishing.

Rehnquist, William R. 1986. "Constitutional Law and Public Opinion." *Suffolk University Law Review*, 20, no. 4: 751–770.

Reid, Brad. 2016. Fourteen Ways to Interpret the Constitution. *Huffington Post.* October 31, 2016. https://www.huffpost.com/entry/fourteen-ways-to-interpre_b_12735744

Religious Freedom Restoration Act. 1993. Public Law No. 103-141, 107 Stat. 1488 codified at 42 USC § 2000bb through 42 U.S.C. § 2000bb-4.

Roberts, John. 2005. "Transcript: Opening Statement before Senate Panel." *New York Times*, September 12, 2005.

Roberts, John. 2016a. "Inside the Supreme Court." Interview with John O'Brien at New England Law School, Boston, MA. *C-Span*, February 3, 2016. https://www.c-span.org/video/?404131-1/discussion-chief-justice-john-roberts&start=375

Roberts, John. 2016b. "2016 Year-End Report on the Federal Judiciary." https://www.supremecourt.gov/publicinfo/year-end/2016year-endreport.pdf

Roberts, John. 2019. "2019 Year-End Report on the Federal Judiciary." https://www.supremecourt.gov/publicinfo/year-end/2019year-endreport.pdf

Roberts, Steven V. 1987. "Ginsburg Withdraws Name as Supreme Court Nominee, Citing Marijuana 'Clamor.'" *New York Times*, November 8, 1987.

Rosen, Jeffrey. 2017. "Not Even Andrew Jackson Went as Far as Trump in Attacking the Courts." *The Atlantic*, February 9, 2017.

Rosen, Jeffrey. 2018. "Is There a Supreme Court Legitimacy Crisis?" *We the People Podcast.* October 18, 2018. https://constitutioncenter.org/podcast-is-there-a-supreme-court-legitimacy-crisis

Rosenberg, Gerald N. 2008. *The Hollow Hope: Can the Courts Bring about Social Change?* 2nd Edition. Chicago, IL: University of Chicago Press.

"Rules of the Supreme Court of the United States." 2019. https://www.supremecourt.gov/ctrules/2019RulesoftheCourt.pdf

Saad, Lydia. 2019. "Supreme Court Enjoys Majority Approval at Start of New Term." *Gallup*, October 2, 2019.

Scalia, Antonin. 2002. "God's Justice and Ours." *First Things*, May 2002. https://www.firstthings.com/article/2002/05/gods-justice-and-ours

Scheingold, Stuart A. 1974. *The Politics of Rights: Lawyers, Public Policy, and Political Change.* New Haven, CT: Yale University Press.

Scheingold, Stuart A. 1989. "Constitutional Rights and Social Change: Civil Rights in Perspective." In *Judging the Constitution: Critical Essays on Judicial Lawmaking*, edited by Michael W. McCann and Gerald L. Houseman. Glenview, IL: Scott, Foresman & Company.

Schmidt, Chris. 2017. "This Day in Supreme Court History—August 8, 1793." Blog. *ISCOTUSnow*. August 8, 2017. http://blogs.kentlaw.iit.edu/iscotus/day-supreme-court-history-august-8-1793/

Segal, Jeffery A., and Albert D. Cover. 1989. "Ideological Values and the Votes of U.S. Supreme Court Justices." *American Political Science Review*, 83, no. 2: 557–565.

Segal, Jeffery A., and Harold J. Spaeth. 1993. *The Supreme Court and the Attitudinal Model.* New York: Cambridge University Press.

Shaw, Kate. 2019. "The Future of the Supreme Court." Robert Barnes interviews Kate Shaw, Gary Lawson, and Jed Shugerman, *WGBH Forum Network*, October 9, 2019. https://forum-network.org/lectures/future-supreme-court/

Siegel, Reva B. 2016. "Same-Sex Marriage and Backlash: Constitutionalism through the Lens of Consensus and Conflict." Lecture presented at Max Weber Lecture Program for Postdoctoral Studies, European University Institute, Florence, Italy. Lecture No. 2016/04.

Silverstein, Helena. 1996. *Unleashing Rights: Legal Meaning and the Animal Rights Movement.* Ann Arbor: University of Michigan Press.

Silverstein, Helena. 2007. *Girls on the Stand: How Courts Fail Pregnant Minors.* New York: NYU Press.

Slotnick, Elliot E., and Jennifer A. Segal. 1998. *Television News and the Supreme Court: All the News That's Fit to Air?* New York: Cambridge University Press.

S.M. 2018. "Why Supreme Court Justices Serve Such Long Terms." *The Economist*, July 4, 2018.

Snell, Kelsey. 2019. "Senate Rewrites Rules to Speed Confirmations for Some Trump Nominees." *National Public Radio*, April 3, 2019.

https://www.npr.org/2019/04/03/709489797/senate-rewrites-rules
-to-speed-confirmations-for-some-trump-nominees

Stone, Geoffrey R. 2008. "The Roberts Court, Stare Decisis, and the Future of Constitutional Law." *Tulane Law Review*, 82: 1533–1559.

Supreme Court Case Selections Act of 1988, June 27, 1988, Public Law No. 100-352, 102 Stat. 662 codified at 28 U.S.C. §§ 1254, 1257–58, 2104 (1994).

"Supreme Court Nominations (1789–Present)." 2020. United States Senate. https://www.senate.gov/legislative/nominations/SupremeCourtNominations1789present.htm

"Supreme Court Packing: Where 2020 Democrats Stand." 2020. *Washington Post*. https://www.washingtonpost.com/graphics/politics/policy -2020/voting-changes/supreme-court-packing/

"Supreme Court Survey." 2018. *C-SPAN/PSB*. https://www.c-span.org /scotussurvey2018/

Taylor, Stuart, Jr. 1987. "A.B.A. Panel Gives Bork a Top Rating but Vote Is Split." *New York Times*, September 10, 1987.

Thomson-DeVeaux, Amelia. 2019. "The Supreme Court Might Have Three Swing Justices Now." *FiveThirtyEight*, July 2, 2019. https:// fivethirtyeight.com/features/the-supreme-court-might-have-three -swing-justices-now/

Thomson-DeVeaux, Amelia, and Oliver Roeder. 2018. "Is the Supreme Court Facing a Legitimacy Crisis?" *FiveThirtyEight*, October 1, 2018. https://fivethirtyeight.com/features/is-the-supreme-court-facing -a-legitimacy-crisis/

Tocqueville, Alexis de. 2012. *Democracy in America*. Vol. I. Edited by Eduardo Nolla. Indianapolis, IN: Liberty Fund.

Toobin, Jeffrey. 2017. "How to Stop a Trump Supreme Court Nominee." *The New Yorker*, January 4, 2017.

Totenberg, Nina. 2019a. "Covering the Supreme Court." Interview with Bill Press at Hill Center at the Old Naval Hospital, Washington, DC. *C-Span*, January 22, 2019. https://www.c-span.org/video /?457152-1/nina-totenberg-covering-supreme-court

Totenberg, Nina. 2019b. "From Cover-Ups to Secret Plots: The Murky History of Supreme Justices' Health." *National Public Radio*, January 23, 2019. https://www.npr.org/2019/01/23/686208930/from-cover -ups-to-secret-plots-the-murky-history-of-supreme-justices -health

Totenberg, Nina. 2019c. "Retired Justice John Paul Stevens Talks History, His New Book and Ping-Pong." *This American Life*, May 10, 2019. https://www.kunc.org/post/justice-john-paul-stevens-talks-history -his-new-book-and-pingpong#stream/0

Tushnet, Mark V. 1987. *The NAACP's Legal Strategy Against Segregated Education, 1925–1950*. Chapel Hill: University of North Carolina Press.

"U.S. Senate Statistics on Party Division." 2020. United States Senate. https://www.senate.gov/history/partydiv.htm

Voeten, Erik. 2013. "Public Opinion, the Court, and Justice Kennedy." *Monkey Cage. Washington Post*, June 28, 2013. https://themonkeycage .org/2013/06/public-opinion-the-court-and-justice-kennedy/

Whittington, Keith E. 2006. "Presidents, Senates, and Failed Supreme Court Nominations." *Supreme Court Review*, 2006: 401–438.

Withers, Rachel. 2018. "Watch Ruth Bader Ginsburg Do Her Impression of Kate McKinnon's Impression of Her." *Slate*, January 22, 2018.

Yourish, Karen, Sergio Peçanha, and Troy Griggs. 2018. "Kavanaugh Is One of Only 114 to Join the Exclusive Club of Justices. Here's How He Fits In." *New York Times*, October 8, 2018.

LEGAL CASES

Abbott Laboratories v. Gardner, 387 U.S. 137 (1967).

Adair v. United States, 208 U.S. 161 (1908).

Adkins v. Children's Hospital, 261 U.S. 525 (1923).

Alberts v. California, 354 U.S. 476 (1957).

Altitude Express Inc. v. Zarda, Docket No. 17-1623 (2020).

Atkins v. Virginia, 536 U.S. 304 (2002).

Baker v. Carr, 369 U.S. 186 (1962).

Barron v. Baltimore, 32 U.S. 243 (1833).

Benton v. Maryland, 395 U.S. 784 (1969).

Bostock v. Clayton County, Ga., Docket No. 17-1618 (2020).

Bowers v. Hardwick, 478 U.S. 186 (1986).

Brown v. Board of Education of Topeka (Brown I), 347 U.S. 483 (1954).

Brown v. Board of Education of Topeka (Brown I), Transcript of Oral Argument, December 9, 1952. https://www.lib.umich.edu/brown-versus -board-education/oral/Marshall&Davis.pdf

Brown v. Board of Education of Topeka (Brown II), 349 U.S. 294 (1955).

Burnet v. Coronado Oil & Gas Co., 285 U.S. 393 (1932).

Bush v. Gore, 531 U.S. 98 (2000).

Chicago & G.T. R. Co. v. Wellman, 143 U.S. 339 (1892).

Chicago, Burlington & Quincy Railroad Company v. Chicago, 166 U.S. 226 (1897).

Chisholm v. Georgia, 2 U.S. 419 (1793).

Citizens United v. Federal Election Commission, 558 U.S. 310 (2010).

City of Boerne v. Flores, 521 U.S. 507 (1997).

Clinton v. City of New York, 524 U.S. 417 (1998).

Clinton v. Jones, 520 U.S. 681 (1997).

Cohen v. California, 403 U.S. 15 (1971).

Cooper v. Aaron, 358 U.S. 1 (1958).

Craig v. Boren, 429 U.S. 190 (1976).

Crandall v. Nevada, 73 U.S. 35 (1867).

Cruzan v. Director, Missouri Department of Health, 497 U.S. 261 (1990).

DeFunis v. Odegaard, 416 U.S. 312 (1974).

District of Columbia v. Heller, 554 U.S. 570, 128 S.Ct. 2783 (2008).

Dred Scott v. Sandford, 60 U.S. 393 (1857).

Duncan v. Louisiana, 391 U.S. 145 (1968).

Employment Division, Department of Human Resources of Oregon v. Smith,
     485 U.S. 660 (1988).

Engel v. Vitale, 370 U.S. 421 (1962).

Everson v. Board of Education, 330 U.S. 1 (1947).

Ferguson v. Moore-McCormack Lines, Inc., 352 U.S. 521 (1957).

Fletcher v. Peck, 10 U.S. 87 (1810).

Frontiero v. Richardson, 411 U.S. 677 (1973).

Gamble v. U.S., 139 S. Ct. 1960 (2019).

Gee v. Planned Parenthood of Gulf Coast, 139 S.Ct. 408 (2018).

Gibbons v. Odgen, 22 U.S. 1 (1824).

Gideon v. Wainwright, 372 U.S. 335 (1963).

Gill v. Whitford, 138 S.Ct. 1916 (2018).

Gitlow v. New York, 268 US 652 (1925).

Gratz v. Bollinger, 539 U.S. 244 (2003).

Green v. County School Board of New Kent County, 391 U.S. 430 (1968).

Gregg v. Georgia, 428 U.S. 153 (1976).

Griswold v. Connecticut, 381 U.S. 479 (1965).

Grutter v. Bollinger, 539 U.S. 306 (2003).

Hamdi v. Rumsfeld, 542 U.S. 507 (2004).

Hammer v. Dagenhart, 247 U.S. 251 (1918).

Heart of Atlanta Motel, Inc. v. United States, 379 U.S. 241 (1964).

Heller v. District of Columbia, 399 U.S. App. D.C. 314 (2011).

Helvering v. Hallock, 309 U.S. 106 (1940).

INS v. Chadha, 462 U.S. 919 (1983).

June Medical Services LLC v. Russo, Docket No. 18–1323 (2020).

Kelo v. New London, 545 U.S. 469 (2005).

Lawrence v. Texas, 539 U.S. 558 (2003).

Ledbetter v. Goodyear Tire & Rubber Co., 550 U.S. 618 (2007).

Lochner v. New York, 198 U.S. 45 (1905).

Loving v. Virginia, 388 U.S. 1 (1967).

Lujan v. Defenders of Wildlife, 504 U.S. 555 (1992).

Malloy v. Hogan, 378 U.S. 1 (1964).

Mapp v. Ohio, 367 U.S. 643 (1961).

Marbury v. Madison, 5 U.S. 137 (1803).

Martin v. Hunter's Lessee, 14 U.S. 304 (1816).

Masterpiece Cakeshop v. Colorado Civil Rights Commission, 138 S. Ct. 1719 (2018).

McClaurin v. Oklahoma State Regents, 339 U.S. 637 (1950).

McCulloch v. Maryland, 17 U.S. 316 (1819).

McDonald v. The City of Chicago, 561 U.S. 742 (2010).

Miranda v. Arizona, 384 U.S. 436 (1966).

Muller v. Oregon, 208 U.S. 412 (1908).

National Federation of Independent Business v. Sibelius, 567 U.S. 519 (2012).

National Labor Relations Board v. Jones & Laughlin Steel Corp., 301 U.S. 1 (1937).

Near v. Minnesota, 283 U.S. 697 (1931).

New York Times Co. v. Sullivan, 376 U.S. 254 (1964).

New York Times Co. v. United States, 403 U.S. 713 (1971).

North Carolina v. Rice, 404 U.S. 244 (1971).

Obergefell v. Hodges, 135 S.Ct. 2584 (2015).

Pavan v. Smith, 137 S. Ct. 2075 (2017).

Payne v. Tennessee, 501 U.S. 808 (1991).

Planned Parenthood of Southeastern Pennsylvania v. Casey, 505 U.S. 833 (1992).

Plessy v. Ferguson, 163 U.S. 537 (1896).

Poe v. Ullman, 367 U.S. 497 (1961).

Pollock v. Farmers' Loan and Trust Company, 157 U.S. 429 (1895).

Powell v. Alabama, 287 U.S. 45 (1932).

Railroad Retirement Board v. Alton Railroad Co., 295 U.S. 330 (1935).

Reed v. Reed, 404 U.S. 71 (1971).

Regents of the University of California v. Bakke, 438 U.S. 265 (1978).

Reynolds v. Sims, 377 U.S. 533 (1964).

R.G. & G.R. Harris Funeral Homes Inc. v. Equal Employment Opportunity Commission, No. 18-107 (2020).

Roe v. Wade, 410 U.S. 113 (1973).

Roth v. United States, 354 U.S. 476 (1957).

Rucho v. Common Cause, 139 S.Ct. 2484 (2019).

Schechter Poultry Corp. v. United States, 295 U.S. 495 (1935).

Shelby County v. Holder, 570 U.S. 529 (2013).

Slaughterhouse Cases, 83 U.S. 36 (1873).

Smith v. Allwright, 321 U.S. 649 (1944).

South Carolina v. Katzenbach, 383 U.S. 301 (1966).

Sweatt v. Painter, 339 U.S. 629 (1950).

Texas v. Johnson, 491 U.S. 397 (1989).

Tinker v. Des Moines Independent Community School District, 393 U.S. 503 (1969).

Trump v. Hawaii, 138 S.Ct. 2392 (2018).

United States v. Carolene Products Company, 304 U.S. 144 (1938).

United States v. Lopez, 514 U.S. 549 (1995).

United States v. Morrison, 529 U.S. 598 (2000).

United States v. Nixon, 418 U.S. 683 (1974).

United States v. O'Brien, 391 U.S. 367 (1968).

United States v. Virginia, 518 U.S. 515 (1996).

United States v. Windsor, 570 U.S. 744 (2013).

Vieth v. Jubelirer, 541 U. S. 267 (2004).

Wallace v. Jaffree, 472 U.S. 38 (1985).

Washington v. Glucksberg, 521 U.S. 702 (1997).

Weeks v. United States, 232 U.S. 383 (1914).

West Coast Hotel Co. v. Parrish, 300 U.S. 379 (1937).

West Virginia State Board of Education v. Barnette, 319 U.S. 624 (1943).

Wickard v. Filburn, 317 U.S. 111 (1942).

Williams v. Mississippi, 170 U.S. 213 (1898).

Wisconsin v. Yoder, 406 U.S. 205 (1972).

Wolf v. Colorado, 338 U.S. 25 (1949).

Worcester v. Georgia, 31 U.S. 515 (1832).

Youngstown Sheet & Tube Co. v. Sawyer, 343 U.S. 579 (1952).

Index

About the Author

Helena Silverstein, PhD, is professor and department head of Government and Law at Lafayette College. She is author of *Girls on the Stand: How Courts Fail Pregnant Minors* (2007; named a Choice Outstanding Academic Title for 2008) and *Unleashing Rights: Law, Meaning, and the Animal Rights Movement* (1996). Her research on law and society, constitutional law, social movements, and abortion politics has appeared in several journals, including *Law & Social Inquiry, Law & Policy, Iowa Law Review, University of Pennsylvania Journal of Constitutional Law, Cornell Journal of Law and Public Policy,* and *Law and Inequality.* From 2014 to 2016 she served as program director of the Law and Social Sciences Program at the National Science Foundation. She received her PhD and MA in political science from the University of Washington and BA in political science and economics from the University of Pennsylvania.